Deregulation and the Airline Business in Europe

Over the past twenty years air fares in Europe have fallen steadily. New entrant airlines such as Ryanair and easyJet have become the largest passenger airlines in Europe, old national airlines have become commercialised and staff productivity of airlines and airports now compete. The reason behind these changes was the change in policy from protecting national airlines to market competition. This book documents a dramatic change in the economic policy surrounding the low-cost airlines and the airport industry as a whole.

In this fascinating monograph, Dr Sean Barrett provides a full deregulation case study from market control by national airlines through regulatory capture of governments to the transformed competitive market today. The topics covered include the deregulation of Europe's busiest route – London to Dublin, the market entry of Ryanair and its sustainability, the outlook for full-service airlines, the commercialisation of national airlines and the impact of airports on competing airlines.

Through a discussion of controversial issues such as the regulatory capture of government protected airlines, the dominance of producers over consumers in protected markets and the costs of protectionism in aviation to the wider economy, Dr Barrett's book will be of interest to anyone involved in the airline business, as well as to wider public or competition policy-makers.

Sean Barrett is currently senior lecturer at the Department of Economics, Trinity College, Dublin, and is a member of the National Economic and Social Council of Ireland.

Routledge studies in the European economy

Deregulation and the Airline Business in Europe

Selected readings

Sean Barrett

Routledge
Taylor & Francis Group

LONDON AND NEW YORK

First published 2009
by Routledge
2 Park Square, Milton Park, Abingdon, Oxfordshire OX14 4RN

Simultaneously published in the USA and Canada
by Routledge
711 Third Avenue, New York, NY 10017

*Routledge is an imprint of the Taylor & Francis Group,
an informa business*

First issued in paperback 2011

© 2009 Sean Barrett

Typeset in Times New Roman by Keyword Group Ltd

British Library Cataloguing in Publication Data
A catalogue record for this book is available from the British Library

Library of Congress Cataloging-in-Publication Data
Barrett, Sean D.
Deregulation and the airline business in Europe / by Sean Barrett.
   p. cm.
   Includes bibliographical references and index.
      1. Airlines–Deregulation–Europe. 2. Airlines–Privatization–Europe.
      l. Title.
   HE9842.A4B37 2009
   387.7'1–dc22   2008043448

ISBN13: 978-0-415-44722-5 (hbk)
ISBN13: 978-0-415-69649-4 (pbk)
ISBN13: 978-0-203-87966-5 (ebk)

To Maeve and Melissa

Contents

Foreword by Professor Alfred Kahn

I first met Sean Barrett in the late summer of 1989 at an ESRC seminar at Worcester College, Oxford, organised by David Banister and Kenneth Button. The papers presented there were published afterwards in *Transport in a Free Market Economy*, edited by Banister and Button and published by Macmillan in 1991.

Those were heady days. We had succeeded in deregulating the industry in the United States a decade previously, setting off waves of discounting that produced net benefits authoritatively estimated shortly thereafter by Steven Morrison and Clifford Winston at some $20 billion a year. (It was only a year or so later, in the early 90s, that the industry's historical susceptibility to waves of destructive competition reasserted itself, producing disconcertingly huge multi-billion dollar losses in the four years of the early 90s.)

At the time of our meeting, in 1989, deregulation was still highly controversial in Europe: standard fares remained outrageously high by American standards, leaving the high-elasticity demand to charters. One participant in the conference expressed the view that deregulation in Europe might turn out 'a monopolistic damp squib'. In that atmosphere of scholarly uncertainty, Sean Barrett stood out as a beacon of optimism, with a dramatic story to tell – a fascinating account of the Irish parliamentary revolt in 1984 against legislation to punish discounting of airline tickets by imprisonment and heavy fines, followed by the founding of Ryanair in 1985 and the deregulation of the Dublin–London route in 1986.

The results as he described them then and now chronicles in this volume – with deserved pride – have been almost unbelievably dramatic. Fares on the Dublin–London route fell by 54 per cent on deregulation day and passenger numbers increased by 65 per cent over the first full year. The momentum has been sustained for over two decades. In the last year before deregulation 1985/1986, the protected Irish national airline, Aer Lingus, had 2.2 million passengers; in 2008, four Irish airlines in the deregulated market will have carried some 72 million.

The market leader is that same upstart, Ryanair, whose chief executive, Michael O'Leary, is a former student of Barrett, at Trinity College, Dublin. O'Leary reinvented Ryanair as a low-cost airline in the early 1990s, when it had a little over 1 million passengers. In 2009 it will have 68 million – making it Europe's largest airline – consistently with the lowest air fares and highest staff productivity in the region.

Barrett has become the leading expert on – and enthusiast for – the Ryanair model and its revolutionary impact on aviation in Europe. He also documents in this volume the almost equally dramatic, successful adaptation of Aer Lingus, from the traditional European national carrier to the new deregulated market – in contrast with other former national airlines in Europe that have either left the market or been absorbed by larger carriers. In addition to raising staff productivity to unprecedented levels, Ryanair has both redefined the airline product in Europe to the point-to-point no-frills model and tackled major input costs at airports and in ticketing, sales and distribution.

Most informative to me has been Barrett's description of the growth of competition among airports, of which he has, characteristically, both played a leading role and been the greatest enthusiast/publicist. Europe had large numbers of underused and less congested airports, most of them built for military purposes or by city and regional governments. To my knowledge he was first to analyse the attractions of these smaller, secondary airports for both low-cost airlines – to whom they could offer the 25-minute turnaround time they needed to keep costs down and the ability to expand operations rapidly, without having to acquire slots at high-cost airports.

The decisions to end ticket sales through travel agents in favour of Internet sales and to abolish frequent-flyer points to engage in price rather than non-price competition were also radical in the transformation of commercial aviation in Europe. Barrett has, for decades, advocated the break-up of groups of airports into competing entitites, and competing terminals within airports.

As one involved in the political and economic aspects of airline deregulation in the United States in 1978, I find Barrett's work in Ireland both fascinating and a source of personal vindication, admiration, and indeed envy. He has been, along with Clifford Winston and Steven Morrison in the United States, my principal reinforcement, vindicator and chronicler of the results of our efforts.

In a recent (2008) response to a seminar in Boulder, Colorado on 'Deregulation Revisited', I said that

> it was precisely the failure of the industry under regulation to provide travellers of modest means with a choice of economy over comfort that constituted both the need for deregulation and the essence of its success. The experience wonderfully illustrates the principle that cartelization of a structurally competitive industry – in particular the prohibition of price competition – sets off all sorts of other forms of cost-inflating competition, substantive and non-substantive, the fatal flaw of which is that it denied customers the choice of low-priced service without those amenities.

European air fares, then the highest in the world, had farther to fall than in the United States. The results of deregulation in Europe have been correspondingly dramatic. The gains from policy entrepreneurship by Sean Barrett, his disciples and his supporters in promoting and achieving the deregulation of European aviation have been immense. This volume chronicles that historic process.

References

Kahn, A. (2008) 'A Grateful response and supplement', presented at the Seminar on Deregulation Revisited: A Tribute to Fred Kahn, University of Colorado, 5 September 2008.

Alfred E. Kahn

Former Chairman of the United States Civil Aeronautics Board;

Robert Julius Thorne Professor of Political Economy Emeritus,

Cornell University; Special Consultant,

National Economic Research Associates

About the author

Dr Sean Barrett is uniquely placed to write on the transformation of the regulation of European aviation. He was an early advocate of deregulation both in academic journals and in the public media. He has been a board member of the *Journal of Air Transport Management* since its foundation. He has served on the Air Transport Users Committee of the Chambers of Commerce of Ireland and represented Ireland on the Council of the Federation of Air Transport User Representatives in the European Community. He is a Government of Ireland nominee on the National Economic and Social Council which advises on economic and social policy and has served on review bodies dealing with industrial policy, ports policy and financial controls in the health service. As a director of the Irish Tourist Board (1984–1989) he advocated deregulated access transport in order to stimulate an important but then stagnant sector of the economy.

Preface

Regulating Europe's skies

Almost 117 million passengers travelled on Europe's low-cost airlines in 2006. The market leader in this segment is Ryanair with 29.9 per cent. The other airlines with a market share above 5 per cent are easyJet with 25.9 per cent and Air Berlin/Nikki with 11.8 per cent. For the year 2008 Ryanair and easyJet combined passenger numbers are estimated at over 100 million. Ryanair exceeded 1 million passengers for the first time in 1993. easyJet was founded in 1995.

The UK Civil Aviation Authority report (2006) entitled 'No Frills Carriers: Revolution or Evolution?' found that between 1996 and 2005 international passenger traffic between the UK and the EU increased from 69.1 million to 123.7 million. Low-cost airlines increased from 3.1 million to 51.5 million and accounted for 89 per cent of the increase in passenger numbers compared with 9 per cent on full-service legacy airlines and 2 per cent on charters. The CAA also noted that 'since 2000, both charter and full-service carriers have seen flat or declining demand'.

Ryanair, the largest and longest established low-cost airline in Europe, is based in Ireland. With a strong tradition of support for its national airline, Aer Lingus, Ireland was an unlikely candidate to provide the market leader in low-cost aviation in Europe. A dramatic parliamentary rejection of legislation to fine, imprison and withdraw the travel agent's licence of those discounting airline tickets in 1984 led to the market entry of Ryanair in 1985 and its entry on the major Dublin–London route in competition with Aer Lingus and British Airways in 1986.

The structure of this book is as follows. Chapter 1 deals with the defeat of regulatory capture. It describes the defeat of the Air Transport Bill in 1984. Legislation to protect national airlines was defeated by a rare parliamentary revolt in Ireland. This led to the establishment of Ryanair, and its entry to the Dublin–London route in 1986. It became the market leader on the busiest international route in Europe and was the first new entrant airline in Europe to carry more passengers than the previous national airline. Chapter 2 describes the European aviation system under the regime of one national airline per country, fare collusion or co-ordination and market sharing agreements. Chapter 3 describes the impact of new market entrants to the Dublin–London route in 1986 over the initial three years. The route is the busiest in Europe with 4.3 million passengers in 2006. Chapter 4 describes the development of Ryanair, the dominant new entrant on the Dublin–London route, in the 1990s. British Airways left the Dublin–London route in 1991. Ryanair became the market leader in 1995. Aer Lingus was then in financial difficulties and required a government rescue plan in agreement with the EU. Chapter 5 describes the continued development of Ryanair after 2000. Its anticipated 58 million passengers in 2008 will be almost six times the number carried by Aer Lingus. Chapter 6 analyses the difficult market faced by full-service airlines in competition both with low-cost airlines and legacy national airlines. It is based on Cityjet, a full-service airline now owned by Air France. Chapter 7 is a case study of the commercialisation of Aer Lingus from regulatory dominance and capture through to privatisation in 2006. Chapter 8 illustrates the growth of airport competition in the deregulated European aviation market in response to low-cost airlines. Chapter 9 examines the problems of dismantling a national airport monopoly and promoting competition between and within airports. Chapter 10 summarises the impact of deregulation on European aviation market in 2008.

Sean D. Barrett

Tables

Acknowledgements

On the 25th anniversary of the parliamentary revolt against the restriction of competition in European aviation, this book honours the politicians and economists who opposed the regulatory capture of European aviation by its national airlines. I am indebted to this group and all who have made this publication possible. Alfred Kahn, Marilyn Pettinga, Ken Button, Anne Graham, David Banister, Joseph Berechman, Tim Tardiff, Michael O'Leary, Adele Bannon, Jim Callaghan, Sean Coyle, Pat Byrne, Jack Short, Anne Graham, John O'Connell and Thomas Lawton provided valuable help and inspiration. Kavitha Ashok, Emily Senior, Terry Clague, and Thomas Sutton took charge of publication matters at Routledge and were assisted by Mary O'Neill, Charles Larkin, Colette Ding and Patricia Hughes at Trinity College, Dublin. I am indebted also to my colleagues at the Department of Economics, Trinity College, Dublin and in particular to Dr Andrew Somerville, head of the department. Special thanks go to the students of Trinity College, Dublin where a tradition of student debate on policy issues goes back to Edmund Burke's foundation of the College Historical Society in 1747.

Chapter 2 is from *Transport in a Unified Europe*, edited by David Banister and Joseph Berechman, North Holland Press, 1993 by permission of Elsevier Science Publishers.

Chapter 3, section 1, is from the *Journal of Air Transport Management*, vol. 2, 1997, no. 2 by permission of Elsevier Science Ltd. Chapter 3, section 2, is from *Transportation*, 16, 1990, by permission of Kluwer Academic Publishers.

Chapter 4 is from the *Journal of Air Transport Management*, vol. 5, 1999, by permission of Elsevier Science Ltd.

Chapter 5 is from the *Journal of Air Transport Management*, vol. 2, 2004, by permission of Elsevier Science Ltd.

Chapter 6 is from the *Journal of Air Transport Management*, vol. 7, 2001, by permission of Elsevier Science Ltd.

Chapter 7 is from the *Journal of Air Transport Management*, vol. 12, 2006, by permission of Elsevier Science Ltd.

Chapter 8, section 1 is from the *Journal of Air Transport Management*, vol. 6, 2000, by permission of Elsevier Science Ltd. Section 2 is from the *Journal of Air Transport Management*, vol. 10, 2004, by permission of Elsevier Science Ltd.

1   The defeat of regulatory capture

Ireland was an unlikely source of contestability in European aviation in 1984. There was a long tradition of attachment to the national airline, Aer Lingus, as a symbol of economic nationalism. The airline controlled the regulatory functions of the Department of Transport, as is shown in Chapter 8. While there was growing consumer resistance to the perceived high levels of fares charged by Aer Lingus and British Airways it seemed powerless against the national airline and its hold over the Department of Transport. The Irish parliament, the Dail, had a strong tradition of party discipline with few cases in which the government did not get its way when proposing legislation. On 27 June 1984 however a parliamentary revolt against the Air Transport Bill set in train a policy change which led to the foundation of Ryanair. The first Ryanair route, from Waterford to Gatwick, started in November 1985 and was followed by entry on Europe's busiest route, Dublin to London, in May 1986. The consumer response to competition between Dublin and London was overwhelmingly positive. Ryanair's projected passenger numbers for 2008 are 58 million compared with 10 million for Aer Lingus, the previously protected national airline. In 2006 the Ryanair share of Europe's low-cost airline market of 117 million passengers was 29.9 per cent. A parliamentary revolt in a country with under 4 million population gave Ryanair first mover advantage and had impacts throughout Europe.

The Air Transport Bill 1984 was introduced in the Irish parliament because the Supreme Court had lifted a temporary injunction restraining Transamerica from selling unapproved fares which were lower than those approved by the Minister. The High Court had granted the temporary injunction at the request of the Minister. A full determination of the action was likely to take up to a year. Rather than wait for a full determination the Minister decided to introduce emergency legislation to close off what was presented as a legal loophole. The penalties for discounting airline tickets were a £100,000 fine, two years in prison and the loss of the travel agent's licence. The Bill was introduced because selling tickets below approved prices was 'undermining the system of control'. Without the Bill, 'the Minister's powers to control airfares would be undermined. Discounting and other malpractices could take place on a scale that would undermine approved tariff structures and could have serious implications for airlines generally and for Aer Lingus in particular.'

The parliamentary opposition to the Bill was led by Mr Desmond O'Malley, then an independent member. As a member of the dominant Fianna Fail party he had served as Minister for Justice and Minister for Industry and Commerce. He returned to the latter department in the years 1999–2003 as minister in a coalition government of Fianna Fail and the Progressive Democrats, the party he founded in 1985. Mr O'Malley had been expelled from the Fianna Fail party in 1983 for refusing to support legislation to confine the sale of condoms to pharmacies on medical prescription. He was a highly respected member of parliament and his opposition attracted support from both the government backbenches of the Fine Gael party and the opposition benches of the Fianna Fail party.

The Bill failed to pass all stages when Mr Bertie Ahern, opposition chief whip, and later Taoiseach (prime minister) declined to support it. The newspaper headlines on the following day included 'Air fares Bill anti-consumer, say deputies' (*Irish Times*) and 'Air fares Bill hits turbulence' (*Irish Press*). In the *Irish Times* the Dail Sketch by Maev Kennedy was entitled 'Trying not to agree with Dessie', an acknowledgement of the crucial role of Mr O'Malley in provoking opposition to the Bill.

The Irish economy in the early and mid-1980s was in serious difficulties. The level of unemployment and the national debt doubled between 1982 and 1987. This was in marked contrast to the period since 1987 in which employment doubled and the unemployment rate fell from 17 to 4 per cent. The protection of employment in state companies such as Aer Lingus was espoused as a goal of policy rather than the wider interest of reducing access costs to an outer offshore island. Ten economists in universities and financial services petitioned against the Air Transport Bill 1984. Their petition is shown in Exhibit 1. The petition was circulated to the media and attracted headlines such as 'Top economists attack Aer Lingus "monopoly" '(*Irish Press*, 28 June 1984). In addition the Irish Independent on the morning of the Dail debate carried an interview with the present author by Stephen O'Byrnes under the title 'Air fares bill is anti-consumer'. This is reproduced in Appendix 1 to this chapter.

The decision by the Irish government to licence Ryanair on Waterford–Gatwick at first and then on Dublin–London (Luton) showed a change of heart by the government. The Transport Minister, Mr Jim Mitchell, had been in Japan when the Air Transport Bill was moved in the Dail on 26 June 1984. He readily adopted a more competitive stance on his return. The Taoiseach, Dr Garret FitzGerald, a former economist at Aer Lingus and lecturer in transport economics at University College Dublin also embraced the more competitive era in Irish aviation policy after June 1984. The u-turn from protectionism to competition in Irish aviation was so swift that Ireland moved instantly from being one of the most conservative countries in aviation policy in Europe to being best positioned to avail of the market opportunities when the EU single market developed in the 1990s.

The heavily protected sole Irish airline, Aer Lingus, had 2.2 million passengers in 1983/4. In the deregulated market in 2008 the projected passenger number on four Irish airlines is 72 million. The development of competition in the

---

Exhibit 1: The economists' petition

The Air Transport Bill 1984

We the undersigned regret the hasty introduction of a Bill designed to limit competition among airlines and travel agents to the obvious detriment of the fare paying public. The attempt to pass the Bill by agreement and without proper debate which such a measure requires is wholly at variance with public pronouncements on the need to encourage efficiency and lower costs and further lowers public confidence in our legislators.

The speed with which this Bill was introduced contrasts with the lethargic pace adopted in implementing many other reforms. It would appear that the Government and Opposition care more about the interests of state monopolies than the public as a whole.

We can find no justification for this price increasing legislation in any of the 1982 election manifestos. It is wholly at variance with the commitment in the Programme for Government to make 'a determined and sustained attack on the domestic factors which push our inflation rate far beyond the average EEC level'. It flatly contradicts the Fine Gael manifesto commitment to regulate cost increasing actions by domestic monopolies.

Our present economic difficulties stem as much from the lack of debate over legislation concerning publicly owned bodies as from undisciplined fiscal policies. The current Bill continues the steady rise in concern for the interests of public monopolies as the expense of consumers.

Sean Barrett, Brendan Dowling, Joe Durkan, Tony Garry, Patrick Geary,
Robert Kelleher, John Kennan, Antoin Murphy and Douglas McLernon.

---

sector is described in the following chapters. The impact of the leading new market entrant, Ryanair, is described in Chapters 4 and 5. Chapter 6 describes the development of Cityjet, a new entrant full service airline. Chapter 7 deals with the commercialisation of Aer Lingus in response to deregulation leading to its privatisation in 2006. Chapters 8 and 9 examine the implications for airports of airline deregulation in Europe. Chapter 10 summarises the transformation of Europe's aviation sector since deregulation.

Appendix 1: Interview published on the date of publication of the Air Transport Bill 1984

27 June 1984, **Irish Independent**: *'Air fares bill is anti-consumer' by* **Stephen O'Byrnes**

The Government plans to outlaw cut-price air fares with its Air Transport Bill, which it hopes to get through all stages in the Dail today, has been attacked by Trinity College economist, Sean Barrett, as a negation of any commitment to open policy making.

He also points out that the bill was not available to the public at the Government Publications Office yesterday, and will only go on sale this morning.

In a paper on the impact of the proposed legislation, Barrett points out that it proposes to increase fines on airlines and travel agents who charge fares lower than those authorised by the Minister for Transport.

'The Minister for Communications had previously intervened to prevent price competition on air routes to Britain and Continental Europe. He had failed, however, in the Supreme Court in his case against Transamerica Airlines and apparently feels that it is in the Irish national interest to rush through this legislation at breakneck speed.'

'New legislation is better introduced after calm consideration of all the diverse factors which make up the national interest in aviation, international trade, tourism, regional development and employment. These factors are so diverse and complex that they cannot be dismissed by this hasty bill,' Mr Barrett says.

'International air travel is controlled by a series of bilateral agreements between governments. The Agreements can be highly restrictive in terms of price competition and the entry of new airlines to the. market or permit many carriers to charge different fares. The former type of agreement is usual in Europe, while the United States and Britain favour the latter, Ireland's geography means that we cannot set our trans-Atlantic air fares regardless of current thinking in the United Sates and Britain.'

'The entry to the market of low-cost carriers such as Virgin and People Express, and the availability of lower fares out of Northern Ireland than from the Republic made the market for lower air fares which the Minister now seeks to abolish. By abolishing these fares he will divert business away from Shannon in particular, since the target airline in this legislation, Transamerica, has its Irish operation centred at Shannon.'

Mr Barrett continues: 'In examining the operation of air services within both the United States and Britain, the Minister should note that deregulation has produced far lower fares than the anti-competition policy of the Irish government.'

Dublin–London is a 290 mile air journey compared to 292 for New York to Buffalo. The fares are £95 and $35.19 respectively. The fare are thus 39 cents a mile on Dublin–London, compared to 12 cents in the US. Rather than legislating against competition the Minister should be learning from it.

Is there any case for tightening controls over competition in air fares as this bill seeks? The answer must be that there is not. The pro-competition approach is the better buy.

1   Ireland is the beneficiary of the present Ireland–US air agreement since the Irish carrier has 85 per cent of the traffic. Seeking to increase this even further runs the risk of retaliation which could lose Irish landing rights in the United States. The present air market regulation between the two countries strongly favours Ireland. US airlines come from a market where price competition is the norm. Preventing them from engaging in price competition is obviously designed to reduce their market share further.

2   Tourism is a two-way traffic. If the higher air fares out of Ireland sought by the Minister are achieved traffic will decline. Planes will thus have smaller load factors ex-Shannon for outward passengers and the ability of the carriers to offer lower fares to Ireland undermined. Ireland hasn't lost out continuously to Britain in its share of the US tourist dollar since the US and Britain cut air fares between them.

3   Air ticket retailing should be a competitive business. The bill makes the travel agent an extension of the airline and compels him to charge fees stipulated by the Minister. The travel agent acting in the consumer interest is abolished by the bill. The Minister for Trade, Mr Bruton, recently referred the question of competition among travel agents to the Restrictive Practices Commission. Today's bill re-empts the result of the inquiry and negates the consumer interest in price competition between both travel agents and airline.

4   Government intervention to prosecute people for charging too little for goods and services makes a nonsense of Government policy to reduce inflation.

5   The bill will enlarge the black hole in balance of payments. Those seeking lower air fares will use travel agents in Newry airports in Britain and Northern Ireland, and lower cost foreign airlines.

6   The bill is decidedly anti-consumer. No Irish Transport Minister used his powers to reduce air fares in recent times. Most of them used their powers to retrospectively sanction fares which had already been charged by the airlines.

Irish industry has faced free competition in world markets for many years. Our tourism must also compete with a wide range of destinations. A competition minded Communications Minister would never have introduced the Air Transport Bill 1984.

2 A Europe of national airlines

Introduction

Air transport in Europe has been highly regulated, based on national sovereignty and non-competing national airlines. Air transport between European countries was typically confined to the national carriers of the countries concerned, with independent airlines excluded from the market as were third-country airlines. The fares charged were agreed upon by the airlines in advance and ratified by governments. Market capacity was also decided in advance, as was its division between the airlines. This regulatory system was frequently criticised because it resulted in high fares and high cost airlines. The fares charged by European scheduled airlines have traditionally been the highest in the world and approximately three times those charged by Europe's charter airlines, which operated under a more competitive regulatory system.

Liberalisation measures were introduced between Britain and the Netherlands in 1984 and between Britain and Ireland in 1986. In the remainder of the EC, gradual liberalisation has been under way but the results have not been dramatic. Liberalisation of the EC market is scheduled for completion in 1997. Agreement with the EFTA countries has also been reached for a free-trade area in aviation encompassing both the EC and EFTA members.

Serious difficulties have nonetheless presented themselves in the way of a contestable market in European aviation. These include a series of mergers between airlines which might have been expected to otherwise compete, difficulties in achieving slots at hub airports for new airlines, predatory pricing, computer reservation system bias, ground handling monopolies, frequent flyer programmes and state subsidies to national airlines.

While aviation is not currently included in General Agreement and Tariffs and Trade (GATT) negotiations, countries with large service sectors such as the United States have argued for its inclusion in future trade liberalisation rounds.

The competitive position of a unified European aviation system, compared with regions such as North America and the Asia-Pacific region, is important in any future liberalisation of the sector worldwide. In addition, the economies of Eastern Europe have the potential to play a significant part in a deregulated aviation market because of their lower labour costs.

The efficiency of European airlines

Europe in world aviation

Table 2.1 shows that the share of world aviation performed by European airlines has declined from 36.1 per cent in 1971 to 31.9 per cent in 1990. The American share of world aviation has declined 48.1 per cent to 38.5 per cent although its share increased slightly during the 1980s. The fastest growing airlines are those in the Asia-Pacific region, whose growth of the industry worldwide was 10 per cent and in the 1980s it was 8 per cent.

Passenger traffic generates two-thirds of international airline revenues, with freight accounting for one-third. Freight grew rapidly in the 1960s. While its growth rate declined in the 1980s, it remained ahead of the growth in passenger traffic. Increasingly, freight is carried on passenger aircraft. All cargo operations have declined. Air freight is particularly suited to the long-distance transport of goods with a high value-to-weight ratio. The increased location of world manufacturers in the Asia-Pacific region and the growth of product markets such as computers, cameras, videos and medical and pharmaceutical goods have favoured the development of air freight.

In the last 20 years, integrated carriers such as Federal Express and DHL have grown rapidly. They provide door-to-door service and specialise in carrying small items and documents. The development of just-in-time (JIT) production methods has focused attention on the high cost of holding goods in stocks in warehouses and in transit. Air transport's speed over long distances and its reliability are important JIT advantages.

Table 2.1 Regional distribution of scheduled airline traffic by percentage of total ton-kilometres performed by airlines registered in region, 1971–2000

	1971	*1981*	*1990*	*2000*
North America	48.1	37.5	38.5	41.0
Europe	36.1	34.6	31.9	24.6
Asia/Pacific	8.2	16.5	19.8	26.1
Latin America/Caribbean	3.9	5.4	4.7	2.5
Middle East	1.7	3.1	2.9	4.1
Africa	2.0	2.9	2.2	1.7
World	100	100	100	100

Source: ICAO Annual Reports (1989): Forecast from ICAO Circular 222, The Economic Situation of Air Transport.

Doganis points out that 'within Europe, most regional air freight is trucked by road. Europe's motorways are criss-crossed nightly by heavy lorries carrying "air" freight!' (1992: 318–9). The development of better road and rail networks in a unified Europe is likely to induce some further diversion of air freight over short distances but in a global economy with a liberal trade environment, the market for long distance road freight will remain buoyant.

European air fares

Air fares in Europe have traditionally been the most expensive in the world. ICAO surveys international air fares each September in 17 regional markets and estimates a world average fare for eight journey lengths ranging from 250 to 16,000 kilometres. Table 2.2 shows that in September 1990, the average fare for a 250-kilometre flight was 70 cents per kilometre in Europe compared with a world average of 45.1 cents. The fares for the 250-kilometre journey in the Asia-Pacific and North American regions were 20.8 and 39.7 cents, respectively. The European fare was the most expensive of nine regions and the Asia-Pacific fare the least expensive. The ICAO survey in the 1990 covered 10,281 city pairs of which 3,098 were 'local Europe' services. The rates of exchange used in converting the fares to US dollars were £0.52 sterling, 5.25 French francs and 1.56 DM per dollar.

Table 2.2 Comparison of average economy class normal fares[a] for passenger-kilometre by route group and distance, 1990

Route group	Distance[b]				
	250	*500*	*1000*	*2000*	*4000*
World (average)	45.1	35.5	28.0	22.1	17.4
North/Central America	46.3	32.2	22.5	IS.6	10.9
Central America	34.5	2S.3	18.6	13.6	–
North America	39.7	27.9	19.6	13.8	9.7
North/South America	21.2	18.4	16.0	13.9	–
South America	22.9	19.6	16.8	14.4	12.3
Europe	70.0	S1.8	38.4	28.4	21.0
Middle East	33.2	26.4	21.9	16.7	15.4
Africa	31.1	26.1	21.9	18.4	15.4
Europe/Middle East	–	27.3	25.0	22.8	20.9
Europe/Africa	–	26.2	23.6	21.3	19.2
Mid-Atlantic	–	–	–	–	20.7
South Atlantic	–	–	–	–	14.5
Asia/Pacific	20.8	19.1	17.S	16.1	14.7
Europe/Asia/Pacific	–	–	13.7	13.9	14.0
South Pacific	–	–	–	–	15.7

Source: ICAO, Annual Survey of Air Fares (1990).

Notes
[a]US cents per kilometre;
[b]kilometres.

Table 2.3 Index of European air fares as proportion of world average, 1977, 1985 and 1990[a]

Distance (km)	1977	1985	1990
250	129	126	155
500	122	118	146
1,000	116	111	137
2,000	109	104	129
4,000	115	96	121

Note
[a] World average = 100.

The margin of excess of European air fares over the world average for three decades is shown in Table 2.3.

In addition to being above the world average, European air fares are significantly above fares in North America and the Asia-Pacific region. In 1990 the fares for a 500-kilometre journey were 51.8 cents in Europe, 27.9 cents in North America and 19.1 cents in Asia-Pacific. The European fare was therefore 46 per cent greater than in North America and 171 per cent greater in Asia-Pacific.

Productivity

Tables 2.4 and 2.5 show the ton-kilometres performed per staff member in 17 European and 15 North American airlines in 1990. North American productivity was on average 36.7 per cent higher than in Europe. The ton-kilometre measure covers freight, mail or passengers carried for one kilometre. Passenger ton-kilometres are obtained by multiplying the number of passengers by 90 kilograms, which allows for the weight of the passenger plus luggage.

Measures of physical productivity per person employed should, however, be used in conjunction with wage costs. Doganis points out that:

> many of the Asian carriers now come into their own with labour productivity levels double or triple those of their European or North American counterparts. Airlines like Air India or Pakistan International Airlines (PIA), the least efficient users of labor in physical terms, are now among the most efficient in terms of resource costs. Conversely, among U.S. airlines, the high ATKs (available ton-kilometres) per employee are substantially eroded by the relatively higher wage levels so that their ATK's per $1,000 of labour cost do not look so impressive. (1992: 134)

Table 2.6 shows the available ton-kilometres per US$1,000 labour cost for five North American, five European and five Asia/Pacific airlines in 1988. The Asia-Pacific average is 2.07 times, and the North American 3.15 times the European. In an analysis of the total factor productivity of 41 airlines in 1983, Windle (1991)

Table 2.4 Staff productivity of European airlines, 1990

Company	T-km performed (millions)	Staff (no.)	T-km per staff ('000)
Austrian	316	4,128	77
Sabena	1,045	7,340	142
Finnair	981	7,127	138
Air France	6,873	39,810	173
UTA	1,146	6,787	169
Lufthansa	8,211	47,619	172
Olympic	829	11,906	70
Aer Lingus	402	5,945	68
Alitalia	2,933	19,348	152
KLM	4,328	24,247	178
TAP	794	9,711	82
SAS	2,564	22,180	116
Iberia	2,587	28,843	90
Swissair	2,542	19,296	132
British Airways	5,769	50,008	115
Dan Air	499	3,843	130
Virgin	492	1,399	352
Total	36,037	300,545	120
Average of 17	2,120	17,679	12

Source: ICAO, Civil Aviation Statistics of the World (1991).

Table 2.5 Staff productivity of North American airlines, 1990

Company	T-km performed (millions)	Staff (no.)	T-km per staff ('000)
Air Canada	3,362	22,622	149
American Airlines	12,845	85,915	150
Canadian	2,712	17,832	152
Eastern	2,653	19,075	139
Delta	9,829	64,791	152
Continental	4,857	33,533	145
Alaska	459	5,822	79
Northwest	10,019	35,775	282
Pan American	5,873	28,823	204
American West	1,769	12,764	139
Hawaiian	498	2,808	177
Midway	732	5,171	142
TWA	6,019	33,189	181
United	13,186	70,179	188
US Air	5,559	50,464	110
Total	80,372	488,763	164
Average of 15	5,358	32,584	164

Source: ICAO. Civil Aviation Statistics of the World (1991).

Table 2.6 Available ton-kilometre per $1,000 labour
cost for major airlines, 1988

Region	ATK per $1,000 labour cost
North America	
Pan Am	10,800
Northwest	8,300
TWA	7,600
Air Canada	7,500
United	6,700
Europe	
British Airways	7,000
KLM	6,500
Lufthansa	5,300
Alitalia	4,000
Swissair	3,600
Asia/Pacific	
Thai	24,000
PIA	23,500
Singapore	20,900
Qantas	10,300
JAL	6,500

Source: Doganis (1992: 136).

found that the US airlines had a 19 per cent productivity advantage over European airlines and that a sample of East Asian airlines had a 155 per cent productivity advantage over the US.

European airline regulation and economic rent

The ban on new entrants coupled with output predetermination and price collusion by airlines generated surpluses, or rents, for producers above the revenues necessary to supply air services in a free market. Rent is an allocatively unnecessary payment, not required to attract resources to a particular employment; it is a receipt in excess of opportunity cost (Buchanan, 1980).

Economic rents in aviation could have been eroded by competitive tendering for route licenses (Demsetz, 1968). With revenues determined exogenously, competitive tendering would have eroded supernormal profits for efficient carriers, increased productivity, and reduced costs. The rent to airlines from the operation of air services in Europe has a number of alternative uses. It might, for example, result in increased profits, increased pay, reduced productivity or the operation of non-commercial services.

In European aviation, there is evidence that the economic rents of airlines resulted in higher wages for airline employees. Table 2.7 shows that airlines' average wages in 1989 were lower in airlines which faced more competitive markets, such as those serving the United Kingdom. In markets where new entrants

Table 2.7 Average wage per airline, 1989

Region	US$
Europe	
Sabena	36,785
Finnair	30,714
Air Inter	30,269
UTA	45,204
Lufthansa	46,393
KLM	37,869
TAP	24,786
SAS	47,554
Iberia	37,819
Swissair	48,435
British Airways	19,238
British Midland	19,232
Dan Air	25,657
Air UK	16,530
Virgin	17,727
Average (15)	32,280
North America	
American	44,526
US Air	51,176
America West	27,833
Alaska	47,550
Continental	37,094
Delta	54,219
Eastern	50,404
Hawaiian	43,447
Midway	25,336
Northwest	53,681
Pan Am	46,912
TNA	50,075
United	49,836
Average (13)	44,776

are blocked, 'there will be no dissipation of rents … output will not be forced above monopoly limits and price will not fall' (Buchanan, 1980: 7).

In North America, deregulation has brought a two-tier wage structure. Wages in the established airlines reflect economic rents earned before deregulation while the lower wages paid in new airlines, such as America West and Midway, reflect the more competitive deregulated markets. In the established airlines, the two-tier wage structure links the wages of staff recruited since deregulation to those of the new airlines, thus creating a two-tier wage structure.

The OECD (1992) noted that 'a study by Lehman Brothers Kuhn Loeb Research has shown that during the pre-deregulation era in the United States, the combined effect of government intervention in all its forms, permitted labor costs to increase at a rate which, within the productivity gains made possible by technological advances, was far in excess of the market for comparable skills.'

Pricing and cost structures in European airlines

The causes of high European airline costs

Tables 2.8 and 2.9 show two studies of the excess of European costs over North America in 1981 and 1983, based on research by the Civil Aviation Authority (CAA) and the Association of European Airlines (AEA). In the CAA (1983) study, European costs were 98.5 per cent higher than in North America. Five cost headings accounted for almost four-fifths of the excess costs in Europe. These were: sales costs (22.9 per cent); route and landing charges (18.3 per cent); station and ground (13.8 per cent); fuel (13.4 per cent) and crew (11.2 per cent).

In the AEA (1984) study, European costs were 74.0 per cent higher than in North America. Five costs headings also accounted for almost four-fifths of the excess costs in Europe. These were: ticketing, sales and promotion (26.8 per cent); landing and enroute charges (24.2 per cent); station and ground (12.3 per cent); cabin services (9.7 per cent); maintenance and overhaul (9.0 per cent) and aircraft fuel and oil (8.7 per cent).

Higher sales costs were the leading cost difference in both the CAA and AEA studies. Higher sales costs in Europe reflect the lower productivity of sales staff in European airlines. Barrett found that the number of passengers per airline ticketing, sales and promotion staff in Europe in 1984 was only 47 per cent of the North American level (1987: 45). The second most important cost difference in both studies is landing and enroute charges. Since these are services bought by the airlines they will be examined separately later.

Station and ground crew and cabin costs reflect the lower productivity of European airlines. The Association of European Airlines study concluded that 'the result of the significantly different route network, fleet structure and social

Table 2.8 US and European airline cost levels, 1981

Cost item	Local Europe	Passenger cost[a] US$ domestic trunk	European excess cost (cents)	(%)
Crew	0.99	0.47	0.52	11.20
Fuel	1.98	1.36	0.62	13.40
Maintenance	0.80	0.46	0.34	7.30
Depreciation	0.46	0.28	0.18	3.90
Route and landing charges	1.05	0.20	0.85	18.30
Station and ground	1.36	0.72	0.64	13.80
Passenger service	0.50	0.43	0.07	1.50
Sales	1.63	0.61	1.02	22.00
Other	0.58	0.18	0.40	8.60
Total	9.35	4.71	4.64	100.00

Source: Civil Aviation Authority (1983), Table 7.

Note
[a] US cents per seat/kilometre.

Table 2.9 US[a] and European[b] operating costs, 1983

Operational area	Average cost[c] per ATK for 15 AEA airlines	Average cost[c] per ATK for 11 US major airlines	European excess costs (cents)[c]	%
Aircraft fuel and oil	12.8	10.1	2.7	8.7
Maintenance and overhaul	6.7	3.9	2.8	9.0
Landing and enroute charges	8.1	0.6	7.5	24.2
Cabin services	7.3	4.3	3.0	9.7
Station and ground	10.6	6.8	3.8	12.3
Ticketing, sales and promotion	14.9	6.6	8.3	26.8
General and administration	3.1	1.5	1.6	5.2
Unexplained residual[d]	9.4	8.1	1.3	4.2
Total	72.9	41.9	31.0	100

Source: Association of European Airlines, Comparison of Air Transport in Europe and the USA (1984), Table 2.

Notes
[a]US data: CAB Form 41 costs for American, Continental, Delta, Eastern, Northwest, Pan-American, Republic, TWA, United, US Air and Western;
[b]AEA operating data for 1983 for Air France, Finnair, Alitalia, British Airways, AER Lingus, Iberia, KLM, Lufthansa, Olympic Airways, Austrian Airlines, SAS, Sabena, Swiss Air, Turkish Airlines and TAP-Air Portugal;
[c]US cent;
[d]not examined in AEA study.

environment in the USA compared to Europe is a system-wide rate of personnel productivity, measured in available ton-kilometers per employee, almost twice that achieved by AEA airlines' (1984: 13). Fuel costs per litre in Europe in 1987 were 114 per cent of those in North America (Doganis, 1992: 138). Fuel costs per passenger-kilometre are also a function of the aircraft type used.

Airport and enroute charges

These charges account for a quarter of the cost difference between North American and European airlines according to the AEA and slightly under a fifth in the CAA study. Graham estimates that the average airport cost per WLU (work load unit) in North America in 1989–90 was $3.86 compared to $11.37 in Europe (1992: 201). Table 2.10 breaks down these costs and shows that labour costs are the chief source of extra costs in Europe.

The cost differences between North American and European airports reflect the different ways in which airports are managed and financed. Many airport facilities in the US are built and managed by the airlines themselves. US airports raise a higher proportion of their incomes from concessions for commercial activities such as shops, car parks and car rental desks. Since their customers, the airlines, did not engage in price competition in the past, European airports have had less market incentive to control and reduce costs. Higher airport charges to airlines

Table 2.10 Airport costs in North America and Europe, 1989/90

Cost item	Europe	North America	Index
Staff	4.77	0.85	561
Other operating costs	3.87	1.31	295
Capital	2.73	1.70	135
Total	11.37	3.86	295

Source: Graham (1992: 201).

Notes
US$ per WLU (work load unit).

were easily recouped in higher airline fares where airlines did not engage in price competition.

Dismantling protectionism in European aviation

Three major barriers to competition in European aviation have been in place for almost 50 years. These are the bans on new entrants, price competition and capacity competition. In addition, the industry has many anti-competitive practices which restrict the possibility of competition even if the major barriers were removed.

The Compass Report (1981) by the European Civil Aviation Conference revealed the lack of competition in European aviation. Only 2 per cent of routes had more than one airline operating per state. On 93 per cent of routes there were limitations on the number of flights per airline. Up to 85 per cent of ton-kilometres were performed under revenue-sharing arrangements.

In the first phase of EC liberalisation in December 1987, market access for new airlines was increased by provision for multiple designation of carriers on routes with 250,000 or more passengers. As of 1 January 1993, any EC airlines may operate any international route in the EC. Full access to air markets within other member states will be permitted in April 1997. Fares charged are to be decided by the airline from January 1993, subject to intervention by the EC and Member States in cases of excessive fares or predatory pricing. The 1987 policy reducing the safety net market share to 40 per cent for the protection of weaker airline is abolished in the 1993 policy.

The results of EC liberalisation measures have been limited. Airlines have successfully held the high unrestricted fares that they traditionally charged. Sorensen (1991), reviewing the period 1987–9, states that 'the take-off point for real competition has not yet been reached'. Doganis (1992) also doubted that there would be real competition in European aviation because of infrastructure deficiencies at airports and in air traffic control, the likely dominance of the market by the larger European airlines, and the inability of liberal national regimes (in aviation) to transfer their policies to conservative states. Pryke (1991) stated that 'if liberalization is not to turn out a monopolistic damp squib, it is vital that governments and the EC should do everything possible to foster competition

Table 2.11 Barriers to contestability in a deregulated
European aviation industry

Structural	Strategic
Hub airport dominance	Mergers
Ground handling monopolies	Pricing policy
Computer reservation systems	Frequent flyer programmes
CRS bias	State aids

and make airline routes as contestable as possible'. Therefore, serious obstacles remain to a fully competitive aviation market in Europe. These are shown in Table 2.11.

Hub airport dominance

Hub airport dominance is the control of major airports by incumbent airlines via restriction or exclusion of new entrants. The allocation of airport slots is controlled by committees of airlines rather than by airport management. Allocations are made on a grandfather rights system and new airlines may be allocated slots at unsuitable times or be excluded from hub airports. This occurred at Heathrow between 1977 and 1991. All of the increase in passengers (from 22 to 40 million) was allocated to the incumbent airlines by administrative decision.

It has also proved difficult to promote both new airlines and new airports, such as Luton, Stansted or London City, which in 1989 attracted only 6 per cent of air passengers in the London area compared to 61 per cent using Heathrow and 33 per cent using Gatwick. Airlines lose the possibility of attracting interlining traffic at the hub. It may also be difficult to develop surface transport links between city centres and smaller airports.

Established airlines can earn economic rents at the hub airports in their control. These rents may be used to fund predatory pricing elsewhere. To tackle the problem of hub airport dominance, Bailey and Williams (1988) recommended that 'airport authorities need to make airport access available on fair and reasonable terms that give all carriers an equal opportunity to compete and that conform to the rights of private citizens to enforce these duties. Antitrust authorities need to look at carriers' abilities to extract rents based on local monopoly positions at hub airports, not just at national monopoly characteristics.'

The first step in ensuring the efficient allocation of airport capacity between established and new entrant airlines is to transfer the slot allocation function from scheduling committees of established airlines to airport management, thus ending the grandfather rights of established airlines. Slots could also be allocated by:

• buying and selling slots with and without grandfather rights,
• slot lotteries,

- slot lotteries with ring fences for categories such as regional services, new entrant airlines, or other target categories and
- administrative allocations of current capacity.

The attraction of selling slots would be the allocation of these slots to more efficient users. For example, Heathrow and Gatwick had 31,000 general aviation movements in 1984. If a market transferred these to airlines carrying 100 passengers per plane, an extra 3.1 million passengers could have been handled.

Slot auctions would, however, place low-cost airlines in competitive markets at a disadvantage compared to airlines operating in monopolistic markets. The auction system would also give airport management the incentive not to invest in extra airport capacity where it might drive down the price of the slots at auction. Slot lotteries would distribute airport capacity in a random way between established and new entrant airlines. Constraints on the randomness, such as a share for new airlines, domestic feeder services, or particular international services, could be imposed.

Administrative intervention to allocate airport capacity has included the removal of charter airlines from busy airports, removal of small domestic services with low interline content, curbing general aviation and capping the frequency of services on a route per carrier.

In 1992, American and United Airlines acquired the slots of Pan Am and TWA at London Heathrow. The UK government allocated slots at Heathrow to Virgin Atlantic, thus eroding the advantage enjoyed by British Airways when Virgin operated from Gatwick. In the liberalisation of UK–Ireland services, the competitive position of Ryanair was improved by the allocation of slots at Stansted instead of Luton because of easier surface access and more interlining traffic at Stansted. Nonetheless, the carriers with Heathrow access, Aer Lingus and British Midland, enjoy a considerable market advantage in attracting business traffic. Airlines with grandfather rights regard slot reallocations as confiscation. In economic terms, the airlines are the customers for, rather than the owners of, airports slots.

Ground handling monopolies

Aircraft and passenger handling costs accounted for 12.2 per cent of total airline costs in the EC in 1984. These services are typically provided by authorised airlines only. Since the authorisations are frequently restricted, a new entrant airline may face the prospect of having its ground handling carried out by a competing airline. The option of self-handling requires that a new airline has a sufficient scale of market entry to justify investment in ground handling equipment and staff.

An example of problems facing airlines in this area is the case of British Midland at Heathrow. In providing evidence to the Monopolies and Mergers Commission (1985) the airline stated that

from its experience of handling at Birmingham, it thinks that it could have provided the services itself at just over half the amount paid … It believes that this difference is a substantial element in its competitiveness, and that it should be able to pass on the benefits of lower handling charges to its customers.

An open market in handling at airports should be permitted. The Monopolies and Mergers Commission (1985) proposed that 'any airline without rights to handle its own traffic has a choice of at least two handlers neither of whom is an airline with which it is in direct competition'. This falls short of a full competitive market. The avoidance 'of unnecessary duplication of share and handling facilities' is the case made against competition. The case is weak because the number of ground vehicles required to handle each aircraft will not necessarily change and competition will increase the overall efficiency of the system. Parking areas for vehicles not in use could be financed by a type of 'road tax' on such vehicles.

Ground handling in Europe varies from monopolies to duopolies and more competitive arrangements. It is currently under examination by the Competition Policy Directorate of the EC. An illustration of the problems remaining in the area is the award, in 1992, by the Spanish Government of a seven-year monopoly at all Spanish airports to Iberia. In 1993, the Competition Policy Directorate of the EC began an investigation of ground handling under Article 90 of the Treaty of Rome.

Computer reservation systems (CRS)

Travel agencies use CRS to access information from airlines on flights and fares available and to make reservations. Since deregulation in the United States, the proportion of seats sold through travel agents has increased from 50 to 80 per cent (Borenstein, 1988). An airline owning a CRS can use it to supply information biased in its favour. It may also earn economic rents for use of the CRS by other airlines. Saunders (1985: 176) found that 'the return on investment for a CRS ranges from 24 per cent to 95 per cent'. Despite attempts to achieve neutrality in the presentation of CRS information by the US Civil Aeronautics Board in 1984, complaints have continued (OECD, 1988).

The EC regulations for CRS require neutrality in their operation. CRS vendors must rank flights by departure or arrival time for non-stop direct flights; for non-direct flights, they must add the elapsed journey time for stopping and for connecting flights by order of departure or arrival time and/or elapsed journey time. Fees are to be non-discriminatory and cost-related. There is to be no discrimination on the basis of different airports serving the same city.

The EC code of conduct for CRS is policed by an Article 85.3 exemption from the Treaty of Rome. The CRS owners would risk loss of this exemption by a breach of the code of conduct. In addition to EC protection for the consumer, it is important that there be two CRSs in Europe. Pelkmans (1991) notes that 'the new CRSs are owned by groups of airlines and hence would not seem to generate problems of market power (via control of information about competitors) as might be the case in the United States'. In early 1993, however, British Airways admitted that it had used CRS access to approach the customers of Virgin Atlantic. Stricter safeguards or divestiture may be required in order to ensure contestability.

Mergers and concentrations

The tradition of price collusion among Europe's national airlines means that new market entrants have a vital role in increasing the contestability of European aviation. In recent years, however, national airlines have increased their share of home markets by absorbing their domestic rivals. Borenstein (1992: 58) found that in the US, 'the short run welfare effect of mergers between direct competitors was probably significantly negative'.

The acquisition of UTA and Air Inter by Air France in 1989 reduced the independent airlines to 3 per cent of scheduled aviation performed by French airlines. UTA had been refused permission by the French government to operate European services. The contestability of European aviation was thus reduced by removing two independent airlines, potential entrants to international routes currently operated only by colluding national airlines. Within France, Air France had total dominance over its remaining small competitors on busy routes such as Paris–Nice. Airlines from other countries will thus find it difficult to enter the French market when the right of cabotage within France is opened up under the third EC liberalisation package.

There are several other examples of increasing mergers and concentration in European aviation. KLM acquired an 80 per cent controlling interest in Transavia; the contestability of the market was further reduced when Air Holland collapsed. In Belgium, TEA collapsed. In Britain, British Caledonian (1987), Air Europe (1991) and Dan Air (1992) have left the market, thus increasing the dominance of British Airways. In Germany, the collapse of German Wings in May 1990 gave Lufthansa a 98 per cent share of German aviation. The remaining German independent airlines are confined to small regional services and charter routes. In Scandinavia, the SAS takeover of Linjeflyg in 1992 reduced contestability. However, potential competitors such as Maersk, Transwede and Sterling remain.

Pricing policy

Airlines with large networks can selectively lower fares in response to new market entry and raise fares on uncontested routes. Kahn describes this process in the case of Capitol Airways as follows:

> I take perverse satisfaction in having predicted the demise of price-cutting competitors like Capitol Airways if we did nothing to limit the predictable geographically discriminatory response of the incumbent carriers to their entry, and in having rejected the conventional wisdom that predation would not pay because any attempt to raise fares after the departure of the price-cutting newcomers would elicit instantaneous competitive re-entry. (1988: 319)

Europe also provides examples of geographically discriminatory responses of incumbent airlines to new market entrants. The European Commission (1989) found that while the average economy fare between Dublin and major European cities other than London increased by 3 per cent between 1987 and 1989, the London fare declined to 51.9 per cent of the 1987 level. The Dublin–London route had new market entrants while the other routes did not.

The EC liberalisation package of 1992 gives the Commission powers to investigate fares which are either too high or too low. The former provision seeks to protect the consumer while the latter examines cases where pricing is predatory in order to eliminate a low-cost producer from the market. A study prepared for the Commission found that 'there have not been detailed formal investigations of predation in the airline industry' (Dodgson *et al.*, 1991).

Frequent flyer programmes

Frequent flyer programmes give passengers free air mileage or other gifts. Airlines with a large route network enjoy an advantage over smaller airlines. Frequent flyer programmes are thus a barrier to entry. Humphreys (1991) notes that

> a passenger maximises his benefits by concentrating his flying on a single airline, thereby increasing the difficulties of a new entrant in competing with a price-matching incumbent. Incumbent airlines can also vary the bonus awards, for example by increasing them on routes operated by a new entrant, or even before a new entrant starts a service.

Levine (1987) proposes that the frequent flyer programme benefits be treated as taxable income of the recipients. He states that 'it is difficult to defend as efficient those practices which reward undisclosed distortion of choices by agents at the expense of principals. The principal risk is intervening to control them in a way that does more harm than good. Regulating these programmes in detail would entangle the regulatory agency in a morass of complicated marketing decisions about which it possesses little information.' There are at present no EC plans to regulate frequent flyer programmes.

State aid

Two schemes of state assistance for national airlines has been approved by the EC in 1991–2. These include US$2 billion aid for Sabena from the Belgian government and US$2 billion for Air France from the French government. The EC is also examining a US$1.2 billion recapitalisation of Iberia while Aer Lingus has also sought assistance.

Subsidies to state aviation companies distort competition between the recipient and non-recipient state and private sector airlines. The subsidies to state airlines have supported the economic rents of producers. Lower cost airlines are placed at a competitive disadvantage compared to the assisted airlines. The protection of state airlines from the consequences of mistakes in investment, labour policies, pricing and resource allocation, reduces overall economic efficiency.

The gains from liberalising European aviation

The large margin between scheduled air fares in Europe and the world average indicates significant potential gains from liberalising the market. The first major liberalisation was the UK–Netherlands market in 1984. Doganis found that 'on London–Amsterdam the club and economy fares were only marginally higher than they had been in 1983 before deregulation. This means that in real or constant value terms they actually declined' (1992: 104). He also noted 'a dramatic proliferation of low promotional fares'. In 1983 the lowest promotional fare was £82 return and there were only three other reduced fares available. By 1989 there were around 30 fares, and the cheapest return fare was £62. In 1986 the Ireland–UK routes were deregulated. Average yields dropped by a third.

Traffic on Dublin–London grew only 2.9 per cent between 1980 and 1985 but doubled between 1986 and 1988 (Barrett, 1990, 1992). Significant new traffic was generated and about 6 per cent of the growth was at the expense of sea carriers. Elsewhere in Europe, road and rail transport are strong competitors with the airlines. Doganis feels that 'it is unlikely that deregulation elsewhere in Europe will have such a profound effect as the doubling of traffic in two years' (1992: 105).

EFTA countries

The European Civil Aviation Conference (ECAC) incorporates both the EC and EFTA states. As of 1987, the EFTA states have participated in ECAC agreements to liberalise capacity and fare-filing arrangements. They also participated in the ECAC code of conduct for CRS. The EFTA states also sought negotiations with the EC to have the 1987 package of reforms applied to EFTA as well in 1993.

Switzerland and Austria have obvious geographical reasons for wanting to participate in EC liberalisation. Since SAS is jointly owned by Denmark (an EC member), Sweden and Norway, these countries also wish to be associated with the development of EC policy.

Sweden deregulated domestic routes in 1992, with a 30 per cent fall in fares on the Stockholm–Malmo route and a 15 per cent increase in passenger numbers. The domestic Swedish monopoly of SAS and Linejflyg was broken by domestic competitors such as Transwede, Malmo Aviation and City Air Scandinavia. Early in 1992, SAS bought 50 per cent of Linjeflyg for US$50.2 million. Norway's domestic market is shared between SAS and Braathens. As SAS has high labour costs, the liberalisation of the Copenhagen–Stockholm–Oslo routes in 1993 will put pressure on it from both domestic and Scandinavian rivals and other lower cost EC airlines. Swissair, Finnair, Austrian Airlines and Icelandair are also high cost producers who faced increasing competition after 1993.

European charter airlines

Charter airlines in Europe developed in a less rigid regulatory regime because of the wish of some countries to develop their tourism sector. Charter airlines have traditionally charged fares of about one-third of scheduled airlines and have served mainly the Mediterranean basin. In 1986, 18.8 million people flew from Britain to Spain, Portugal, Italy and Greece. The charter share was 78 per cent, ranging from 52 per cent on the Italian routes to 90 per cent between Britain and Spain. The market success of charter airlines is based on high load factors, high productivity and aircraft utilisation. Doganis notes that the charter airline Monarch 'got more than twice as many flying hours out of its Boeing 757s than British Airways did' (1992: 182).

There are also large savings in ticketing, sales and promotion costs. Rather than operate expensive retailing offices and travel agents, charter airlines sell to tour operators. The Civil Aviation Authority data for 1988 show ticketing sales and promotion costs per passenger of £28.33 for British Airways, £6.09 for British Midland and 18 pence for the charter airline Monarch.

Charter airlines fill 85 per cent of their seats as compared with only 65 per cent for scheduled. Charter airlines have 15–25 per cent more seats than scheduled airlines operating the same aircraft. Charter airlines also generate higher duty free sales per passenger than scheduled airlines.

The cascade studies examined cost differences between scheduled and charter airlines. Table 2.12 shows the steps in a cascade study. Table 2.13 shows the cascade analysis for British Airways and a UK charter airline in 1975–6. The studies deduct the various components of the scheduled air fare from the cost

Table 2.12 Basic steps in a cascade study

Step	Description
1. Sales commission	These costs are not relevant to the charter service and are thus deducted.
2. Tourist class	A first class service does not exist on charter flights and the effects are eliminated.
3. Seating density	Allowance is made for the different seating pitch in scheduled and charter flights.
4. Load factor	Account is taken of the effect of increasing the passenger load factor from 55 per cent for scheduled services to 85 per cent, which is typical for charter operations.
5. Peak–trough ratio	Charter airlines have a larger seasonal variation in passenger numbers and allowance is made for their resulting higher costs.
6. Utilization	Charter services are assumed to be able to achieve 25 per cent higher utilization of both crew and aircraft than scheduled airlines and appropriate adjustments are made.
7. Standards	Account is taken of the costs attributable to the higher standard of service provided by the scheduled airline.
8. Not applicable	Adjustment of those costs and revenues that occur for scheduled services but not for charter ones. These relate to two main areas: sales, reservations and advertising costs, and cargo revenue and bar profit.

Source: European Commission, Scheduled Passenger Air Fares in the EEC (1981: 42–7).

Table 2.13 British Airways cascade analysis[a]

Cascade steps	Route A	Route B	Route C
Total scheduled cost per passenger	100	100	100
1. Deduct commission	92	92	91
2. Tourist class	86	84	87
3. Seating density	77	80	83
4. Load factor	56	59	60
5. Peak–trough ratio	60	62	63
6. Utilization	57	60	61
7. Standards	51	51	53
8. Not applicable	36	37	39
Derived charter	36	37	39
Actual charter	34–37	32	35

Source: European Commission, Scheduled Passenger Air Fares in the EEC (1981: 42–7).

Note

[a] The table indicates the reductions in cost in each step of moving from the cost of scheduled to charter aviation.

differences between the scheduled and charter airlines. Table 2.13 shows that by adjusting down the services of the scheduled airlines they could produce a charter-type product at a cost broadly comparable with the actual cost of charter airlines.

The scheduled airlines have used the cascade studies to support the case that there are no significant efficiency differences between scheduled and charter airlines which cannot be explained by differences in the two types of product; that is, scheduled and charter flights. Other interpretations of the cascade studies have raised issues such as why the scheduled airlines have not produced the charter product given the greater profitability of charter than scheduled airlines. The claimed extra costs of scheduled services may also be due to the lack of price competition among providers of the services. Sales, reservations and marketing costs may be high because of non-price competition. Unbundling the items in the cascade study and selling them separately would test the market to see if passengers wish to trade the purported benefits of scheduled aviation in the cascade study in return for lower fares.

Charter airlines in a deregulated market

The existence in Europe of a large charter airline sector operating in a high cost environment but charging fares only a third of the scheduled airlines is an important source of potential contestability. The competitive impact of the charter airlines is reduced, however, by their lack of experience of scheduled aviation on the major routes in Northern Europe, where the potential gains from competition are greatest. The charter airlines would have to develop marketing networks to match those of the scheduled airlines. They require access to slots at hub airports.

While the regulatory distinction between scheduled and charter airlines has been blurred by the introduction of group inclusive fares on scheduled services and 'seat only' fares on charter services, in general, the movement of charter airlines into scheduled aviation has not been a success. World Airways failed in the US in 1986; Air Europe and Dan Air failed in 1990 and in 1992. Britannia discontinued its limited scheduled services in 1990 in order to concentrate on its extensive charter network. While the scheduled and charter airlines appear unlikely to compete directly on the main scheduled routes, the extent of the competition between them depends on the development of pro-contestability policies by European regulatory authorities after deregulation.

Eastern Europe

The major airlines in Eastern European are Aeroflot International (Russia), Balkan Bulgarian (Bulgaria), CSA (Czechoslovakia), Malev (Hungary), LOT (Poland) and Tarom (Romania). Eastern European airlines in general have a significant opportunity for growth because of their cost advantage over Western European airlines, due to markedly lower wage costs. Eastern European airline salaries average US$4,000 as compared with $53,000 for employees of Western European airlines. The former would save $268 million a year over a Western counterpart assuming a common work force of 5,000 (*Airline Business*, June 1992: 71).

However, there are also significant problems facing Eastern European airlines. These consist mainly of (1) a lack of hard currency and/or a Western partner; (2) ageing fleets, as many of their aircraft were made in the former USSR; (3) a need to upgrade services in the air and on the ground, including airport terminals and (4) low airline staff productivity when compared with the West. To illustrate the opportunities and problems facing Eastern European airlines, the airlines operating in the former USSR and Hungary are contrasting case studies. Of the 10,000 jet aircraft in service worldwide in 1988, almost 2,000 were Soviet built and used for domestic flights within the former Soviet Union. Aeroflot had a monopoly on all air traffic operations within the former USSR and had over 400,000 employees. It handled almost 125 million passengers in 1988 (Economist Intelligence Unit, 1990: 109). Table 2.14 shows details of Aeroflot operations in 1988, and Table 2.15 shows the traffic output and fleet data for seven East European airlines in 1988.

Aeroflot's monopoly has been broken up with almost 70 registered airlines in its place, all of them laying claim to former Aeroflot assets. Among these are Air Russia, Russian International Airlines and Golden Stars. However, there still remains a quasi-monopoly with over 40 of these new airlines owned by official Russian structures such as the Ministry of Transport. In addition, not all of the newly independent airlines have their own aircraft (*Airline Business*, May 1992: 28).

Foreign partners are needed by airlines in the former Soviet Union to provide capital, services and marketing experience. In addition, demand is expected to

Table 2.14 Aeroflot operations, 1989

	International	*Domestic*	*Total*
Passengers (million)	4.3	127.3	131.6
Revenue pass.-km (billion)	16.6	211.1	227.7
Available seat-km (billion)	23.0	237.8	260.8
Passenger load factor (%)	72.0	88.8	87.3
Freight tons (000)	68.0	3,162.0	3,230.0
Available ton-km (billion)	2.7	30.7	33.4
Revenue ton-km (billion)	1.9	21.8	23.7

Table 2.15 East European airlines, 1988

Country	*Airline*	*Pass.-km (mn)*	*Employees (no.)*	*Jet aircraft (no.)*
Bulgaria	Balkan	2,279	3,954	48
Czechoslovakia	CSA	2,242	5,675	32
East Germany	Interflug[a]	1.6	7,500	32
Hungary	Malev	1,178	4,595	22
Poland	LOT	2,701	6,067	29
Romania	Tarom	1,669	3,250	32
USSR	Aeroflot	213,192	400,000	1,910

Source: Wheatcroft and Lipman (1990).

Note
[a] 1.6 million passengers.

rise by around 20 million a year for domestic and international passenger services (*Airline Business*, January 1991: 44). The shortage of hard currency is further exacerbated by the fact that ruble-paying citizens travelling abroad and connecting with foreign carrier services must be paid for by Aeroflot in hard currency.

Provisional figures filed with IATA in 1989 show that Aeroflot made net profits of US$19.4 million on revenues of $1,884 million on international services only. However, in order to build up revenues from foreign services, the airlines must improve their image among westerners in terms of quality of service.

Most of the former regional Aeroflot divisions have little hard currency to invest in their operations. Because of this, they are hampered in attempting to secure foreign investment and it is likely that some of these independents will fold. In addition, poor management and lack of infrastructure have made these carriers unattractive investments.

In contrast to Aeroflot, the Hungarian airline Malev is proving to be an attractive investment for Western airlines. It has been in profit since 1988 and is now less dependent on Eastern European revenues, having restructured its network to tap into the more profitable markets within the EC. Malev's situation is helped by Hungary's relative economic development. In addition, Budapest is a convenient geographical regional hub. At the end of 1992, the airline had proposals from five potential partners. KLM wished to buy a 30 per cent stake in the airline. Malev planned to sell 19 per cent of its equity directly to private investors on the Stock Exchange, with Government and employees holding the remaining 51 per cent. A partner would help Malev expand into long-haul flight operations (to New York and Seoul) and, in addition, enable it to get support from the European Bank for Regional Development. CSA had developed a similar link with Air France in early 1992 with assistance from the European Bank for Reconstruction and Development.

Because the Eastern European market collapsed and Malev had to focus on Western markets, traffic declined, with revenue-passenger-kilometres (RPKs) falling from 1.63 billion to 1.23 billion between 1990 and 1991. In addition, passenger numbers dropped to 1.04 million from 1.47 million (*Airline Business*, May 1992: 57). However, a five-fold increase in local currency fares and a rise in hard currency revenues saw sales increase from $211.5 million to $289.4 million. Pre-tax profits rose from $21.7 million to $26.5 million in 1991. Part of Malev's success can be put down to the fact that Western aircraft make up 46 per cent of its capacity. It has also made advances in terms of its services. It introduced business class on intra-European flights and extended its frequent flyer program to include foreign passengers. Malev has increased the Western European share of its capacity from 66 per cent in 1989 to 91 per cent in 1992.

CSA, LOT and Balkan Bulgarian are adopting a three-pronged development approach similar to that of Malev. This involves (1) seeking a partner, (2) developing an Eastern European hub and (3) expansion of long haul services. However, some analysts have pointed to declining yields in Western Europe as one potential difficulty with this strategy (*Airline Business*, May 1992: 59). Another problem, referred to earlier, is that of the need to replace older aircraft within these fleets. FitzGerald estimated that Eastern European countries (excluding the former Soviet Union) would require at least 300–450 Western aircraft during this decade (Economist Intelligence Unit: 167). However, early currency convertibility has helped carriers to restructure their fleets. This makes these airlines more attractive propositions for foreign investors.

Liberalisation of European and world aviation

Europe has the highest scheduled air fares in the world and a tradition of non-competing high-cost national airlines. While the EC has taken steps to liberalise market access, price competition and capacity competition, the gains have been minimal apart from markets such as UK–Netherlands and UK–Ireland. Europe's low-cost charter airlines are likely to confine their operations to holiday sun destinations.

New airlines in Europe face an array of obstacles to market entry such as control of hub airports by incumbent airlines, predatory pricing, state aid to national airlines, control of CRS by incumbents, and frequent flyer programs which favour large airlines. In addition, several potential independent competing airlines, such as UTA, Air Inter, Transavia, Air Europe, British Caledonian, Dan Air, TEA and

German Wings, have left the market either through takeover or liquidation. The loss of these potential competitors has concentrated aviation around the national carrier in most European countries. National airlines have not yet competed with one another. If such competition were to occur, the loss of the independent airlines would be a less serious obstacle to contestability.

The application of EC liberalisation policies to the EFTA states after 1993 is unlikely to produce major changes. The EC and EFTA states have traditionally had close aviation links. The EFTA airlines have had high costs but liberalisation in Sweden may have some restraining effect.

Eastern European airlines presently have a substantial labour cost advantage over Western Europe. Liberalisation of the total European market would present significant market opportunities for Eastern European airlines to become exporters of air transport with low fares based on low labour costs. The cost advantage would face erosion over time as Eastern Europe's airline staff sought wages and conditions now enjoyed in Western Europe. The cost advantage would also face erosion by EC policies of labour market harmonisation such as is mentioned in the Social Chapter of the Maastricht Treaty.

The inclusion of services such as aviation, telecommunications, shipping, banking and insurance in future GATT rounds has been proposed by the United States, whose economy is dominated by the service sector. Aviation has traditionally been treated as a special case in international trade but the sector's argument that it differs from other international trade enjoys declining support. Widening the scope of international trade negotiations to include services such as aviation increases the potential gains from trade liberalisation. Whereas in sectoral negotiations the potential loser or high cost producer seeks some compensating gains within that sector, trade negotiations across several sectors allow for compensation elsewhere in the economy in sectors where the country has a comparative advantage.

Europe's high-cost aviation sector is unlikely to change as a result of EC and EFTA liberalisations. The impact of new low-cost airlines and charter airlines is likely to be diluted by the structural and strategic obstacles to contestability. While a potential source of competition exists in Eastern Europe, this may also be reduced by factors such as general economic difficulties there. There are fears that a 'fortress Europe' policy might emerge to defend Europe's high-cost airlines from outside competition.

The main sources of such competition are North American and Asia-Pacific airlines. The latter enjoy a substantial cost advantage over European airlines and a reputation in many cases for high service standards. Their home market is the fastest growth area in world aviation and will exceed Europe by 2000. The overall efficiency of European aviation would be increased by competition from North American and Asia-Pacific airlines. A potential free-trade area in aviation could combine both the European market and the North American Free Trade Area of the United States, Canada and Mexico. This would allow North American airlines to develop their limited fifth freedom services within Europe on a fully competitive basis. It would allow European airlines the market access to routes within North America which they have frequently sought. However, Europe's greatest cost disadvantage in aviation is with the Asia-Pacific airlines.

Global airlines are likely to replace airlines identified with one country. Transnational corporations have achieved dominance in many sectors of the world economy but historically there have been few in aviation. The exceptions were SAS, which is jointly owned by Norway, Sweden and Denmark and Air Afrique, which is owned by ten African states.

The adoption of policies of deregulation and privatisation in the late 1970s and 1980s brought acceptance of foreign ownership of airlines. For example, SAS acquired 24 per cent of Airlines of Britain, which includes British Midland. KLM acquired 14.9 per cent of Air UK which feeds its Amsterdam hub from many points in Britain.

The movement towards a multilateral rather than bilateral regulatory system for aviation has also weakened the identification of airlines with individual countries. In late 1992, British Airways acquired 35 per cent of Qantas in its privatisation by the Australian government. It also unsuccessfully sought a 44 per cent stake in US Air. The maximum permitted share of foreign ownership of US airlines has increased from 24 to 49 per cent in 1992. BA also had stakes in Air Russia, Deutsche BA and TAT (France).

In addition to acquiring a stake in overseas airlines, global alliances have been formed by agreements between airlines. For example, SAS formed an alliance with Continental, Thai International, All Nikon, Canadian, LAN Chile. Lufthansa, Air France and Iberia also have an alliance, and Air France acquired a stake in Sabena. Delta has an alliance with Swissair and Singapore Airlines and KLM has an alliance with Northwest.

Conclusion

Europe's high-cost airlines have enjoyed protection from competition for many decades. However, market liberalisation and the change to multilateral rather than bilateral aviation agreements are increasing market pressures on the protected airlines. In addition, the privatisation of airlines has paved the way for globalisation, when airlines will no longer be identified with a single country. The advantages of the global airline lie in marketing and the ability to survive setbacks in particular markets.

However, there are still many barriers to contestability remaining in European aviation. The most serious of these are the control of airport slots at Europe's major airports and the use of geographical price discrimination against new market entrants. Barriers to new entrants in European aviation should be a focus for EC competition policy. New market entry is important because Europe's national airlines have traditionally not been willing to compete with other national airlines.

In the evolving regulatory framework towards free trade, the EC market will be among the first to be liberalised. The potential efficiency gains are large given the high fares charged and the economic rents earned by producers under protectionist policies. The addition of the EFTA countries to this area of free trade is unlikely to have significant price implications because the EFTA airlines also have high costs. Europe's charter airlines have achieved major cost savings over scheduled airlines but appear likely to concentrate on their traditional inclusive tour market. Eastern European airlines have major potential labour cost savings over those in Western Europe. A full free-trade area in aviation throughout Europe offers Eastern Europe airlines important market opportunities in the short and medium term until their costs approach those in Western Europe. A free-trade area in aviation between all of Europe and the North American Free Trade Area of the USA, Canada and Mexico would achieve the long-sought goal of European airlines operating within North America. It would also protect consumers from a fortress Europe policy. In a global free-trade market in aviation, the market leaders are likely to be the Asia-Pacific airlines, which at present have significant cost and standard of service advantages over European airlines. There will be strong market pressures on the airlines in a Unified Europe to meet the service and price standards of the Asia-Pacific region airlines.

In facing competitive pressures, European airlines will not be able to rely on government intervention to the degree enjoyed in the past. The most profitable large European airlines, such as British Airways, are likely to become global airlines. Smaller national airlines, accustomed to protection and state subsidy, are likely to be absorbed by larger airlines in a liberalised market. Independent airlines will seek market niches where they can survive in the presence of large multinational airlines. In an aviation world of liberalisation, privatisation and globalisation, many of the instruments and targets of market regulators will be subject to changes even more revolutionary than those facing the airlines.

References

Association of European Airlines (1984) *Comparison of Air Transport in Europe and the USA*. ABA: Brussels.

Bailey, E.E. and Williams, J. (1988) Sources of rent in the deregulated airline industry, *Journal of Law and Economics* 31: 173–202.

Barrett, S. (1987) *Flying High: Airline Prices and European Regulation*. Avebury: Aldershot.

Barrett, S. (1990) Deregulating European aviation – a case study, *Transportation* 16: 311–27.

Barrett, S. (1992) Barriers to contestability in the deregulated European aviation market, *Transportation Research A* 26A: 159–65.

Borenstein, S. (1988) The competitive advantage of a dominant airline. Discussion paper no. 280, Institute of Public Policy Studies, Ann Arbor: University of Michigan.

Borenstein, S. (1992) The evolution of U.S. airline competition, *Journal of Economic Perspectives* 6: 45–53.

Buchanan, J. (1980) Rent seeking and profit seeking, in *Toward a Theory of the Rent Seeking Society*. College Station, TX: A&M University Press.

Civil Aviation Administration (1983) A comparison between European and United States air fares. Paper no. 83006, London: Civil Aviation Administration.

Demsetz, H. (1968) Why regulate utilities?, *Journal of Law and Economics* 11: 55–65.

Dodgson, J., Katsuoulacos, Y. and Pryke, R. (1991) *Predatory Behaviour in Aviation*, Brussels: Competition Directorate of the European Communities.

Doganis, R. (1992) *Flying Off Course*. London: Routledge.

European Commission (1989) *Report on the First Year (1988) of the Implementation of the Aviation Policy Approved in December 1987*. European Commission, COM (89) 476.

European Civil Aviation Conference (1981) *Report of the Task Force Oil Competition in Intra-European Air Services (The Compass Report)*. Paris: ECAC.

Economist Intelligence Unit (1990) *European Liberalization and World Air Transport*, in Wheatcroft, S. and Lipman, G. (eds). London: Economist Intelligence Unit.

Graham, A. (1992) Airports in the United States, in Doganis, R. (ed.), *The Airport Business*. London: Routledge.

Humphreys, B. (1991) Frequent flyer programs, *Avmark Aviation Economist* 8: 12–15.

Kahn, A. (1988) Surprises of airline deregulation, *American Economic Review* 78: 316–22.

Levine, M. (1987) Airline competition in deregulated markets: theory, firm strategy and public policy, *Yale Journal of Regulation* 4: 394–494.

Monopolies and Mergers Commission (1985) *The British Airports Authority*. CMND.9644, London: Monopolies and Mergers Commission.

OECD (1988) *Deregulation and Airline Competition*. Paris: OECD.

OECD (1992) Forum for the future, in *New Policy Approaches to International Air Transport*, Paris: OECD.

Pelkmans, I. (1991) The internal EC market for air transport, in Banister, D. and Bunon. K. (eds), *Transport in a Free Market Economy*. London: Macmillan.

Pryke, R. (1991) American deregulation and European liberalization, in Banister, D. and Bunon, K. (eds), *Transport in a Free Market Economy*. London: Macmillan.

Saunders, D. (1985) The antitrust implications of computer reservation systems, *Journal of Air Law and Commerce* 51: 157–96.

Sorensen, F. (1991) The changing aviation scene in Europe, in Banister, D. and Button, K. (eds) *Transport in a Free Market Economy*. London: Macmillan.

Wheatcroft, S. and Lipman, G. (1990) *European Liberalisation and World Air Transport*, London: Economist Intelligence Unit.

Windle, R. (1991) The world's airlines. A cost and productivity comparison, *Journal of Transport Economics and Policy* 25: 31–50.

3 Deregulating the Dublin–London route

(I) The implications of the Ireland–UK airline deregulation for an EU internal market

> It is appropriate to announce now that I have approved in principle a new air service from Dublin to Luton, costing £99.
>
> (Minister for Communications, Parliamentary Debates,
> 4 December 1985, Vol. 352, Col. 1052)

The deregulation of air transport between Ireland and Britain was announced during a parliamentary debate on the Air Transport Bill 1984 (Government of Ireland, 1984) measure to impose penalties on those discounting airline tickets. The Irish government had sought in the High Court to prevent Trans America Airlines and travel agents from selling tickets for travel between Ireland and the United States at less than the price approved by the Minister for Communications. The High Court found that the Air Transport and Navigation Act 1965, which gave the Minister power to control air fares did not apply to travel agents (High Court decision 1984 No. 2762, 9 April 1984). The High Court granted the injunction against Trans America Airlines. The Supreme Court subsequently upheld the appeal of Trans America Airlines against the High Court injunction restraining the airline from selling tickets for travel between Ireland and the United States at less than the price approved by the Minister. Whether the airline was in breach of the law would have to be determined by trial rather than injunction.

The government introduced the Air Transport Bill 1984 to Parliament on 27 June 1984 in order to control the discounting of air fares because a final determination of a legal action against Trans America might take 12 months and in the meantime powers to control air fares could be severely undermined.

> This could lead to considerable instability in the market with discounting and other malpractices emerging on a scale that would undermine approved tariff structures and could have serious implications for airlines generally and Aer Lingus in particular.
>
> (Parliamentary Debates, Vol. 362, Col. 855)

The Bill proposed penalties of up to two years in jail, a fine of £100,000 and the loss of a travel agent's licence for the sale of airline tickets below prices set by the Minister. Opponents of the Bill were sufficiently strong to prevent it being passed before the summer recess. The deregulation of Ireland–Britain air services, as announced on 4 December 1985, came in the context of hostility to a Bill to prevent price competition. The deregulation announcement contradicted the Bill then before the parliament, a point noted by the Speaker. On the new Dublin–Luton licence the Speaker stated that 'the Minister has announced it, the Deputy has welcomed it and neither was in order' (Col. 1055). Britain had negotiated a liberalisation of the air services market with the Netherlands in 1984. Within the EC, Britain 'has been the main advocate of reform' in aviation regulation (Dobson, 1995: 187). The policy change in Ireland to deregulation on air routes to Britain was readily accepted in Britain.

The performance of Ireland–UK air routes prior to deregulation

Public dissatisfaction with the performance of the air transport sector caused a legislative measure intended to restrict competition when introduced in parliament in June 1984, to become by December 1985, a pro-competition measure. The dissatisfaction was primarily caused by the high fares charged on the Dublin–London route.

Table 3.1 shows the performance of the Dublin–London route over the period 1980–5 according to a CAA study. Of the 11 routes studied, London–Dublin had the largest fare increase at 72.6 per cent and the smallest passenger growth, 2.8 per cent. The London–Dublin fare increase was 74 per cent greater than the increase in the retail price index and 66 per cent greater than the average fare increase, 43.7 per cent on the 11 routes studied by the CAA.

The Dublin–London route accounted for 55 per cent of air travel between Britain and Ireland in 1985. The remaining routes of importance were London–Cork, with 10 per cent of the Britain–Ireland air passenger market, London–Shannon (8 per cent), Dublin–Manchester (6 per cent) and Dublin–Birmingham (5 per cent).

Table 3.2 shows the stagnation of air travel between Britain and Ireland during the period 1980–5. Only Italy of the main European markets showed a lesser performance, with a 5 per cent fall in passenger numbers compared to 3 per cent on the Irish routes. Table 3.2 also shows that charter airlines played a smaller role on Britain–Ireland routes, 1 per cent, than on any of the major routes to Europe from Britain. In the typical European air transport market national airlines enjoyed protection from competition. While some states wishing to promote tourism allowed charter airlines to tourist destinations, Ireland did not.

The low expectations for traffic volumes on the Ireland–Britain routes under regulation are indicated in the Aer Lingus Annual Report for 1993/4. The report noted 'a return to modest growth levels' but stated that 'the prospects for any significant growth in passenger numbers over the next few years are limited' (p. 11).

Table 3.1 Fare increase and passenger growth London–Dublin and major routes from London compared, 1980–5

London to ...	Passenger numbers 1985 (000s)	Load factor 1985 (%)	Fare increase 1980–5 (%)	Growth 1980–5 (%)
Glasgow	1080.8	62.6	31.9	40.4
Edinburgh	1033.9	62.7	31.9	58.3
Belfast	895.3	60.8	40.9	30.7
Manchester	869.1	59.8	45.5	41.9
Aberdeen	460.3	64.6	29.2	34.5
Newcastle	313.2	58.0	38.8	18.4
Paris	2438.3	73.9	63.2	17.1
Amsterdam	1312.5	70.8	38.5	24.1
Dublin	994.3	75.2	72.6	2.8
Frankfurt	977.4	70.6	43.2	40.1
Brussels	719.0	61.7	43.6	20.4
Average (11)	–	65.5	43.7	29.9

Fare comparison note: retail price index increase 1980–5: 41.5 per cent.

Source: CAA Competition on the Main Domestic Routes, Paper 87005 (1987).

Note
London–Dublin indices as proportion of II major routes from London (average = 100).

Passenger growth	1980–5	9
Fare increase	1980–5	166
Load factor	1985	115

Table 3.2 Growth of main European air routes ex Britain 1980/5 and 1985 charter shares

	Growth 1980–5 (%)	Charter share 1985 (%)
Spain	38	82
France	21	12
Germany	16	18
Ireland	−3	1
Greece	56	81
Italy	−5	51
Netherlands	17	2
Switzerland	39	28
Portugal	120	78

Source: CAA Annual Reports.

European air fares have traditionally been the highest in the world in the annual surveys of ICAO. The survey for 1985 reported that 'in US dollar terms, these average "local Europe" fares remain among the highest in the world at shorter distance; in September 1985 they were 26 per cent higher than the world average at 500 km'. Table 3.3 shows the level of international air fares in 1985 in Europe

Table 3.3 International air fares, 1985 US cents per passenger km

	Distance km				
	250	500	1000	2000	4000
Europe	36.3	27.9	21.5	16.6	12.8
North America	25.3	19.1	14.4	10.9	8.2
World Average	28.7	23.6	19.4	16.0	13.2
	Index (world = 100)				
	250	500	1000	2000	4000
Europe	126	118	111	104	96
North America	88	81	74	68	62

Source: ICAO Annual Survey of International Air Transport Fares and Rates.

Table 3.4 Staff productivity of European airlines in 1984

Company	tkm performed (millions)	Number of staff	tkm per staff (000s)
Austrian	153	2,831	54
Sabena	1,038	8,592	121
Finnair	481	5,532	87
Air France	4,932	35,232	140
UTA	961	6,589	146
Lufthansa	4,700	32,535	144
Olympic	664	10,313	64
Aer Lingus	363	5,789	63
Alitalia	1,952	18,144	108
KLM	3,054	19,230	159
TAP	520**	9813	53
SAS	1,502	18,258	82
Iberia	2,061	22,769	91
Swissair	1,855	16,147*	115
British Airways	4,744	36,180	131
British Midland	131	1,306	100
British Caledonian	977	7,144	137
Dan Air	499	2,945	169
Total	30,587	259,349	118
Average of 18	1,699	14,408	118

Source: ICAO, Civil Aviation Statistics of the World, 1984.
* 1983; ** estimate.

and North America, the two mature aviation markets in the world. The world average is also shown.

The high fares charged by European airlines were absorbed by a combination of low productivity and high costs rather than reflected in high profits. Tables 3.4 and 3.5 show the productivity of European airlines in 1984 and average remuneration compared with GNP per head. Average productivity for 16 North American major

Table 3.5 Airline staff remuneration per head and GNP per head, 1984

Company	$ per employee	Ratio to GNP per head	Index
Aer Lingus	19,968	4.0	156
Air France	19,631	2.2	86
Alitalia	27,189	4.4	172
Austrian	24,740	3.1	121
British Airways	15,117	2.0	78
British Midland	13,755	1.8	70
British Caledonian	15,194	2.0	78
Dan Air	13,297	1.8	70
Finnair	14,672	1.4	55
Iberia	15,739	3.8	148
KLM	22,654	2.6	102
Lufthansa	27,128	2.7	105
SAS	25,611	2.3	90
Sagbena	21,406	2.8	109
Swissair	33,459	2.4	94
TAP	11,646	6.0	234
UTA	29,531	2.7	105
US Majors (16)	41,085	2.7	105
Air Canada	27,335	2.1	82
Average (19 Countries)		2.56	100

Source: ICAO, Civil Aviation Statistics of the World, 1984; OECD National Accounts.

airlines in 1984 was 160,000 tonne-kilometre (tkm) per staff member, 35 per cent greater than the average for the 18 European airlines in Table 3.4. The dominant airline on Ireland–Britain routes before deregulation was Aer Lingus. Table 3.4 shows that its productivity was only 53 per cent of the European average. It shared a low productivity performance with other small national airlines such as Austrian, Olympic and TAP. Table 3.5 shows that while the average ratio of airline staff remuneration per head to GNP per head was 2.56, this was exceeded by Aer Lingus where the ratio was 4. Alitalia, TAP, Iberia and Austrian also exceeded a ratio of 3 of airline staff remuneration to GNP per head.

The protection afforded to European state airlines by their governments allowed them to engage in rent-seeking behaviour to enhance the earnings of airlines through government control of competition. In Tables 3.4 and 3.5 the performance of Aer Lingus, a protected airline, contrasts with British Midland whose scope for rent-seeking behaviour was nil because the airline did not participate in the high-cost cartel of national airlines operating on international routes in Europe. Output per staff member in British Midland was 54 per cent greater than in Aer Lingus but remuneration was 31 per cent lower. Unit wage costs in British Midland were therefore only 45 per cent of those at Aer Lingus.

On the eve of deregulation the Ireland–Britain air routes were characterised by very low growth rates in passenger numbers, high fare growth and low productivity and high costs for the dominant airline, Aer Lingus. Strong public opinion pushed the government towards deregulation despite the strong protectionist stance in both the courts and the legislature by the government. The Ryanair Dublin–Luton service began on 23 May 1986 at a fare of £95 unrestricted, a reduction of 54 per cent on the £208 fare from Dublin to Heathrow.

The impact of deregulation

Market size impact

The impact of deregulation on market size in Ireland–Britain aviation has been dramatic. The contracting market from 1980 to 1985 became the fastest growing European market over the years 1985–94, with growth of 184 per cent. This was 1.95 times the growth rate to France, 2.16 times the growth rate to the Netherlands and 2.62 times the growth rate to Germany. Table 3.6 shows the growth of UK air traffic on major European routes over the years 1985–94. The monthly distribution of traffic growth on Dublin–London in 1987, the first full year of deregulation, is compared to 1985, the last full year of regulation, in Table 3.7. The highest growth occurred in August, 91.7 per cent compared to 64.9 per cent over the year as a whole.

The established airlines operated a differentiated pricing policy with a range of discounts for advance booking and staying away on Saturday. Yield maximisation programmes reduced the availability of the discounted fares at times of peak demand. Ryanair, on the other hand, charged the same fare to all passengers and did not restrict demand by charging higher fares at times of peak demand. Deregulation promoted therefore a large increase in summer traffic, an important consideration in the development of the Irish tourism industry in the absence from the market of the Charter airlines which promoted tourism in other countries.

The division of the 91.7 per cent market growth in August 1997 between established and new entrant airlines was equal. The new entrants had 24.1 per cent

Table 3.6 UK international air traffic on major European routes 1985/94

Country	Passengers 1994 (000s)	Growth 1985/94 (%)
Spain	17,645	85
France	7,261	94
Germany	6,190	70
Ireland	5,126	184
Greece	4,963	73
Italy	4,188	62
Netherlands	4,013	80
Switzerland	2,647	31
Portugal	2,692	63

Source: Civil Aviation Authority.

Table 3.7 Dublin–London passenger numbers under
regulation and deregulation

	Passengers (000s)		
	1985	1987	Increase (%)
January	63.2	87.4	38.2
February	59.4	89.0	49.9
March	80.8	108.4	34.2
April	76.4	124	62.3
May	82.0	118.4	44.4
June	92.3	*147.0	59.3
July	97.2	177.6	82.7
August	106.7	204.5	91.7
September	93.3	168.7	80.8
October	85.3	157.6	84.7
November	75.8	122.3	61.4
December	78.9	130.7	65.7
Year	991.7	1635.5	64.9

New airlines' share of Dublin–London traffic, 1987

	Share (%)
January	12.9
February	13.5
March	14.0
April	14.1
May	14.5
June	21.7
July	23.4
August	24.1
September	23.2
October	22.5
November	21.8
December	20.7

Source: CAA, Monthly Airport Statistics.

* Second new entrant to market

of the 1987 market, some 49,300 passengers out of a total increase of 97,800 on the route over the 1985 volumes.

An important factor in the benefits from deregulation is the response of incumbents to new market entrants. The 50 per cent increase in the outputs of incumbents airlines on the Dublin–London route which had expanded output by only 2.5 per cent over the previous five years illustrates the change from a predetermined market size which was shared to one where new entrants increased the size of the market by reducing fares.

Price impact

The initial impact on the unrestricted fare was a 54 per cent reduction from the incumbent's fare of £208 unrestricted to £95 for the same ticket on Ryanair.

The competitive response of Aer Lingus to this fare reduction was the London Business Bonus, a hotel voucher in London worth up to IR£115 (£95 at the 1988 exchange rate) and a 55 per cent reduction from the £208 fare. In the restricted fare groups the established airlines reduced the 28-day Apex from £95 to £63 (a 33 per cent reduction), the 14-day Apex from £119 to £77 (a 35 per cent reduction). In addition, late saver (standby) and special saver fares of £69 and £75 were introduced and a Super Budget of £123, a three-day business fare, which was a 41 per cent reduction on the £208 fare.

In 1995 some 80 per cent of passengers on Ryanair, the largest carrier on Dublin–London route, travelled on fares of £59/£69 return and some 6 per cent on a fully flexible fare of £99. Taking the medium fare of £69 in Ryanair and noting that the £208 fare before deregulation in 1985 is the equivalent of £270 at 1995 prices, its passengers would have experienced fare reductions of as much as 75 per cent. This contrasts with estimates of a 15 per cent reduction due to deregulation in the United States (Williams, 1994: 59). Yield information is not available for all airlines on the routes but the Ryanair savings contrast with estimates of a 15 per cent overall reduction in fares due to deregulation in the United States. Williams also notes that in the EU

> the continuing gradual removal of economic controls has not produced any dramatic changes. There has been neither a general lowering of fares nor a rapid influx of airlines onto routes previously the preserve of the associated flag carriers. (1994: 144)

The non-price improvements generated by deregulation included increased frequency of service, fewer conditions attached to budget type fares and a greater choice of airports. For example, in the London area, Stansted, London City and Luton are now served in addition to Heathrow and Gatwick before deregulation.

The standard of in-flight service before deregulation was minimal. That remains the case on Ryanair which emphasises low fares. British Midland and Virgin Cityjet have operated a high standard of service and Aer Lingus has raised its standard above the pre-deregulation services, especially in business class.

Market share impact

Prior to deregulation in 1986 the market shares of the Dublin–London route were Aer Lingus 65 per cent and British Airways 35 per cent. In 1995 the market shares were Ryanair 37 per cent, Aer Lingus 35 per cent, British Midland 19 per cent, Virgin Cityjet 5 per cent and BA Express 4 per cent. The major market exit was British Airways in 1991. The airline left the market because of low yields and wished to use its valuable slots at Heathrow on more remunerative long distance routes.

Impact on incumbent airlines

The beneficiaries of protection from competition in air transport between Ireland and Britain were British Airways and Aer Lingus. British Airways retains a market presence through code-sharing with independent UK airlines. Aer Lingus was the leading airline between Ireland and Britain under protectionism. Tables 3.4 and 3.5 show that under protection the airline had low labour productivity and high labour costs. As a high labour cost airline based in a country with high unemployment it was vulnerable to start-up airlines such as Ryanair. It also had considerably higher unit labour costs than British Midland, its major British competitor under deregulation. Aer Lingus experienced serious financial problems from 1988 to 1994 but became profitable again in 1995.

The airline lost $313 million in 1993 and had a net margin of minus 23 per cent. This was worse than all other European airlines with the exception of Olympic. In 1994 the loss was $187 million and the net margin was minus 8.8 per cent. The restructuring of the airline under the Cahill–Owen Plan was approved by the Dail (parliament) on 6 July 1993. The plan as drawn up by the company chairman Bernie Cahill and Peter Owen who had worked on the restructuring of British Airways prior to privatisation in 1986.

Under the plan, subsidiary activities such as hotels and computer companies were sold. The redundancy of 1000 staff, a two-tier employment structure and changes in work practices produced annual savings of £50 million. EU approval was secured for a £175 million capital injection over a three-year period. The airline withdrew from a number of fifth freedom services at Manchester and reduced its services on Dublin–London where its market share fell from 63 per cent in 1992 to 40 per cent in 1994. It also reduced some Irish regional services.

Nuutinen envisaged small profits for Aer Lingus in 1995/6 and 1996/7 but notes that

> some industry analysts believe that the equity injections and associated measures can only prolong Aer Lingus' life by a few years after which structural changes in the industry and greater competition within Europe will have made it very difficult for a small low-yield peripheral carrier to survive as an independent entity. (1993: 19)

Aer Lingus was ill-prepared for deregulation and was too successful a lobbyist for protection to face market competition. Its opposition to deregulation is shared by most European state airlines. It is in a stronger position to meet further competition as a result of its restructuring under the Cahill–Owen plan and its experiences under the Ireland–Britain deregulation. Since the protection of national airlines is enjoyed at the expense of the remainder of the economy the gains elsewhere from deregulation of air services are next examined.

Macroeconomic impact

The rapid increase in the availability of low-cost airline seats following deregulation coincided with rapid growth in Irish tourism which had stagnated for almost two decades. In 1994 the Irish government Green Paper on Aviation Policy estimated that airline deregulation had generated a 60 per cent increase in visitor numbers, additional tourist earnings of £560 million and an additional 25,000 jobs in tourism over the years 1987–93. In addition the volume of outward business travel increased by 50 per cent. The overall impact of deregulation was to increase the competitiveness of an island economy. The sea cartel ended as a result of the ending of the air cartel and sea fares are estimated to have fallen by 40 per cent in real terms in 1995 compared to 1987 (Stena Sealink, 1995).

The policy implications of Ireland–UK airline deregulation for other European air services

The results of deregulation of the Ireland–Britain air routes have been spectacular in terms of fare reductions and volume increases. With the introduction of a deregulated air market within the EU from April 1997 the wider implications of the Ireland–Britain case study are important.

The circumstances which favoured the Ireland–Britain deregulation's positive impact were as follows:

1   Large fare increases in the five years before deregulation.
2   A stagnant market over the seven years prior to deregulation.
3   The inherent advantages of air over surface travel between islands. The one-hour flight between Dublin and London competed with a nine-hour journey by sea and rail. There was thus a large pent-up demand for low-cost air travel between Britain and Ireland.
4   Charter air services which met the demand for low-cost air travel elsewhere in Europe held less than 1 per cent of the Ireland–Britain market.
5   The large Irish ethnic population in Britain created a market for travel between the islands.
6   Ireland became a fashionable tourist destination compared to sun destinations. Prior to 1986, the cartel choked off demand by restricting the availability of excursion fares through yield management programmes whereas under competition supply increased radically.
7   New entrants were readily available on a scale required to make deregulation effective. British Airways left the market thus leaving a share available for new entrants. The scale of entry of Ryanair, the largest new entrant, was significant and it became the market leader.
8   Ireland's high unemployment allowed the recruitment of airline staff at competitive wages where the incumbent airline wages incorporated a rent element.

By contrast with the factors which favoured the success of the Ireland–Britain deregulation the following factors would indicate less dramatic results from airline deregulation in other European markets.

1   low fare increases;
2   high market growth;
3   availability of road and rail alternatives to air transport;

4   a large charter market share;
5   a small ethnic travel market;
6   a small tourist trade;
7   lack of new airline entry on a large scale and lack of market exit by present national airlines and
8   inability to undercut the costs of established airlines by new entrant airlines based in countries with low unemployment and high labour costs.

Doganis (1992) attributes 'the phenomenal growth' of Ireland–Britain air services under deregulation to

> the special characteristics of this market, notably the large Irish population in the UK and a very substantial volume of seaborne ferry traffic which was ripe for diversion to air as fare levels fell. It is unlikely that deregulation elsewhere in Europe will have such a profound effect of doubling traffic in two years.

The number of passengers by sea between Britain and Ireland increased from 2.9 million in 1985 to 3.6 million in 1994. This 24 per cent growth was far less than the 184 per cent growth in air travel shown in Table 3.6 but deregulation increased both the air and sea passenger numbers. On the other hand there are factors which indicate large potential gains from further European deregulation. European air fares are the highest in the world and the industry is characterised by low productivity and high costs. European aviation is thus vulnerable to new entrants and to competition from airlines from North America and the Asia-Pacific region. The latter is likely in a globalised aviation market with trade liberalisation in services.

Post-deregulation barriers to contestability

In addition to its positive aspects the Ireland–Britain airline deregulation highlighted problems which are likely to occur elsewhere in Europe. These problems are outlined below.

Lack of slots at hub airports

The largest new entrant, Ryanair was the market leader in 1995 on Dublin–London. It has no slots at Heathrow. In its initial phase it used Luton as its London base. Because of difficulties of surface access to Luton from central London, Ryanair transferred its emphasis in the London market to Stansted in 1991 while retaining some services at Luton. The problems of developing a new airline while excluded from a major slot constrained airport are illustrated by comparing the Ryanair experience on Dublin–London where it took nine years to become market leader and its routes to Birmingham, Manchester and Glasgow, entered in 1993/4.

Ryanair entered Dublin–Birmingham in November 1993. It became the market leader in December 1993 with 53 per cent of the market which grew by 67 per cent over the previous December. Ryanair entered Dublin–Manchester in May 1994. It became market leader in June with 55 per cent of the market which grew by 56 per cent compared to June 1993. Ryanair entered Dublin–Glasgow in May 1994. In June it became the market leader with a 46 per cent share of a market which grew by 112 per cent over June 1993. The other shares were 41 per cent for Aer Lingus and 13 per cent for Manx. Ryanair used Prestwick airport to serve the Glasgow market as it was able to negotiate lower airport charges there. In 1995 it commenced a Prestwick–Stansted service in advance of the EU market in cabotage services in 1997. The Ireland–Britain deregulation illustrates the potential for competition between airports in a deregulated market.

Predation

The US experience of deregulation indicates that incumbent airlines with a network of services are likely to respond to new entrants by selectively cutting fares on routes where they face new entrants. In the Aer Lingus case, the executive chairman in his restructuring plan cut the airline's capacity on Dublin–London by 20 per cent and sought to increase yields. Before cutting capacity the airline lost £12 million on the route. Reducing its market share from over 60 per cent to 48 per cent, inter alia, converted this to a profit of £2 million (Cahill, 1993, 1994). Before its restructuring Aer Lingus thus engaged in below-cost selling on the Dublin–London route incurring losses which were 12 times the profits of Ryanair, its major competitor.

In contrast to the normal pattern of a decline in air fares per mile as distance travelled increases, Aer Lingus under deregulation charges substantially higher fares on its Ireland–mainland Europe routes than on its Ireland–UK routes, where it has faced more competition. Within its airline operation, therefore, it has the potential to charge fares above cost on its uncontested European mainland routes in order to subsidise its operations on the deregulated Ireland–UK routes. It has also used the profits from its hotel and other ancillary services to subsidise the airline and received state aid.

State aids

In 1993/5 Aer Lingus received £175 million from the Irish government as part of a restructuring programme. The aid was approved by the EC as a one-off measure. Similar aid programmes have been approved for Olympic, TAP, Sabena, Alitalia, Iberia and Air France.

Since ease of market exit is an assumption of contestability theory, the state aids to European national airlines are an obstacle to deregulation and its benefits. The aid programmes have been opposed by Europe's private airlines and national airlines required to operate to a commercial mandate. In the present case study the impact of state aid on the market was significant when compared with the estimated profit of Ryanair in the early 1990s of about £1 million a year. The Commission has sought to limit state aids to one round. Since the high costs of

European aviation have been known for decades but the airlines have continued to recruit extra staff, the commitment of both airline managements and governments to the restructuring of many state airlines must be questioned. Until governments are willing to restructure loss-making state airlines, and managements do so, it is unlikely that the EC will be able to confine subsidisation of airlines to the present limits. Attempts to reform loss-making airlines lack creditability when failure does not lead to market exit.

Regulation and contestability

As national barriers to entry in European aviation have been removed, the role of regulator has passed to the EC. Its policy on slots has been timid and confined to allocating unused slots to new entrants. Entry on the scale achieved in Ireland–Britain required far larger availability of slots than proposed by the EO.

The commission has powers to examine fares in order to adjudicate on whether they are predatory. The commission conducted a dawn raid on Aer Lingus in 1994 in order to ascertain the airline's pricing policy on the routes from Dublin–Manchester, Birmingham and Glasgow in response to the arrival of competition on these routes, thus fares between Dublin and Birmingham, Manchester and Glasgow did not fall at the prospect of potential new entrants in 1986 but with the arrival of actual new market entry in 1993/4. Between 1986 and 1993/4, Aer Lingus operated a policy of high fares on the uncontested, but contestable routes and low fares on the contested services to London.

The Ireland–Britain experience echoes the US where potential competition is no substitute for actual competition. While contestability theory suggests that the number of actual competitors should have no effect on prices many studies have found that the number of airlines actually competing on a route has a significant effect on the price level (Borenstein, 1992: 53).

Conclusion

The implications of the successful derogation of Ireland–UK air services for the remainder of the EU market may be examined under two categories of routes, domestic and international.

De Witt notes that '17 out of 25 of the highest density routes in the EU are domestic routes (1995: 177). Until April of 1997 these routes are protected against direct competition.' The results of the deregulation of the Dublin–London route, the second busiest international route in the EU after London–Paris, are therefore relevant. The Dublin–London experience indicates that new entrants are attracted to high-density routes and that alternative airports such as Stansted, Luton and London City can be developed if new entrants are excluded from slot constrained airports such as Heathrow. The alternative airports can however reduce the market share of new entrant airlines. The Ireland–UK experience indicates however that the restriction of new entrant airlines to alternative airports in direct competition with incumbents on routes such as Birmingham–Dublin and Dublin–Manchester achieved a larger market share faster than on Dublin–London where alternative London airports had to be served.

The results of the liberalisation of EU international routes, other than Ireland–UK, have been disappointing. De Witt (1995: 176) notes that 'over a period of 2 years freedom of fares, not one single EU carrier has been inspired to start extensive fare competition in the European market'. The cost structure of European national airlines is high by world standards although Oum and Yu (1995: 194) state that 'European aviation liberalization which began in 1987 appears to have produced substantial productivity gains'.

The lesson of the Ireland–UK experience is that new entrants are the key to achieving the gains from airline deregulation both in the introduction of price competition and increasing capacity to serve the expanded market. In the Ireland–UK case the market prospects of new entrants were increased by the withdrawal from the market of one of the former cartel members, British Airways. On the other hand the remaining member of the cartel, Aer Lingus, was rescued by the Irish government with an IR£175 million injection over the years 1993–5. The undertaking has been given that no further rescue will be allowed. On routes where both national airlines are protected by their governments the market prospects for new entrants would be reduced compared with those on Ireland–UK routes. The greater the amount of subsidy and other support from governments the lesser the prospects for new entrant airlines. The protection of national airlines by their governments reduces their incentive to tackle their high cost base in Europe. In the Ireland–UK case the requirement to face new market entrants has secured some reforms in Aer Lingus compared to its conduct under protection. It remains to be seen however if the corporate culture of the airline has changed.

The impacts on price and market size from the Ireland–UK deregulation of 1986 may not be as dramatic elsewhere in Europe because of the special characteristics of the Ireland–UK market. Nonetheless there are strong indications that removing the barriers to new market entrants will yield significant economic benefits both on other EU international routes and the domestic routes to be deregulated in April 1997.

(II) Deregulating European aviation – a case study

The highly restricted European aviation market has been criticised for its high costs and low productivity (Bailey, 1986; Barrett, 1987; Doganis, 1985; OECD, 1988; Sawer, 1987). The London–Dublin route is the second busiest international scheduled air service in Europe. This article examines its deregulation in May 1986 and the implications for other routes in Europe's tightly regulated scheduled aviation scene.

International scheduled aviation in Europe is controlled by inter-governmental agreements which restrict market entry and price competition and predetermine output shares. A European Civil Aviation Conference report ('The Compass Report') in 1981 found that only 2 per cent of European international routes had more than one airline per state, that 93 per cent of routes had limitations on the number of flights per airline and that between 75 per cent and 85 per cent of tonne-kilometres were performed under revenue-pooling agreements. Inter-governmental restrictions were accompanied by collusion between national airlines. The Compass Report (1981) also found that

> airlines often on their own initiative, and usually without direct government influence, enter into inter-airline commercial agreements which reflect the capacity, scheduling and tariff provisions of the bilateral agreements and also provide for each airline to act as the other's agent for other aspects such as baggage and cargo handling, reservations and ticket sales, and also for pooling and sharing the revenues obtained from the operation of a route or routes.

The results of restrictive governmental regulation and inter-airline collusion are that international scheduled aviation in Europe is expensive and is produced by high-cost airlines. The International Civil Aviation Organisation (ICAO) annual surveys of international air transport fares and rates have typically found European fares to be the highest in the world especially at shorter distances. Table 3.8 shows the ICAO fare comparisons for Europe, North America and the world average in 1977 and 1985. Table 3.9 shows that the cost per passenger seat kilometre in European aviation in 1981 was 64 per cent above that of the US domestic trunk carriers. European scheduled aviation is characterised by the absence of price competition and new market entrants, and by low productivity

Table 3.8 European, North American and international air fares 1977–85 per passenger-kilometre (US cents)

	Distance				
	250	*500*	*1000*	*2000*	*4000*
			1977		
Europe	21.9	17.5	14.1	11.3	10.1
North America	12.1	9.4	7.4	5.3	4.5
World average	16.9	14.3	12.2	10.4	8.8
			1985		
Europe	36.3	27.9	21.5	16.6	12.8
North America	25.3	19.1	14.4	10.9	8.2
World average	28.7	23.6	19.4	16.0	13.2
		Index 1977 (World = 100)			
Europe	129	122	116	109	115
North America	79	66	61	51	51
		Index 1985 (World = 100)			
Europe	126	118	111	104	96*
North America	88	81	74	68	62

Source: Annual Survey of International Air Transport Fares and Rates, International Civil Aviation Authority, Montreal.

* This group accounted for only 0.6 per cent of the 2,310 European air routes in the ICAO survey.

Table 3.9 Local Europe and US domestic trunk airline costs, 1981

	Cost item passenger cost (US cents per seat km)			
	Local Europe	US domestic trunk	European excess cents	Cost (%)
Crew	0.99	0.47	0.52	11.2
Fuel	1.98	1.36	0.62	13.4
Maintenance	0.80	0.46	0.34	7.3
Depreciation	0.46	0.28	0.18	3.9
Route and landing charges	1.05	0.20	0.85	18.3
Station and ground	1.36	0.72	0.64	13.8
Passenger service	0.50	0.43	0.07	1.5
Sales	1.63	0.61	1.02	22.0
Other	0.58	0.18	0.40	8.6
Total	9.35	5.71	4.64	100.0

Source: Civil Aviation Authority, 1983, A Comparison between European and United States Air Fares, London, table 7.

Table 3.10 The 'cascade' analysis of the costs of scheduled and charter airlines in Europe

Cascade steps	Route A	Route B	Route C
Total scheduled cost per passenger	100	100	100
Deduct commission	92	92	91
Tourist class	86	84	87
Seating density	77	80	83
Load factor	56	59	60
Peak/trough ratio	60	62	63
Utilisation	57	60	61
Standards	51	51	53
Not applicable	36	37	39
Derived 'charter'	36	37	39
Actual charter	34–37	32	35

Source: Report on scheduled passenger air fares in the EEC, EEC, Brussels, 1981.

and high sales and airport costs. This can be seen both from comparing scheduled aviation in Europe and other parts of the world and from comparing scheduled and charter airlines within Europe. Charter airlines in Europe operate under a more liberal regime than the scheduled airlines with easier market entry and price competition. Table 3.10 shows that the charter airlines typically charge fares between 32 per cent and 37 per cent of the scheduled airlines. It also shows the steps by which the scheduled airlines might match the charter fares. A result of regulation of aviation in Europe therefore is to prevent the supply of an alternative low-cost product in the market for inter-city air travel. The charter airlines have not in the past been permitted to operate between the main cities in

Northern Europe but dominate vacation services to the Mediterranean basin. While it is possible that the lower priced charter service might be rejected on non-price grounds this trade-off was not usually permitted on services between the major European cities.

While the 'cascade' analysis in Table 3.10 purported to explain the differences in scheduled and charter air fares through quality factors, its main impact subsequently was to show that, even in Europe's high-cost environment, scheduled airlines could have significantly reduced fares had they chosen to emulate the charter product.

The regulation of European aviation in the post-war period thus resulted in a two-tier aviation industry comprising a low-fare less-regulated holiday charter sector and a high-fare scheduled sector with regulation of prices, capacity and market entry. Evidence from markets not subject to these regulations indicated lower fares and costs.

In the US, airline deregulation removed these barriers to competition. Jordan (1970) found that intra-state travel, in California, not subject to federal government regulation, was 47 per cent cheaper than interstate travel. Morrison and Winston (1986) estimated that US deregulation in 1978 'has led to at least a $6 billion (in 1977 dollars) annual improvement in the welfare of travellers, with the greatest benefit going to business travellers from increased flight frequency. It has also led to at least a $2.5 billion (in 1977 dollars) annual increase in industry profits.' Morrison and Winston (1989) estimated that mergers in the mid-1980s reduced the gains to consumers from deregulation by $423 million per year by giving the airlines the market power to charge higher fares.

The theory of contestable markets renewed interest among economists in removing barriers to entry in the promotion of efficiency. The regulated airlines serving the London–Dublin route were heaving criticised over a number of years for high fares. The alternative to regulated air travel was a ship and train journey taking nine hours. The policy change to deregulation in 1986 resulted from consumer pressures and the wish of new entrants to serve the route.

The 1986 deregulation on the Dublin–London air route

The system of banning new entrants, price collusion, and capacity controls was changed in May 1986 on the Dublin–London route. In the table, the fare difference between scheduled and chartered airlines is attributed to differences in service standards such as seat pitch, load factor, lower service standards and so on. The scheduled airlines could produce a charter-type product for between 36 per cent and 39 per cent of their present fares thus almost matching the charter airlines who charge between 32 per cent and 37 per cent of the scheduled airlines' fares. The eight steps purport to explain the difference between charter and scheduled airline fares because charter airlines do not incur travel agents' commission when they sell directly to a tour operator; they do not incur the extra costs of operating business class, lower seat density and lower load factors of the scheduled airlines; they have 25 per cent more fleet utilisation because charter night flying is more common than for scheduled airlines and because, under the 'not applicable' category, the scheduled airlines have greater sales, advertising and reservations costs while they lack the extra bar profits of the charter airlines.

- New entrants were permitted. Ryanair entered the route in May 1986 and Virgin Atlantic in June 1987.
- Price competition was permitted. The new airlines were not required to engage in tariff co-ordination with British Airways and Aer Lingus, the incumbents.
- Capacity controls were not applied to the new earners. The share of the new carriers in the total Dublin–London market and the relative market sizes of Ryanair and Virgin Atlantic are determined by consumer preference rather than by predetermined capacity limits.

In contrast to the established carriers the new market entrants did not pool revenues. They did not have interchangeability of tickets with other carriers. They did not use the services of other carriers for passenger and baggage handing.

While new market entry occurred on 23 May 1986, output limitation remained in operation until 1 December 1986. Initially Ryanair was restricted to 44-seat 748 aircraft but was allowed to use jet aircraft from 1 December. By the end of 1986 the post-war anti-competitive structure that typified European aviation had been dismantled on the Dublin–London route. The revenue pooling agreement between Aer Lingus and British Airways ended in April 1988.

Table 3.12 compares the Dublin–London route and ten other European international and British domestic routes over the period 1980–5. It can be seen from Table 3.12 and its footnote that the route before deregulation was characterised by low market growth, high fare increases and a higher than average load factor. Ireland–United Kingdom air routes have not been served by charter airlines which have been a restraint on the price and output policies of scheduled airlines in other European markets. In 1986, for example, only 1 per cent of passengers between Britain and Ireland used charter services compared to 82 per cent between Britain and Spain. Nonetheless, Dublin–London was then Europe's third largest international scheduled air route after London–Paris and London–Amsterdam.

The impact of deregulation on price

Table 3.13 shows that the impact of the new market entrants on price has been to reduce the unrestricted fare by between 48 per cent and 66 per cent for peak and off-peak travel, respectively. The pricing policy of the new entrants has been to offer low unrestricted fares. The low fares offered by the incumbents, by contrast, were subject to advance booking requirements, minimum stay-away requirements, cancellation charges, ticket alteration penalties and restricted availability. The Civil Aviation Authority survey, cited in Table 3.11 above, shows

Table 3.11 London–Dublin and major routes ex-London compared 1980–5

	Passenger nos 1985 (000s)	Load factor 1985	Fare increase 1980–5 (%)	Passenger growth 1980–5 (%)	Business share (%)	Interline (%)
London to …						
Glasgow	1080.8	62.6	31.9	40.4	72	25
Edinburgh	1033.9	62.7	31.9	58.3	63	34
Belfast	895.3	60.8	40.9	30.7	44	18
Manchester	869.1	59.8	45.5	41.9	79	44
Aberdeen	460.3	64.6	29.2	34.5	69	33
Newcastle	313.2	58.0	38.8	18.4	73	42
Paris	2438.3	73.9	63.2	17.1	57	15
Amsterdam	1312.5	70.8	38.5	24.1	57	13
Dublin	994.3	75.2	72.6	2.8	45	25
Frankfurt	977.4	70.6	43.2	40.1	58	19
Brussels	719.0	61.7	43.6	20.4	68	31
Average (11)		65.5	43.7	29.9	0.62	30

Source: Civil Aviation Authority, Paper 87005, Competition on the Main Domestic Trunk Routes.

Fare comparison note: Retail Price Index increase 1980–5: 41.5 per cent; interline data refers to interlining in London.

London–Dublin indices as proportion of eleven major routes ex-London (average = 100)

Passenger growth	1980–5	9
Fare increase	1980–5	166
Load factor	1985	115
Business travellers%	1985	73
London interlining%	1985	83

Source: derived from main table above.

that business travel accounted for 45 per cent of the passengers using the established airlines on the route. This category of short-notice passenger has been the major beneficiary from deregulation with a reduction from £104 to as low as £35 in the unrestricted fare.

The reaction by the established carriers against competition for the unrestricted fare category has been to retain the £208 fare but to combine it with London hotel discounts, free car hire and other vouchers worth up to £95 sterling (IR£112). This scheme is known as the London Business Bonus and discounts the £208 fare by up to 68 per cent. It was introduced as a temporary measure when the new airlines started jet service but has remained in operation. It is assumed below that the saving is £50 per trip and that half of those eligible avail of it. Other full-fare passengers may not use it because of day return trips or onward trips.

Table 3.11 indicates that 55 per cent of the passengers on the established airlines travelled on discounted fares subject to the restrictions designed to prevent short-notice passengers availing of the reduced fares. The discounted fare passenger now has access to low unrestricted fares as a result of deregulation and thus enjoys greater flexibility. The discounted fares have also been reduced since deregulation.

Table 3.12 Dublin to London fares before and after deregulation (IR£)

	Fare (summer 1988)	Fare (pre-May 1986)	Fare reduction (%)
New entrants			
Virgin Atlantic one-way peak	38	91**	58
Ryanair one-way peak	54	91**	41
Virgin Atlantic off-peak	35	91**	62
Ryanair off-peak	44	91**	52
Virgin Atlantic round trip	70–76	208**	66–63
Ryanair round trip	88–108	208**	58–48
Established carriers			
Restricted fares			
Maxi-saver (28 day Apex)	63	95	34
Late saver	69	No fare	–
Special saver	75	No fare	–
Apex (14 day)	77	119	35
Excursion (Saturday night away)	89	159	44
Super budget	123	No fare	–
Unrestricted fares			
Budget (Gatwick)	164*	164	68*
Budget (Heathrow)	188*	188	60*
Executive	208*	208	54*
Budget one way (Gatwick)	82	82	0
Budget one way (Heathrow)	94	94	0
Executive one way	104	104	0

IR£1 = £0.85 sterling = $1.45
* London Business Bonus applies. The London Business Bonus entitles passengers at these fares to a hotel voucher in London worth up to £95 sterling (IR£112). Other incentives include a day's free car hire, free airport car parking and complimentary duty-free good or shopping vouchers.
** Comparable fare available on established carriers before May 1986.

Table 3.12 shows that three new restricted fares have been introduced since deregulation and that the previous three discounted fares have been reduced by 34 per cent for 28-day Apex, 35 per cent for 14-day Apex and 44 per cent for the Saturday night stay-away fare. The unweighted average fare reduction for the three discount fare categories available both before and after deregulation is therefore 38 per cent or £20 per trip.

Table 3.13 quantifies the total benefits and is based on the unit savings in Table 3.12. In Table 3.13 the new airlines are assumed to have a 25 per cent market share. The average yield is estimated at £36 for Virgin Atlantic and £51 for Ryanair. Market information is used to weight peak and off-peak travel and the Ryanair/Virgin Atlantic shares.

The benefits per unit of generated traffic are valued at half of the benefits per unit to existing traffic. The growth of 107 per cent in traffic since deregulation means that the benefits to generated traffic in 1988 are estimated at £12.5 million. The total benefit to consumers in 1988 is therefore £37.4 million. The 1985 consumer expenditure on the route was an estimated £80 million. The estimate for 1988 is

Table 3.13 Estimated average yield per passenger
journey on Dublin–London route (IR£)

	£
Regulation	
Unrestricted fare	104
Discounted fare	62
Weighted average	81
Deregulation	
Established airlines unrestricted	79
Established airlines discounted	42
New airlines	47
Weighted average	56

Market shares assumed are 55 per cent unrestricted
fares and 45 per cent discounted fares under regulation.
Under deregulation these proportions are retained but the
established airlines' share is reduced to 75 per cent to
accommodate the new entrants. The average benefit from
deregulation to pre-deregulation traffic is therefore £25
per passenger journey and £24.9 million in total for the
994,000 passengers. As a proportion of pre-deregulation
fares the saving is 31 per cent.

£119 million. Thus, an increase in expenditure of almost 50 per cent has purchased
117 per cent more journeys under deregulation.

Impact of deregulation on market size

The estimated size of the Dublin–London route in 1988 is 2.00 million passengers.
This is 2.01 times the traffic for 1985, the last calendar year of pre-deregulation
policies. Table 3.11 shows that the number of passengers grew by only 2.8 per cent
over the years 1980–5. The impact of deregulation has been to bring strong growth
to a hitherto stagnant market. Fifty-three per cent of the extra traffic in 1987 over
1985 was carried by the new carriers.

Impact of deregulation on market structure

The new entrants had almost a quarter of the market in the latter half of the
1987. The seasonality of the market changed under deregulation to emphasise the
peak. Under regulation the established airlines were able to eliminate discounted
fares at times of peak demand in order to maximise yield per passenger (Levine,
1987). The new entrants' strategy of charging a low unrestricted fare to all
passengers does not reduce peak demand by increasing price. Thus it can be
seen in Table 3.14 that the largest increases in passenger numbers occurred under
deregulation in the busiest months. The increase in August 1987, the peak month,
was 91.7 per cent over August 1985 under regulation. This was also the month
in which the new entrants recorded their highest market share of 24.1 per cent.

Table 3.14 Dublin–London passenger numbers under regulation and deregulation ('000 passengers)

	1985	1987	Increase (%)
January	63.2	87.4	38.2
February	59.4	89.0	49.9
March	80.8	108.4	34.2
April	76.4	124.0	62.3
May	82.0	118.4	44.4
June	92.3	147.0	59.3
July	97.2	177.6	82.7
August	106.7	204.5	91.7
September	93.3	168.7	80.8
October	85.3	157.6	84.7
November	75.8	122.3	61.4
December	78.9	130.7	65.7
Year	991.7	1635.5	64.9

New Airlines' Share of Dublin–London Traffic 1987

	Share %
January	12.9
February	13.5
March	14.0
April	14.1
May	14.5
June*	21.7
July	23.4
August	24.1
September	23.2
October	22.5
November	21.8
December	20.7

Source: Civil Aviation Authority, Monthly Airport Statistics.

* Second new entrant to market.

The peak-to-trough ratio under deregulation was 2.33 to 1 and under regulation in 1985 it was 1.79 to 1.

Rent under airline regulation

Table 3.13 estimates that regulation allowed the two incumbent carriers to charge an average of 31 per cent above the deregulation price on the Dublin–London route. The ban on new entrants coupled with output predetermination and price collusion by the incumbents generated producer surpluses or rents above the levels necessary to supply air services under free market conditions. Rent is an allocatively unnecessary payment not required to attract resources to the particular employment. It is a receipt in excess of opportunity cost (Buchannan, 1980). This economic rent was worth £25 million a year. Based on capacity provided it was split 60:40 between Aer Lingus and British Airways. The rent was important to

Aer Lingus because the Dublin–London route accounted for 40 per cent of its European traffic.

The economic rents could have been eliminated by the price control powers of the governments. They lacked the yield information necessary to make this decision. European governments have traditionally been weak in dealing with their national carriers. On the Dublin–London route fare increases sanctioned were 66 per cent higher than for the average of the 11 routes in Table 3.11 over the years 1980–5. The rate of increase sanctioned was 75 per cent above the UK inflation rate.

The economic rents on the Dublin–London route could also have been eroded by creating competition for the market where bilateral agreement prevented competition in the market. Where two airlines of differing efficiency share a route and charge the same fare the choice facing the more efficient airline is either to earn supernormal profit or to decline to the efficiency of the other airline. Competitive tendering for route licences would have eroded the supernormal profits of efficient carriers or stopped their declining in efficiency to the standard of the less efficient bilateral partner airline (Demsetz, 1968). The sale of route licences was rejected by the Civil Aviation Authority, however, because 'route licences are not property. British Airways did not purchase its licences and the licences fees and charges, which it, like other airlines, has paid in respect of licences over the years do not in any way reflect the profit expectations arising from their use' (1984). A market in route licences could have been created. Since revenues were determined exogenously, the bids for route licences would have reflected the different cost structures of the bidder airlines and the rent would have accrued to the government selling the licence rather than to the airline.

The surplus from the operation of European air routes under regulation has a number of alternative uses. It might, for example, result in increased profits, increased pay and for reduced productivity, or the operation of services on routes which do not satisfy normal commercial criteria.

The evidence from the Dublin–London deregulation does not support the hypothesis that aviation rent increased profits or financed thin routes. Aer Lingus was a marginally profitable aviation operation under regulation. Since deregulation it has paid its first dividend. Its profits were greater under deregulation than under protectionism which insulated the cost structure of the airline from competitive pressures. Under regulation there were three points in the Republic of Ireland with international service. This has increased to seven under deregulation as lower-cost airlines find it possible to serve routes which were not viable in the high-cost environment.

Since deregulation Aer Lingus has introduced a two-tier wage structure. Table 3.15 shows that under regulation the airline's average staff remuneration was one of the highest among airlines in the OECD countries when compared with GNP per head. Whereas the average for the nineteen countries examined was airline pay at 2.56 times the GNP per head the Aer Lingus ratio was 4.0. While Table 3.15 shows that the ratio is generally higher the lower a country's GNP per head, there is evidence in the Irish case that airline pay is high in absolute terms.

Table 3.15 Airline staff remuneration per head and GNP per head, 1984

	$ per employee	*Ratio 10 GNP per head*	*Index*
AerLingus	19,968	4.0	156
Air France	19,631	2.2	86
Alitalia	27,189	4.4	172
Austrian	24,740	3.1	121
British Airways	15,117	2.0	78
British Midland	13,755	1.8	70
British Caledonian	15,194	2.0	78
Dan Air	13,297	1.8	70
Finnair	14,672	1.4	55
Iberia	15,739	3.8	148
KLM	22,654	2.6	102
Lufthansa	27,128	2.7	105
SAS	25,611	2.3	90
Sabena	21,406	2.8	109
Swissair	33,459	2.4	94
TAP	11,646	6.0	234
UTA	29,531	2.7	105
US Majors (16)	41,085	2.7	105
Air Canada	27,335	2.1	82
Average (19 countries)		2.56	100

Source: ICAO, Civil Aviation Statistics of the World, 1984, OECD National Accounts.

The ability of the regulatory system to generate economic rent is less the greater the degree of competition. Two British airlines in Table 3.15 have little possibility of generating economic rent. 'In market systems, all economic rent tends to be eroded or dissipated as adjustments take place through time' according to Buchannan (1980: 5). British Midland is mainly an internal carrier on competitive routes while Dan Air is primarily a charter airline. Table 3.15 shows that in 1984 average Aer Lingus remuneration was 50 per cent greater than Dan Air and 45 per cent greater than British Midland. Historically in European aviation market entry and price competition were not allowed. Where entry is blocked, Buchannan states that 'there will be no dissipation of rents ... output will not be forced above monopoly limits and price will not fall' (1980: 7).

Contestability aspects

The contestability of the Dublin–London route has been increased by new entrants and reduced collusion between the incumbents. Price competition has replaced price collusion and capacity controls have been abolished. In addition to expanding the total market the new entrants have been successful in attracting customers from the incumbents. It has been maintained by the established airlines that the high unrestricted fares charged by them represented an acceptable price for a superior product and seat availability. A Luton Airport survey of Ryanair passengers in

November 1987 found that 45 per cent were on business trips. This is the same proportion as for the established airlines at Heathrow under regulation as shown in Table 3.11.

Scale economies were not important in the London–Dublin deregulation. The new entrants had 400 staff each in the case of Ryanair, Virgin and Capitol and 2,100 in British Midland. This compared with 4,500 staff in Aer Lingus and 38,000 in British Airways. The sunk costs of establishing Ryanair were £2.2 million in 1986. There were profits of £0.9 million in 1987 and losses in 1988/9. Costless exit was not therefore possible in less than a three-year period.

Barriers to contestability

Three new entrants had to develop Luton as their London airport. The main airport, Heathrow, has not accepted new entrants since 1977. The new entrants thus found themselves having to undertake extra marketing expenditures to promote not just new airlines but a new airport. They are also prevented from competing for the 25 per cent of the market which interlines at Heathrow and Gatwick.

The ban on new entrants at Heathrow has allowed the incumbent airlines to increase their traffic at that airport from 23 million to 38 million between 1977 and 1988. Airlines with grandfather rights at many of Europe's hub airports have persuaded airport authorities and governments that scarce capacity should be allocated to them only. More efficient solutions should be sought such as a lottery or auction of airport slots and expansion of airport capacity. In 1989 the Irish government transferred to Ryanair the Aer Lingus Stansted licence, as part of a two-airline policy. Aer Lingus will serve Heathrow and Gatwick and Ryanair will serve Luton and Stansted.

Even where new airlines have access to important airports in Europe they are placed at a competitive disadvantage in the market for passenger and baggage handling. At Heathrow, handling is confined to airlines with grandfather rights. British Midland informed the Monopolies and Mergers Commission that it could provide the services itself for just over half the amount charged by a grandfather rights airline at Heathrow and that 'this difference is a substantial element in its competitiveness and that it should be able to pass the benefits of lower handling charges to its customers' (1985: 107). At Dublin the new entrants were permitted to self-handle but the market in handling for others is restricted to Aer Lingus.

The deregulation of a single route such as Dublin–London within a highly regulated market such as Europe places new entrants at a disadvantage. They lack the sources of rent that are available to carriers within the regulated sector. Geographical price discrimination contributed to the demise of World and Capital Airways, according to Kahn. Reductions in fares by the incumbent airlines on Dublin–London have not occurred on other uncontested routes between Ireland and Britain. While air travel between Britain and Ireland has grown 227 per cent during 1985–9 the uncontested Birmingham route has remained stagnant. The discounts known as the London Business Bonus also exhibit geographical price discrimination. They are available on trips ex-Dublin but not ex-London.

This reflects the greater competitive success of the new Dublin–London entrants in Ireland than in Britain. While traveller survey data indicate that the growth of traffic since deregulation has been evenly divided between residents of Britain and Ireland, airline sources indicate that in Britain residents of Irish birth or descent have responded most to deregulation. The Ireland–UK results might not apply in non-ethnic markets.

The greater success of the new entrants in Ireland than in Britain may indicate economies of scope. In Britain it may be easier to market the London–Dublin route as part of a network serving many cities. The Irish market is much smaller and is heavily dominated by the Dublin–London route.

Inequality of access to yield management computer programmes, which divide aircraft into subunits to be sold at different prices to different market segments, is a barrier to contestability between incumbents and new entrants. Levine points out that such information can 'negate partially or entirely the new entrant's cost advantage and affect its staying power' (1987: 477).

Price-discriminating incumbents can limit their fare reductions to price sensitive segments of the market, can limit apparently unrestricted fares by hidden capacity controls and price discrimination between different routes. This allows the incumbent to match the lower overall simple fares of the new entrant on only a portion of the incumbent's traffic. If a sufficient number of the new entrants' price-sensitive passengers can be won back the load factor of the new entrant will fall. If the new entrant is forced to exit the market the hidden capacity controls over the lower fares can be increased by the incumbents thus replacing real across-the-board savings by restricted reductions which can be confined to a small segment of the market.

The London–Dublin route in 1989

Passenger numbers increased by 15 per cent to 2.3 million or 2.3 times the pre-deregulation traffic in 1985. The value in fare savings from deregulation to passengers in 1989 was therefore £24.9 million to the 994,000 pre-deregulation passengers and £16.2 million for 1.3 million generated passengers over the 1985 base year with benefits to these passengers valued at half the pre-deregulation unit value.

Fares did not increase in the years 1986–9 under deregulation. During these years consumer prices increased by 10 per cent in Ireland and by 18 per cent in the United Kingdom. The fall in real fares under deregulation contrasts with the period 1980–5 when fares ex-London increased by 72.6 per cent compared with an increase in the Retail Price Index of 41.5 per cent, as shown in Table 3.11. Under regulation fares increased 75 per cent faster than the RPI in the UK. Taking 1986 as 100 a fare in the UK would have cost 118 in 1989 if it increased in line with inflation. An actual fare of 69 is therefore a reduction of 42 per cent in real terms. Compared to an index of 110 the Irish actual fare of 69 is a saving of 37 per cent.

British Midland entered the Heathrow–Dublin route in April 1989 and Capital Airways replaced Virgin Atlantic on Luton–Dublin in July 1989. British Midland was the only new entrant with access to slots at Heathrow. It raised service standards with meal service for all passengers and introduced an IR£128 business fare for a three-day return ticket. This was immediately matched by the incumbent airlines who previously charged £208 for that fare category. Service quality also improved in extra frequency from 16 flights daily in the summer of 1985 to 45 in 1989 and the initiation of services to Luton and Stansted which were not served in 1985. British Midland's market entry had a significant impact in raising the market share of the new entrants (British Midland, Ryanair and Capital) to 28 per cent in the second half of 1989. In the same period the share of the Luton airlines (Ryanair and Capital) fell to 15 per cent.

Conclusions

The deregulation of the Dublin–London route has brought significant benefits in fare savings and generated traffic on a high-cost stagnant route. Collusion between the established airlines has been reduced and a two-tier wage structure has been introduced. The gains have been achieved despite the exclusion of two new entrants from Heathrow and the lack of competition in the services to airlines at the London and Dublin airports.

Other important obstacles to contestability also persist. They include geographical price discrimination by established airlines operating partly in regulated and partly in deregulated markets. Economies of scope are indicated by the lesser success of the new entrants in the market ex-London than ex-Dublin. Computer technology which allows incumbent carriers to segment the market but apparently offering fares lower than the new entrants while retaining their high yield traffic has been a major obstacle to new market entrants under deregulation in the United States. The European national carriers have the advantage of having seen how the major US airlines used this technology to remove new entrants. There are therefore many areas of economic rent in European aviation which require policy responses in the application of European Community competition policy to the aviation sector as part of a single European market by 1992. The Dublin–London deregulation has brought significant gains to users but left several important sources of rent unaddressed (Bailey and Williams, 1988).

Hub airport access for new airlines and their protection from the abuse of a dominant position by established airlines will be required at government and EC level to ensure that the gains from competition are retained. The role of new entrants is vital. On Dublin–London there has been no obvious increase in competition between Aer Lingus and British Airways since 1986. There have, however, been periods of frenzied competition between Aer Lingus, as market leader, and Ryanair and British Midland, the important new market entrants. Airlines with a large network have the ability to engage in geographical price discrimination against competitors on a limited number of routes. While EC competition policy forbids the abuse of a dominant position it has not been applied in aviation. Since new entrants are essential in eliminating collusion between established airlines they are critical in promoting and retaining contestability in European aviation.

References

Bailey, E.E. (1986) Price and productivity change following deregulation: the US experience, *Economic Journal* 96: 1–17.

Bailey, E.E. and Williams, J.R. (1988) Sources of rent in the deregulated airline industry, *Journal of Law and Economics* 31: 173–202.

Barrett, S.D. (1987) *Flying High: Airline Prices and European Regulation.* Aldershot: Avebury.

Borenstein, S. (1992) The evolution of US airline competition, *Journal of Economic Perspectives* 6: 45–730.

Buchannan, J. (1980) Rent seeking and profit seeking, in *Toward a Theory of the Rent Seeking Society.* College Station, TX: A&M University Press.

Cahill, B. (1993) Evidence to the Joint Committee on Commercial State Sponsored Bodies, 8 July, pp. 1–28.

Cahill, B. (1994) Managing change in changing times. Address to Trinity College Business Alumni, 29 November 1994.

Civil Aviation Authority (1984) *Airline Competition Policy.* London: CAP 500.

Demsetz, H. (1968) Why regulate utilities?, *Journal of Law and Economics* 11: 55–65.

de Witt (1995) An urge to merge, *Journal of Air Transport Management* 2: 173–80.

Dobson, A. (1995) *Flying in the Face of Competition.* Aldershot: Avebury.

Doganis, R. (1985) *Flying off Course, The Economics of International Airlines. Unwin European Civil Aviation Conference (1981).* Report of the Task Force on Competition in Intra-European Air Services (The Compass Report), p. 41.

Doganis, R. (1992) *The Airport Business.* London: Routledge.

Government of Ireland (1984) *Air Transport Bill.* Dublin: Government of Ireland.

Government of Ireland (1994) *Green Paper on Aviation Policy.* Dublin: Government of Ireland.

Jordan, W. (1970) *Airline Regulation in America.* Baltimore: Johns Hopkins, p. 226.

Kahn, A.E. (1988) Surprises of airline deregulation, *American Economic Review* 78: 316–22.

Levine, M.E. (1987) Airline competition in deregulated markets: theory firms strategy and public policy, *Yale Journal of Regulation* 393: 477.

Monopolies and Mergers Commission (1985) *The British Airports Authority.* London: HMSO, p. 107.

Morrison, S. and Winston, C. (1986) *The Economic Effects of Airline Deregulation.* Brookings Institution, Chapter 1.

Morrison, S. and Winston, C. (1989) Enhancing the performance of the deregulated air transportation system, *Brookings Papers on Economic Activity* Special Issue: 80.

Nuutinen, H. (1993) Aer Lingus – a radical restructuring, *The Avmark Aviation Economist* June 16–19.

OECD (1988) *Deregulation and Airline Competition.* Paris: OECD.

Oum, T.H. and Yu, C. (1995) A productivity comparison of the world's major airlines, *Journal of Air Transport Management* 2: 181–95.

Sawer, D. (1987) *Competition in the Air.* Institute of Economic Affairs.

Williams, G. (1994) *The Airline Industry and the Impact of Deregulation.* Aldershot: Avebury.

4 Ryanair's market entry

Peripheral market entry, product differentiation, supplier rents and sustainability in the deregulated European aviation market – a case study

We will now examine the market entry of Ryanair, a startup airline based in Ireland and the first new entrant airline in the EU likely to exceed the passenger numbers carried by its national airline. The implications for contestability policy are examined.

In 1985 Ryanair commenced service from Waterford in the southeast of Ireland to Gatwick, using a 15-seat Bandeirante. In May 1986, the company commenced service between Dublin and Luton using HS 748 aircraft and charging £94.99 return compared to £208 charged by Aer Lingus and British Airways on the Dublin–Heathrow route. Table 4.1 shows the passenger numbers carried by Ryanair and Aer Lingus since 1985. In 1998, Ryanair will carry an estimated 86 per cent of the passengers carried by Aer Lingus. Table 4.2 shows that this relative performance is about five times as successful as the typical second airline in Europe compared with its national carrier.

Ireland had one of the most stagnant markets in aviation from Britain between 1978 and 1985. It was perceived an unattractive market for new entrants. Many foreign airlines did not take up their entitlements under bilateral aviation agreements so that in 1979/80 Aer Lingus accounted for 72 per cent of passengers at Irish airports. Irish air routes also showed a high rate of growth of fares. The charter market between Ireland and Britain was minimal. The emphasis in policy in Ireland was to protect the national airline. Airline costs in Ireland were high because of low productivity and high wage costs. The deregulation of Irish aviation policies in 1986 occurred because of hostile reaction to legislation to fine, imprison and remove travel agent licences from those discounting airline tickets (Barrett, 1997). The evidence of the cascade studies was that basic charter-type air services could be provided for about a third of the European scheduled fares. Many economists in Ireland believed that competition would reduce fares and that in turn this would generate extra air traffic because of Ireland's island location and the low speed and high cost of sea travel. Over the entire period since 1986 the evidence has been that Ryanair entry to a market, by catering for those who did not previously fly, has expanded the market by more than the number of passengers carried by Ryanair. While the passenger numbers on the incumbent airlines have not declined, the advent of Ryanair on a route has reduced the yields of established airlines. Ryanair's virtual parity with its national airline contrasts with an average

Table 4.1 Passenger numbers on Aer Lingus and Ryanair 1985–98 (000s)

	Aer Lingus	Ryanair	Ryanair/Aer Lingus (%)
1985	2,267	5	0.2
1986	2,280	82	4
1987	2,670	318	12
1988	3,523	600	17
1989	3,970	660	17
1990	4,067	750	18
1991	3,786	711	19
1992	4,062	945	23
1993	3,706	1,120	30
1994	3,736	1,600	43
1995	4,189	2,387	57
1996	4,785	2,950	62
1997	5,300	3,730	70
1998 (est.)	5,800	5,000	86

Table 4.2 Passengers (millions) carried by national airlines and second airlines, Europe, 1997/8

National airline		Second airline		Second airline index[a]
Aer Lingus	5.3	Ryanair	4.1	77
British Airways	40.9	British Midland	5.7	14
Air France	33.5	AOM France	3.4	10
KLM	14.7	Martinair	2.0	14
Lufthansa	44.4	LTU	7.2	16
Austrian	3.9	Lauda	1.4	36
SAS	20.8	Brathens	5.7	27
Iberia	16.1	Air Europa	6.3	39
Alitalia	24.6	Meridiana	2.7	11

Source: Airline Business, September 1998.

Note
[a]National airline = 100.

of second airline performance of 21 per cent of its national airline for the eight other national airlines and second airlines compared in Table 4.2.

There have been four main stages in the development of Ryanair.

1   1985–90: the startup phase. The Ryanair chief executive describes this phase as 'considerable initial enthusiasm and public support by introducing low fares and competition on the Dublin–London route'. This was followed by a period in which 'we made the traditional airline mistakes, over-expanded into a broad

network of unsustainable routes, an unmanageable fleet, which despite having only eight aircraft included four different aircraft types'. By 1990 the airline was losing £7 million a year on a revenue of £40 million and had eaten up £20 million of equity in the previous four years (O'Leary, 1994).

2 The 1991 restructuring and relaunch as a 'no frills' airline. This stage involved a downsizing from 18 to 4 routes, reducing staff numbers from 570 to 525, eliminating business class and complimentary in-flight services and abolishing the airline's frequent-flyer programme. The airline chose a standardised Boeing 737-200 fleet. The airline does not have lounges at airports and does not use airbridges. The emphasis of the relaunched airline was cheap point-to-point transport. Ryanair does not offer interlining and is not involved in alliances with other airlines. Average yield was reduced by 50 per cent between 1991 and 1994. The four routes served were Dublin to Stansted, Liverpool and Luton and Knock to Stansted. The model chosen for the relaunch was Southwest in the United States. The London base operation was moved from Luton to Stansted. The corporate headquarters was moved from Dublin city centre to the airport.

3 The 1993–7 expansion programme on UK routes. This stage involved service between Dublin and Birmingham (1993), Manchester, Gatwick and Glasgow (1994), Leeds–Bradford, Cardiff and Bournemouth (1996) and Teesside (1997). In addition, Cork (1995) and Kerry (1997) were served from Stansted. Ryanair introduced a Stansted–Prestwick service in 1996 before the removal of the ban on cabotage on 1 April 1997. By 1997, Ryanair was the dominant airline on every route it served between Ireland and Britain. It then changed its emphasis for expansion to mainland Europe.

4 The 1997–8 expansion programme on mainland Europe routes. In this phase new routes from Dublin to Paris and Brussels and Stansted to Oslo and Stockholm opened in 1997 and routes from Stansted to Kristianstad/Malmo, Venice, Rimini, Pisa, St Etienne/Lyon and Carcassone/Toulouse were added in 1998.

The Ryanair route network in 1998 comprised 26 routes:

Dublin–UK	12 routes
Stansted–mainland Europe	8 routes
Stansted–Irish regions	3 routes
Dublin–mainland Europe	2 routes
Internal UK	1 route

In contrast to its startup phase the financial performance of Ryanair in recent years has been impressive. In the first quarter of 1998/9 profits were IR£9.2 million on sales of £57.8 million and 1.2 million passengers were carried. For the year 1997/8 the Ryanair net margin of 16.5 per cent was the second highest of 175 airlines worldwide in the annual *Airline Business* analysis (1998). Profits have increased from £1.4 million in 1992 to £8.4 million in 1993, £12.0 million in

1994/5, £13.4 million in 1995/6, £15.3 million in 1996/7 and £28.3 million in 1997/8.

Causes of the Ryanair success

The success of Ryanair is based on several important policy decisions. The airline had to assess the profitability of Irish aviation in the mid-1980s in a manner which was quite different from the views of both public policy makers and incumbent airlines. It had to end the regulatory capture of public policy making in aviation by the national airline. It had to assess the potential of market segments not served by the incumbent airlines and the impact of factors such as Ireland's island location on those markets. It had to devise a new product in order to achieve an impact differing from the products available before deregulation. It had to tackle the high cost base of Irish aviation, both the factors internal to airlines such as low productivity, and external factors such as airport charges, travel agency fees and computer reservation system costs. The critical Ryanair decisions were as follows.

Reassessing the potential profitability of Irish aviation

Ireland in the mid-1980s was not an obvious location for establishing a new airline. The economy was in recession throughout much of the decade. Unemployment was high. Tourism had stagnated for 20 years. Table 4.3 shows that the dominant Ireland–UK route, Dublin–London, had in the first half of the 1980s the lowest growth in passenger numbers (2.8 per cent) and the highest growth in fares (72.6 per cent) of 11 routes examined by the Civil Aviation Authority.

A gloomy view of the profitability of Irish aviation was held by the dominant airline in that market, Aer Lingus. The chief executive of the airline wrote in

Table 4.3 Stagnation and fare increases on Ireland/UK aviation before deregulation. London–Dublin and ten major routes compared, 1980–5

London to ...	Passenger growth (%)	Fare increase (%)
Edinburgh	58.3	31.9
Manchester	41.9	45.5
Glasgow	40.4	31.9
Frankfurt	40.1	43.2
Aberdeen	34.5	29.2
Belfast	30.7	40.9
Amsterdam	24.1	38.5
Brussels	20.4	43.6
Newcastle	18.4	38.8
Paris	17.1	63.2
Dublin	2.8	72.6
Average (11)	29.9	29.9

Source: Civil Aviation Authority (1987), Competition on the Main Domestic Trunk Routes (CAA Paper 87005), London.

1988 that 'the traditional Aer Lingus view was that the shorthaul and seasonal nature of our European network was inherently not economic, or at least only marginally so, and would have to be supported by a profitable Atlantic operation' (Kennedy, 1998: 174). It was also company policy, with Irish government support, to build up ancillary activities such as hotels, to cross-subsidise the airline. The Aer Lingus chairman's report for 1985/6 stressed also the uneconomic nature of aviation services to Ireland when he described the entry of Ryanair as follows:

> The decisions of the regulatory authority at home have the utmost significance for us. The awarding of a licence to an additional recently founded Irish carrier between Dublin and London was a critical decision. With the possible exception of the Atlantic route at some time in the future, Dublin–London is the only route on the Aer Lingus network that has the volume of business to allow of itself a reasonable return on capital. The decision to put a fourth carrier on the route will have an effect on Aer Lingus' ability to earn enough profit to attract capital needed for fleet renewal and for further development. It will also affect Aer Lingus' ability to operate those marginal Cross-Channel and Continental routes where little or no return can be earned. The advent of this carrier on the route has brought about the usual predatory pricing phase while it attempts to take over market share and this phase has yet to run its course. Further applications have, as we expected, now come for relaxation of conditions set out in the Dublin-London licence and for operations on further segments of Aer Lingus' few profitable routes ... We also request consideration from the licensing authorities at home of further dilution in the precarious markets we serve.
>
> (Aer Lingus Annual report, 1985/6: 8)

In March 1985, the Aer Lingus chief executive stated that the economics of services on its smaller thinner routes – mainly between Dublin and provincial British cities – had it very poor indeed, with traffic falling, the service then being cut back and this leading in turn to the traffic falling again (Share, 1988: 269).

It was thus necessary for a new entrant Irish airline in the mid-1980s to have a radically different view of the market to that held by the dominant airline and the regulatory authorities. A positive factor in assessing the prospects for investment in Irish aviation is the country's island location. The alternative of sea journeys to Britain was also expensive as both aviation and sea transport were operated by cartels. The surface transport journeys were time-consuming; for example, a nine-hour ship and train journey from Dublin to London contrasted with a one-hour flight. An indication of the attractiveness of islands for aviation is seen in the impact of the Channel Tunnel. Passenger numbers between Heathrow and Charles de Gaulle fell from 2.7 million in 1994 to 1.8 million in 1997. A rail tunnel to Ireland is highly unlikely in the foreseeable future.

Even in the era of high fares before deregulation, aviation was a more important sector of the economy in Ireland than in the European Community as a whole.

Eurostat data for 1983 indicate that the ratio of air trips per head of population in the then European Economic Community was 0.74, based on 202.4 million air trips from a population of 272.4 million in the ten member states. The Irish ratio was 0.97, based on 3.4 million journeys in a population of 3.5 million. There was in Ireland therefore a propensity to undertake air journeys some 31 per cent greater than in the EEC as a whole, notwithstanding the high fares charged and Ireland's lower incomes.

In assessing the market, a new entrant in the mid-1980s would have noted considerable resentment of the high fares charged by the incumbent airlines. The resentment was justified by the gains to consumers from competition. The Dublin–London fare of £208 and the Cork–London fare of £240 were cut by some 70 per cent based on comparing the 1998 fares with those charged before competition on these routes.

The growth of traffic after deregulation confirmed that there was a large pent-up demand for air travel between Ireland and Britain. For example, traffic on the Dublin–London route in August 1985, the first full year of deregulation, was 87 per cent higher than in August 1985, the last full year of pre-deregulation policies.

The dynamic impact of Ryanair's market entry is seen in Table 4.4. In 1985 Ireland was the seventh largest market in Western Europe for air travel from Britain but by 1997 it ranked second. The contrast with the German market is striking. In 1985 the German market was twice the size as the Irish but in 1997 Irish traffic was 9 per cent greater. In passenger numbers a margin of 1.8 million in favour of the German routes was replaced by a margin of 0.7 million in favour of the Irish routes. Before deregulation the Irish traffic in Table 4.3 lagged behind all other routes. After deregulation, as Table 4.4 indicates Ireland became the leading growth market.

Table 4.4 Air passengers from UK to main EU countries, 1985–97

	1985	*1997*	*Index*
Austria	364	1152	316
Belgium	988	2339	232
Denmark	613	1673	273
Finland	183	604	330
France	3736	6443	172
Germany	3644	7125	196
Greece	2875	3774	131
Ireland	1807	7786	431
Italy	2583	5234	203
Netherlands	2227	5773	259
Portugal	1547	2888	187
Spain	7571	19,558	258
Sweden	511	1589	310

Source: Civil Aviation Authority Annual Statistics.

Ending regulatory capture

The Irish regulatory authorities were frequently described as 'the downtown office of Aer Lingus' in the era before 1986. In the years 1936 to 1986 the airline achieved substantial regulatory capture and succeeded in having its interest defined as the Irish national interest. The patriotic connotations of Aer Lingus are captured in Share's account of the launch of the New York service in 1960: 'You saw for the first time an Irish plane with a shamrock. There was a great deal of emotional pride in the thing' (1988: 95).

The Air Navigation (International Lines) Order of 1935 required ministerial authorisation for air services 'with a view to the limitation or regulation of competition as may be considered necessary in the public interest' (Share, 1988: 3). For example, a company seeking to operate air services between Ireland and Britain, Crilly Airways, was informed in 1935 that 'the Minister was unable to entertain his proposals. The reason given was the Government's intention to set up a national airline at the earliest possible date' (Share, 1988: 3). Several other proposals were turned down before the Air Transport Act 1936 'enshrined the position of the State as the sole international carrier. KLM has been set up in 1919, Lufhtfhansa in April 1926 and Air France in 1933, all State entities benefiting from official restriction of competition' (Share, 1988: 22). In 1949 a proposal for an air service from Cork to Britain was turned down by the government on the grounds that air transport policy did not contemplate that airlines other than Aer Lingus would operate scheduled services between the two countries' (Share, 1988: 69). From 1946 to 1957 Aer Lingus had a monopoly of air services between Britain and Ireland. British European Airways (BEA) and British Overseas Airways Corporation (BOAC) held 40 per cent of the shareholding in Aer Lingus. The shareholding arrangement ended in 1965. The official history of Aer Lingus acknowledges that changes in aviation policy were driven by popular dissatisfaction with Aer Lingus as the market leader and defender of high fares on Ireland–Britain air routes.

The pessimism of Aer Lingus about the future of Irish aviation may have been a strategic decision by the company to deter new entrants and regulatory change by disseminating the view that Irish aviation routes were chronically uneconomic. In retrospect it can be seen that the pessimism of Aer Lingus was not justified. International Civil Aviation Organization (ICAO) data show that the Dublin–London was the sixth busiest international route in the world in 1985 when Aer Lingus was describing its market in most pessimistic terms. The dynamic effects of deregulation were hugely greater than Aer Lingus believed and than even the advocates of deregulation expected. In 1997 Dublin–London was the second busiest international route in the world after Hong Kong–Taipei (ICAO: Civil Aviation Statistics of the World).

The monopoly was defended by the regulatory authorities:

> In October 1950 the Minister for Industry and Commerce informed the Independent Air Transport Association of Britain that in his view Aer Lingus

was providing adequate services between Ireland and that country and that where additional services were justified the company would provide them in due course. One of the independents, Silver City, was proposing to start a car ferry from Liverpool, and Aer Lingus asked the Minister to protect the company's position as they were considering the opening of a similar service on the route.

In retrospect, those in Aer Lingus and the regulatory bodies who saw little prospect for airline services failed utterly to see the stimulus which competition would provide to the size of the market. They also failed to see the harm done to an island economy by a high-cost aviation policy. No analysis was undertaken by the government of the gains to Aer Lingus and its staff from protectionism and the losses to the economy at large. Irish tourism grew faster than any other country in the OECD in the decade after access deregulation. The period after 1993 saw economic and employment growth in Ireland which was unprecedented.

The gains to Aer Lingus from protectionism up to 1986 are illustrated in a combination of a low-productivity high-wage airline as shown in Table 4.5. Aer Lingus as a protected airline had one of the lowest productivity figures in Europe and one of the highest ratios of airline pay to GNP per head. The comparison

Table 4.5 Average airline staff remuneration, ratio to GNP per head and cost per unit of output, European Airlines, 1984

Company	Wage $	GNP ratio	tkm per staff (000s)	Wage cost ($) per 000 tkm
Aer Lingus	19,968	4.0	63	370
Air France	19,631	2.2	140	140
Alitalia	27,189	4.4	108	251
Austrian	24,740	3.1	54	504
BA	15,117	2.0	131	115
British Midland	13,755	1.8	100	138
B. Caledonian	15,194	2.0	137	111
Dan Air	13,297	1.8	169	79
Finnair	14,672	1.4	87	169
Iberia	15,739	3.8	91	173
KLM	22,654	2.6	159	142
Lufthansa	27,128	2.7	144	188
SAS	25,611	2.3	82	312
Sabena	21,406	2.8	121	177
Swissair	33,459	2.4	115	291
TAP	11,646	6.0	53	220
US Majors (16)	41,085	2.7	–	–
Air Canada	27,335	2.1	–	–
Average	–	2.56	–	–
Average (Europe)	–	–	–	211

Source: ICAO, Civil Aviation Statistics of the World, 1984; OECD National Accounts.

with British Midland shows that Aer Lingus wages were 45 per cent higher. The ending of the era of protectionism in Irish aviation some 11 years before the realisation of this goal in the EU as a whole was a major plus in locating a new airline in Ireland. The crucial decision in 1985 to enter the market contradicted the conventional wisdom in the established industry which had accomplished regulatory capture.

Ryanair's startup costs were reduced by the recession in the Irish economy in the 1980s. Unemployment in 1986 was 17.6 per cent and there was a ready supply of labour. This was not the case in 1998. Unemployment was officially measured at 9.2 per cent, which is lower than in Germany, France and Italy and the EU average unemployment rate. GDP per head has increased from 70 per cent of the EU average to 103 per cent. From an initial low-cost labour market at startup Ryanair has moved to wage parity with Aer Lingus but with far higher productivity in return. In 1998, for example, some 1,000 staff in Ryanair will handle 5 million passengers while 5,000 staff in Aer Lingus will handle 5.8 million.

Ryanair, having convinced investors and government regulators that the era of protectionism in aviation had not served the public interest, then had to seek the support of passengers and potential passengers for its market emphasis on the budget-sensitive passenger. The key elements were those who did not travel by air at all because of high basic fares and the restricted availability of discounted fares to a small number of seats which had to be booked long in advance of the journey.

Defining a new aviation market

Porter (1996) examines three sources of strategic market positions: variety-based, needs-based and access-based. Lawton (1998) emphasises Ryanair's choice of needs-based positioning, as opposed to variety-based or access-based positioning, in explaining the airline's success. 'A focussed competitor such as ... Ryanair thrives on groups of customers who are overpriced by more broadly targeted competitors' (1998: 5). The success of Ryanair has been based on expanding the market rather than diverting a static market from other airlines. This strategy was based on the gaps in the market left by established airlines. For example, the absence of a low fare for the short-notice passenger annoyed Irish people living in Britain who wished to go home at minimal notice for funerals, family illnesses, and so on. Before Ryanair these passengers were compelled to pay a business fare or to predict by as much as 28 days the illnesses and deaths of family members. As Ryanair expands its services to the European mainland this Irish ethnic factor will diminish and the airline will have to develop markets such as leisure visits, and sectors of the business market where passengers pay for their own tickets and/or do not consider traditional business class airlines good value for money. An indication of dissatisfaction in the business community with business class as marketed by the incumbent airlines was a survey by the Chambers of Commerce of Ireland which indicated that over 90 per cent of the chief executives of the top thousand Irish companies regarded business class as bad value for money. The leisure passenger elsewhere in Europe is served by charter airlines or in the back of the aircraft run by the incumbent scheduled high cost airlines. Airlines such as Ryanair have to establish in the market a reputation for the lowest fares which traditional airlines cannot match. The incumbent airlines will seek to counter this by charging some passengers low fares but preventing their high-fare passengers from diluting the yield by transferring to these fares. Porter notes that Southwest Airlines serves price and convenience sensitive passengers in a way in which full-cost airlines could not emulate. Southwest has chosen to perform its activities differently and to perform different activities than its rival (Lawton, 1998: 5). Ryanair chose the Southwest model (O'Leary, 1994: 14).

Ryanair has achieved significant economies in tackling the problem of monopolistic service suppliers to airlines. It has secured far higher productivity from its staff than the incumbent airlines as Table 4.7 indicates below. It has reduced travel agents margins from 9 to 7.5 per cent and developed its own telemarketing arm, Ryanair Direct, which retails over a third of its tickets thus eliminating both the CRS and travel agent costs of these passengers.

Tackling the other elements in the aviation value chain

In addition to securing regulator and passenger support for the new airline product the new entrant airline must tackle the problem of costs arising elsewhere in the aviation value chain. Borgo and Bull-Larsen (1998) state that 'an airline can improve its bargaining power in two ways; by increasing its importance to its suppliers, or by diminishing its suppliers' importance to itself'. They note that support services to the airlines such as ground handling, catering, airports and CRS 'have been able to achieve returns of 15–16 per cent on capital' (1998: 54).

The policy implications for airlines of this analysis are that 'in the whole of the airline value chain, the only participants not making attractive returns are the airlines themselves. To capture their rightful share of the value, the carriers must set about restructuring the value chain to improve their own position within it' (1998: 59). Three steps are recommended in this strategy: examine the structure and returns of the airline's suppliers, challenge the significant excess returns of labour groups and find new ways to leverage the airline asset base.

Ryanair has developed services at lesser-used airports, and availed of competitive markets in handling. Table 4.6 shows the airports served by Ryanair and the incumbent carriers. Ryanair operates at only two slot-controlled airports, Gatwick and Manchester. It is thus able to expand output quickly and to become a major operator on its routes. In addition the lesser-used airports have offered inducements to Ryanair passengers such as free parking at Kristianstad, Rimini, Carcassone, Charloi and Beauvais and low-cost train and bus connections such as those at Stansted and Prestwick.

Airport charges are a higher proportion of the ticket price of low-cost short-haul airlines than for high-cost and long-haul airlines. Ryanair's campaigns for lower airport charges have frequently been strident. The official investigation of

Table 4.6 Secondary airports served by Ryanair and alternatives
served by incumbents, 1998

Ryanair airport	Incumbents' airport
Stansted, Luton, Gatwick	Heathrow
Prestwick	Glasgow
Charleoi	Brussels
Beauvais	Paris CDG
Torp	Oslo
Skavasta	Stockholm
Caracssone	Toulouse
St Etienne	Lyons
Kristianstad	Malmo
Teesside	Newcastle
Knock, Kerry	Shannon

the March 1998 strike at Dublin Airport notes that 'it was said that Ryanair's attitude to the airport authorities had not always been cordial or respectful' (p. 58). Where low-cost airlines demand a sharing of the ticket price in a way that is more favourable to the airline and its passengers than to the traditional earners of economic rent at airports, travel agents, and CRS there has been predictable opposition from the latter groups.

Cutting the airline's internal costs

The major internal cost faced by airlines is staff costs. Borgo and Bull-Larsen estimate that airline workers have 'made an accumulated excess return of approximately $13 billion over and above what the market would have compensated them' (1998: 59). Ryanair has a policy of matching the wages paid by its competitors but at a far higher level of productivity. Pay at Ryanair includes attendance and productivity bonuses.

Table 4.7 compares the labour and aircraft productivity of EU national airlines with that of Ryanair. The performance of Ryanair of 48 staff per aircraft and 4,800 passengers per staff member is remarkable compared to the 14 members of the Association of European Airlines. Ryanair has only 41 per cent of the AEA average staff per aircraft while the number of passengers per staff member, at 4,800, is over six times larger than the AEA average, at 752.

The Ryanair figures for staff per aircraft and passengers per staff member also compare strongly with Southwest, the airline on which it has chosen to model itself. Ryanair has just over half the Southwest number of staff per aircraft and carries over two and a half times as many passengers per staff member as Southwest.

The Ryanair productivity data indicate that the no-frills product with many inputs bought in rather than supplied in-house is an aviation service which AEA members have chosen not to produce. It would be difficult for these airlines to change their corporate culture to produce the Ryanair product. The Ryanair

Table 4.7 Labour productivity of European National Airlines,
1997 compared with Southwest and Ryanair

Airline	Staff per aircraft	Passengers per staff per year
Aer Lingus	159	819
Air France	116	450
Alitalia	146	1293
British Airways	140	600
British Midland	133	1178
Finnair	94	597
Iberia	132	739
KLM	118	505
Lufthansa	124	969
Olympic	125	820
Sabena	95	559
SAS	126	923
Swissair	140	578
TAP	112	510
Average (14)	116	752
Southwest	91	1893
Ryanair		
1992	61	1936
1993	59	2389
1994	52	2259
1995	58	3453
1996	58	3767
1997	58	4377
1998	48	4800

Source: Association of European Airlines Yearbook 1997; Ryanair
Prospectus, 1997, Airline Business, September 1998.

comparison with Southwest has to be qualified in respect of the latter's higher service levels and longer stage lengths.

The low-cost no-frills product of Ryanair was found to be quite acceptable to passengers on short-haul flights. By contrast, incumbent airlines operated business class and served meals, drinks and newspapers. Staff time was saved both in not providing in-flight services and not having to clear up refuse such as newspapers and spillages from tea and coffee.

By operating a single aircraft type, the 737-200, the airline was able to achieve better fleet utilisation, and higher staff productivity. The airline does not incur hotel overnight costs for staff. Aircraft are based at Dublin, Prestwick and Stansted and cockpit and cabin staff work from these airports only.

Ryanair achieves a standard 25-minute turnaround time on international services. Compared to turnaround times of 45–60 minutes for rival airlines its quicker turnaround saved the airline between 50 and 70 minutes on a round trip between Britain and Ireland. The saving is the equivalent of the typical taken time on a journey between Britain and Ireland and allows Ryanair to achieve more rotations per day per aircraft than its competitors. The ready availability of slots at all its other airports facilitates quicker turnaround in competition with Aer Lingus at airports such as Heathrow (65 minute turnaround), Paris (50 minute), and Brussels (60 minute). Where the airlines share the same airport, as at Stansted, Manchester and Birmingham, the Aer Lingus turnaround at 45 minutes, is 80 per cent greater than the Ryanair turnaround of 25 minutes. The absence of boarding cards has speeded up check-in. It also led to quicker boarding times and increased punctuality. Passengers board early because the penalty for delaying boarding is to occupy the least popular seats.

The Ryanair success is based therefore on a low-cost product catering for a substantial market which was underserved before deregulation. The low number of staff per aircraft and the high number of passengers per staff member indicate that the Ryanair product is produced in a way which contrasts with the traditional European national airline. The product is low cost because the cost base has been strongly tackled, productivity of staff is high and many aspects of the traditional full service airline have been discarded. The airline has also reduced the impact of external costs for services such as airports, handling, and booking systems. The sustainability of the Ryanair product and performance is examined below.

Factors affecting the sustainability of Ryanair

In assessing the sustainability of Ryanair's market success factors such as management mistakes, the consumer response to the Ryanair product and the airline's relationships with other segments of the aviation value chain such as labour, airport authorities, the owners of reservation systems and travel agents are important factors. These are examined below and also the regulatory environment for the sector.

Managerial error

Each enterprise faces the risk of mistakes. Ryanair admits that in the initial years 'we made the traditional airline mistakes' (O'Leary, 1994). The airline's UK base was in Luton and it was difficult to persuade some travellers that it was a substitute for Heathrow. Ryanair ran turboprop services to Irish regional airports at Waterford, Kerry, Galway, Sligo and Donegal. Unsuccessful services were also provided from Dublin to Brussels and Amsterdam via Luton, and to Paris, Manchester and Munich and from Knock to Manchester and Birmingham. The regional services were expensive to operate but passengers on those routes expected fares comparable to those charged by Ryanair on the Dublin–London jet services. Ryanair was not successful in marketing both low fares and a business class product in the same aircraft.

Ryanair underestimated the response to its market entry by the major incumbent airline. Table 4.8 shows losses which Aer Lingus incurred between 1991 and 1995 and which only the inevitability of bankruptcy halted. Much of these losses

Table 4.8 Net losses and approved subsidies (1991–5) for airlines in competition with Ryanair in 1998 ($billion)

	Net losses	*Subsidies*
Aer Lingus	0.5	0.3
Air France	2.8	3.7
Alitalia	0.4	1.0
Sabena	0.3	1.8
Total	4.0	6.8

Source: Smith (1997) Table 1.

were incurred in competition with Ryanair in markets such as the Irish regions and London services. Ryanair made several other mistakes such as locating its headquarters in a high-rent neighbourhood in the city centre, lack of attention to costs, lack of a marketing focus and the development of an unwieldy network.

Consumer response

The development of a low-cost airline requires large consumer support in order to achieve the economies of high aircraft utilisation and high local factors. Ryanair, as the first European airline to rival the size of its national airline, has been an obvious success in attracting passengers to its very low fares without free in-flight services and, on some routes, the use of secondary airports.

Some, perhaps small, but sometimes vocal, segments of the market dislike the Ryanair product because of lack of service and lack of compensation if there are delays. Incumbent airlines typically have responded to low-fare airlines by discounting heavily some seats while retaining a high-fare business class for late bookings. Full service airlines also stress this aspect of their product compared to the minimal service provided by low-cost airlines. While in recent years passengers have accepted that service on low-cost airlines is related to the fare paid there is an occasional expectation that a low-cost airline should provide full service. Disaffected passengers generate adverse publicity for low-cost airlines. The low-fare product may be less acceptable to passengers on longer journeys.

Labour market opposition

Before deregulation the aviation sector in Ireland was able to combine high wages and low productivity because fares were high. Ryanair has sought to achieve wage parity with other airlines and handling agents and to combine its low fares with high staff productivity. This has attracted strong opposition from trade unions in Ireland culminating in the closure of Dublin Airport on 7 March 1998. The actions taken included the blockading of aircraft on the tarmac at the airport. In a traditionally heavily unionised sector such as European aviation the presence of non-union firms is especially irksome to trade unions. The report on the airport closure by official Irish government investigation (Flynn and McAuley, 1988: 14) states that in their interviews with Ryanair staff, 'the majority of those who met with the Enquiry appear to have a negative attitude to trade union recognition within the Company. Some are not even very tolerant of the right of a minority to join a union.' The report also found that 'it is clear that most employees in Ryanair identify strongly with the Company and its management. They are proud of its achievements and success. They are confident that the Company will continue to grow and this will provide additional career opportunities for them.' They also found that 'most employee groups consider that they work hard for the Company, harder and more effectively than workers in other airport-based companies' and that 'one of the principal advantages of working for Ryanair was stated to be the prospect of promotion, which is regarded as being considerably better in Ryanair than in other airport companies. The Company's policy of promotion from within is highly regarded by employees' (1988: 13). The report cites a Ryanair management letter to the trade union SIPTU, which states that 'neither they (the employees) nor we, require the assistance of any third parties, particularly SIPTU, "the Aer Lingus union" at Dublin Airport, which would happily sacrifice Ryanair and our people at any time, if it benefited your many thousands of members in Aer Lingus' (1988: 30). While only 3 per cent of Ryanair staff have joined SIPTU the union was able to close the airport because of its strength in membership of other airlines, in particular Aer Lingus, and the airport operator, in particular the airport police and fire services. The enquiry in its summary noted that 'it has been said that as Ryanair expanded, employees at other airline companies became concerned about the effect of this on their own future employment prospects, remuneration and working practices and that this had given rise to tension' (1998: 58).

Suppliers of services to the airline

The emergence of low-cost airlines has also attracted opposition from travel agents. Low fares lead to lower income to the travel agent per ticket sold. Travel agent income per ticket sale was also reduced when Ryanair reduced commission from 9 to 7.5 per cent. In July 1998, the Competition Authority of Ireland successfully obtained a court injunction to prevent travel agents collectively boycotting the sale of Ryanair tickets. The combination of a lower commission for travel agents and low fares has reduced the attractiveness of selling Ryanair tickets. Gill (1988: 32) notes for example that Lunn Poly ceased to sell Ryanair tickets.

Low-cost airlines have brought pressure on airport costs. In the era of non-competing airlines airport pricing was a matter of cost recovery by airports. Ryanair operates at only two airports, Gatwick and Manchester, which are slot constrained. As airports become slot constrained in the future airport managers may seek to review special incentive programmes for low-cost airlines. Airport charges are a higher proportion of low-cost airlines ticket price than either high cost airlines or long distance routes. Ryanair aggressively and loudly campaigns against airport charges and this has led to tensions between the airline on the one hand and airport managers and airport staff on the other. According to the Flynn–McAuley

Report, 'it was said that Ryanair's attitude to the airport authorities had not always been cordial or respectful' (1998: 58). The key airports in the Ryanair network are Dublin and Stansted. Dublin, after eight years of stagnation, was happy to facilitate Ryanair in 1986 but relationships between the airport and Ryanair have deteriorated in recent years because of Ryanair criticism of Dublin's costs. The unused capacity at Stansted provided Ryanair with a similar market opportunity in 1991. The success of Ryanair depends critically on the availability of airport capacity at low cost.

Regulatory policy and contestability

Aviation has traditionally been among the most heavily regulated sectors of the economy. Ryanair has been a beneficiary of liberalisation in the markets it serves but barriers to contestability remain. Levine (1987) points out that while deregulation removes the ban on new entrants maintained by governments at the behest of incumbent airlines, there are many other ways in which the incumbents can deter market entry. He proposes that regulators should pursue post-deregulation pro-contestability policies in order to increase overall economic efficiency and to remove obstacles to new entrants such as

- hub airport dominance,
- predatory pricing,
- ground handling monopolies,
- state aids,
- CRS bias,
- price collusion,
- anti-competitive mergers and
- frequent-flyer programmes.

With regard to the general applicability of contestability theory to the Ryanair case two preliminary points are of interest. Potential market entry did not affect price in the markets served by Ryanair. Price reductions by incumbents required actual market entry. The possible fare reductions on UK provincial routes did not occur with the London deregulation in 1986 but with actual market entry in 1993/4. Similarly, fare reductions to Paris and Brussels by incumbents occurred only with actual market entry in 1997 rather than potential market entry.

Contestability also requires ease of market exit. There were two major examples of this during the period. The market exit of British Airways from Ireland in 1991 and the partial exit of Aer Lingus in order to reduce its heavy losses on the London routes in 1994 both improved the contestability of the market. Table 4.8 shows however that four airlines with which Ryanair currently competes received $6.8 billion in subsidies and incurred $4 billion in net losses between 1991 and 1995.

In regard to airport access, the scale of market entry required by the Ryanair development strategy requires significant access to airports. Ryanair has sought to develop the use of secondary airports in order to bypass slot-constrained airports. Route entry thus involves two components: promoting a new airline and a new airport. For example, Ryanair initially sought to develop Luton as an alternative to Heathrow, a slot-constrained airport from which it was excluded. The strategy failed, mainly because of Luton's poorer surface access to Central London. It was decided in 1991 to retain Luton for local services and to transfer the bulk of the London operation to Stansted. The ready availability of capacity at both Dublin and Stansted, the airline's main hubs, has been a crucial factor in the development of Ryanair.

The bypassing of slot constrained hub airports has also occurred in the services to Oslo, Stockholm, Malmo, Brussels, Paris, Lyon, Glasgow and Toulouse. The Ryanair product, cheap point-to-point transport without interlining, is suited to lesser-used airports. The lack of congestion for both passengers and airlines using secondary airports may be perceived as an advantage by some categories of passenger.

Predatory pricing has been a feature of many Ryanair markets. Aer Lingus, the main competitor of Ryanair, incurred losses of $0.5 billion between 1991 and 1995, as shown in Table 4.8. It engaged in below-cost selling on Irish regional routes in 1990/1991 and on the London routes up to 1994. The services on the Irish regional routes from Dublin, launched by Aer Lingus against the Ryanair direct services to London, were subsequently successfully submitted to the Irish government for a public service subsidy. Aer Lingus also admitted in 1994 that it had sold seats on the London routes at a loss of £12 million per annum and decided to cut its capacity in order to eliminate these losses. On the other hand Ryanair was fortunate that British Airways left the Irish market in 1991 thus creating the space in which Ryanair expanded. Other less commercially oriented airlines might have stayed on the routes for prestige reasons or because there was no shareholder pressure to cut losses.

In ground handling Ryanair has been a beneficiary of measures to deregulate ground handling. It has thus avoided the problems which monopolies and cartels in handling caused for previous new entrant airlines, such as British Midland at Heathrow. Ryanair has typically availed of competitive handlers such as Servisair while using its own staff at Dublin.

Ground handling has been an area of conflict between incumbents and new entrants. For example, Dublin airport was closed for a day in March 1998 because the union representing handlers in Aer Lingus sought to recruit some Ryanair handling staff. Deregulating handling is an essential part of airline deregulation and is thus likely to be opposed by incumbent airlines and their staff and trade unions.

Table 4.8 shows the considerable state aid given to Aer Lingus and other Ryanair competitors between 1991 and 1995. It is an objective of EU policy that such aid should cease. The market prospects of airlines such as Ryanair will improve if subsidies to state airlines are removed.

In tackling the problem of reservation system costs Ryanair raised the proportion of its sales made direct to the public through its telemarketing company, Ryanair

Direct, from 25 per cent in 1996 to 35 per cent in 1997 (Ryanair, 1998: 9). Lavere (1998) cites a prediction by the former general manager of Galileo in North America that 'the rising popularity of electronic ticketing, booked directly with the airline either by phone or through its web site makes GDS (global distribution systems) extremely vulnerable' (1998: 43). Ryanair claims that its CRS cost is excessive because the charge is levied per transaction, and is therefore higher as a proportion of revenues for low-cost than for high-cost airlines. EU rules had earlier sought neutrality in the CRS treatment of host and user airlines. This included the designation of Luton as a London airport.

The tradition of price collusion between Europe's national airlines has continued despite deregulation. New entrants such as Ryanair are therefore essential in order to secure the benefits of competition for passengers and efficiency gains in airlines which did not traditionally compete in either price or quality of service.

EU aviation has seen mergers such as Air France, UTA and Air Inter, and the Sabena take over of Air Europe and the KLM takeover of Transavia. These national takeovers and mergers increase the importance of international competition on both international and internal routes. In the Ryanair case a takeover by an incumbent national airline would have serious anti-competitive implications. It has been EU policy to release slots for other airlines where there are mergers or alliances. Successful frequent flyer programmes tie passengers to the airlines operating these programmes. Ryanair has reduced fares to such an extent that it does not wish to operate a frequent-flyer programme.

Conclusion

The successful market entry of Ryanair involved ignoring the pessimistic official and incumbent airline views of the profitability of Irish aviation. As an island, Ireland was a correct choice of location for a new airline offering substantially lower fares than the incumbents. The results have been dramatic. Ryanair has catered for markets not previously served and increased trip frequency. The very high productivity of its staff combined with cost reductions achieved both within the airline and in services such as airports, reservation and retailing costs, make it unlikely that the established airlines could compete on price with Ryanair. The airline has been able to attract passengers for whom the full service airline product provided at high fares by European national airlines is not an attractive option.

References

Barrett, S.D. (1997) The implications of the Ireland–UK airline deregulation for an EU internal market, *Journal of Air Transport Management* 3: 67–74.

Borgo, A. and Bull-Larsen, T. (1998) Strategy losses, *Airline Business* 14(6): 54–9.

Flynn, P. and McAuley, D. (1998) *Report of Enquiry into the Industrial Dispute at Dublin Airport*. Dublin: Government Publications.

Gill, T. (1998) Ryanair, passing go in Europe, *Airline Business* 14(6): 30–2.

Kennedy, D. (1988) Aer Lingus, in Nelson, R. and Clutterbuck, D. (eds), *Turnaround*. London: Mercury.

Lawton, T. (1998) Hard choices and low prices: positioning for sustainable advantage in the airline industry, the case of Ryanair, presented at the Air Transport Research Group Symposium, Dublin.

Levere, J. (1998) CRS Rocky Relations, *Airline Business* 14(8): 40–3.

Levine, M. (1987) Airline competition in deregulated markets, *Yale Journal on Regulation* 4: 393–494.

O'Leary, M. (1994) The challenge of replicating Southwest Airlines in Europe, in *Proceedings of the 2nd International Aviation Conference*, London: Institute of Economic Affairs.

Porter, M. (1996) What is strategy?, *Harvard Business Review* 6: 61–78.

Ryanair (1997) Prospectus for American Share Issue, May.

Ryanair (1998) Prospectus for London Stock Exchange, July.

Share, B. (1988) *The Flight of the Iolar, The Aer Lingus Experience, 1936–1986, Dublin*. London: Gill and Macmillan.

Smith, H.G. (1997) The European Airline Industry, a banker's view, *Journal of Air Transport Management* 3(4): 182–96.

5   The sustainability of the Ryanair model

Introduction

The projected Ryanair passenger number for the year ended 31 March 2005 is 28 million. In the European international scheduled airline market Ryanair will rank third after Air France/KLM at 45 million and Lufthansa at 30 million passengers respectively. In April 2004 the market capitalisation of Ryanair was €3747 million. This compares with €1206 million for easyJet, its main low-cost rival, and €4155 million for Air France/KLM, €4961 million for British Airways, €5428 m for Lufthansa and €2584 million for Iberia. This article examines the sustainability of the Ryanair model which differs substantially from the traditional European national airline model that dominated the sector before deregulation.

We examine the Ryanair airline product and discusses how it differs from the traditional airline product in Europe in terms of price and service standards. We will then deal with the use of secondary airports and their impact on passenger choice and airline economics. We then examine the low cost base of Ryanair both in terms of high productivity of the airline's staff and its cost control over inputs from other, and discuss the sustainability of the Ryanair model in terms of its product, consumer attitudes, secondary airport acceptability, its low cost base, and some external factors.

The Ryanair product

The average Ryanair fare in 2003/4 was €40 and the expectation is a €38 average fare in 2004/5. The net margin fell from 28 per cent in 2002/3 to 21 per cent in 2003/4 and is predicted to fall to 18 per cent in 2004/5. The net margin has thus fallen by ten points in two years. While the margin exceeds the industry average, it may come under pressure from factors such as further falls in yields and the lack of scope for more reductions in an already low cost base.

Ryanair has achieved the lowest cost base by a combination of product changes, which unbundled the traditional European national airline product, by high staff productivity compared to the European average and by reducing the costs of airport services bought in by the airline. The following sections examine these factors in turn. In conclusion the factors affecting the sustainability of the Ryanair model are examined.

The list below illustrates a possible 17 aspects in which the Ryanair product is inferior to the traditional European airline product. The tradeoff in choosing the Ryanair product is major price savings and, perhaps surprisingly, some quality improvements (Barrett, 1999). Customer service items dropped from the traditional European airline product by Ryanair include:

1. In-flight service items: No sweets, newspapers, free food or beverage service. No seat allocation. No business class service. More seats per aircraft and a higher load factor.
2. Airport service items: Secondary airports are typically served. No interlining or connecting journey tickets are issued. Passengers and baggage must be checked in at each airport on a multi-sector journey. No airport lounge service.
3. Ticket restrictions: Tickets are not sold through travel agents. There are no company retail ticket outlets; no frequent-flyer programme; stricter penalties for 'no show' passengers.

Fare reductions have been the key feature in the public mind of greater competition in European aviation. Deregulation enabled Ryanair to enter the Dublin to London route in 1986 resulting in a reduction in fares of 55 per cent, from IR£208 (€264) to IR£95.99 (€121). The 2004 fare of €80 charged by Ryanair, the market leader on Dublin–London, contrasts with the 2004 value of the pre-deregulation fare of over €500, giving a fare reduction of over 80 per cent in real terms. Fare reductions have been a feature of the Ryanair operations as it grew from four routes in 1991 to 180 in 2004 with the number of passengers increasing from 200,000 to 28 million.

There are also some service improvements from the Ryanair product. These are better punctuality, fewer lost bags, and no overbooking (see Table 5.1, which also includes the flight completion rates; i.e. the extent to which flights in the timetable are actually operated).

The punctuality performance of Ryanair is high because of the customer product characteristics and the airports served. The simple point-to-point airline product is not delayed by interlining passengers. Check-in is quicker because the point-to-point journey is less complex than an interline one. Boarding is quicker because seat choice is greater for earlier passengers at the departure gate. Because Ryanair operates from lesser-used non-hub airports the airline encounters less airport congestion than airlines serving major hubs. The low rate of missing bags per passenger is also a function of a simple point-to-point journey and less congested airports served. The completion rate indicates that any impression that Ryanair amalgamates flights in order to increase load factors is incorrect.

A further service improvement in the Ryanair product is not overbooking. Because of the problem of 'no shows' traditional European airlines overbook flights. When the 'no show' predictions exceed the actual number of 'no show' booked passengers then the passengers arriving last at check-in are

Table 5.1 Customer service levels, 2004 (Q1)

	Punctuality (%)	Missing bags per 1000 passengers	Completion (%)
Ryanair	93.0	0.6	99.7
SAS	90.6	10.0	98.8
Air France	84.7	12.8	97.6
Lufthansa	83.6	16.9	98.8
easyJet	82.5	n.a.	n.a.
Iberia	81.9	9.9	99.0
British Airways	80.5	16.7	99.0
Alitalia	75.5	11.6	97.7
Austrian	65.1	22.5	98.0

Source: Association of European Airlines, Punctuality Report, March 2004 with Ryanair and CAA data. Punctuality data refer to arrivals within 15 min of published time. Completion rate refers to actual performance of flights listed in timetable.

denied boarding. The burden of the 'no show' problem is therefore borne by the passengers denied boarding. It is likely that these passengers will have a higher value of time than those who check in earliest. It is also likely that there is considerable loss of goodwill when booked passengers are denied boarding by traditional airlines. The Ryanair policy contrasts with traditional airline policy by transferring the cost of 'no show' passengers to the passengers who do not show and from those 'bumped' from overbooked flights. Where airlines do not have incentive payments to persuade those with a lower value of time to take a later flight, the passengers who dislike being denied boarding will find the Ryanair product superior. Those who value the flexibility of the traditional airline ticket and accept the risk of being denied boarding from time to time will continue to fly with the traditional airlines.

New airports and European airline competition

While much of the Ryanair business model is based on the Southwest model (O'Leary, 1994) in the United States a radical adaptation of the model to Western European circumstances has been to serve secondary airports. According to Fewings (1999) in a study of 13 Western European countries there were 431 airports. The vast majority of these were under-utilised because national airlines concentrated on hub airports. At these hubs the national airlines engaged in interlining, market sharing and price coordination. Slots at hubs acquired a scarcity value and were typically allocated to incumbent airlines in order of seniority at the airport by a scheduling committee presided over by the home country national airline.

The first secondary airport promoted by Ryanair was London–Luton in 1986. Slots were not then available at Heathrow. The Dublin–London route prior to the 1986 deregulation was virtually a Heathrow monopoly. Since deregulation the Heathrow share has fallen to 46.9 per cent as other airports have competed for what is the busiest international route in Europe with over 4 million passengers per year.

Prior to deregulation there was little incentive for airlines to serve new airports because traffic on these routes was taken into account when allocating market shares on trunk routes. There was little service to non-hub airports which had been developed by various city and regional governments and some private interests. Many developed from former military airfields.

Bringing Europe's underused secondary airports into greater use has been a vital part of the success of low-cost airlines, in particular Ryanair. Access to hub airports was either prohibited or heavily restricted for new entrants. The high cost base of hub airports would have been a large portion of the low-cost airline ticket price. The grandfather rights of incumbent airlines at hub airports would have restricted the supply of slots available to new entrant airlines seeking slots at hubs. Secondary airports became part of the low-cost airline product.

The quick turnaround time achieved by airlines at secondary airports would not have been possible at congested hub airports. The change in the airline product from the full-service airline integrated interline product to the low-cost airline point-to-point trip product would inevitably have brought pressure from low-cost airlines for price reductions at hub airports in respect of facilities which they did not require. An early example of low-cost airlines declining to use airport facilities which were separately priced was the use of airbridges. As low-cost airlines and their passengers redefined the traditional airport product they put pressure on airports to reduce their cost base and unbundle their prices.

Deregulation of European aviation required therefore the development of more services at many under-utilised secondary airports. The combination of new entrant airlines seeking airport access slots frequently not available at hubs and a lower cost product than provided by the hubs and the continent's large supply of underused secondary airports in effect deregulated the European airport market. The low-cost airlines required a low-cost airport product with quick turnaround times. The low-cost airline requirement at airports ruled out paying for services such as airbridges and business lounges and required fewer check-in desks per passenger because check-in times were reduced by the point-to-point product compared with multi-journey check-in and the added check-in delay in registering frequent-flyer points. For secondary airports the deregulated market brought the opportunity to develop business with the new market entrants rather than remain under-utilised. Since the new airlines sought substantial reductions from published lists of charges the managers of secondary airports had to examine whether an expansion of passenger numbers by low-cost airlines would be financially worthwhile and whether the expansion would generate non-aeronautical revenues through shop, restaurant, car parking, car hire, ground transport sales, and so on. The secondary airport managers also had to estimate the impact of extra passengers on their cost base compared to their pre-deregulation underused cost base. While most of the secondary airports had significant spare runway capacity the change from being almost empty to taking scheduled flights with 737-800 aircraft with 189 seats in the high density configuration might require some changes to terminal buildings and extra airport staff. There might also be a need for longer airport opening hours.

The case against secondary airports stressed their remoteness compared with hub airports and the difficulty of access from them to major destinations. In the event, passengers transferred with alacrity to the new airports. The initial attraction was the low fares charged by the new entrant airlines and the initial market share for the combination of new airline and new airport ranged between 20 per cent and 25 per cent. In the case of the most mature market deregulation, Dublin–London, deregulated in 1986 with five competing airlines and five competing London airports, the market share of once secondary airports is over 50 per cent. Table 5.2 shows the market shares of secondary airports on a number of Ryanair routes in June 2004.

The right hand column in Table 5.2 indicates the market shares of secondary or new airports in competition with hub airports in June 2004. It shows in the Glasgow case, for example, almost two-thirds of passengers on the Dublin route chose Prestwick, the new airport market entrant, in preference to the main Glasgow airport.

In addition to fare savings generated by both low-cost airlines and low-cost airports, passengers at secondary airports are attracted by benefits such as short walking distances, less congestion, crowding, confusion and stress and less time waiting for baggage. In addition the new airports may have their own catchment areas providing more convenient air access to passengers who previously spent much time on surface transport journeys to a small number of hub airports. At any rate passengers have transferred strongly to new airports in Europe. Some managers of slot-constrained hub airports may be happy enough to lose low-yield short-haul point-to-point passengers who did not require the full infrastructure of hub airports and may choose instead to concentrate on interlining and longer distance higher yield passengers and airlines. A new division of labour among airports may develop as a result of airline deregulation.

Table 5.2 Market shares of Ryanair competing secondary airports, June 2004

Route	Hub airport	Competing airports	Non-hub share (%)
Dublin–London	Heathrow	Stansted, Gatwick, Luton, City	53.1
Dublin–Glasgow	Glasgow	Prestwick	66.4
Dublin–NW England	Manchester	Liverpool, Leeds, Blackpool	45.5
Dublin–Paris	CDG	Beauvais	34.0
Ireland–Brussels	Brussels	Charleroi	66.0*
Dublin–Birmingham	Birmingham	East Midlands	31.8
London–Frankfurt	Frankfurt	Hahn	20.7
London–Stockholm	Stockholm	Skavsta, Vasteras	36.5
London–Oslo	Oslo	Torp	25.8
London–Venice	Venice	Treviso	40.4
London–Milan	Milan	Orio al Serio	28.2
London–Rome	Rome	Ciampino	34.1

Source: Airline data.

Note
* 2003 data.

In assessing the consumer impact of secondary airports four case studies present particularly impressive results. Stansted had just over 1 million passengers in 1988, the year before Ryanair commenced services there. By 2002 it had 16 million passengers of which Ryanair accounted for 8.3 million or 52 per cent. Stansted was developed because of congestion at Heathrow but the Heathrow airlines were reluctant to transfer and the development of Stansted required new entrant airlines.

Prestwick had declined to 10,000 passengers in 1993 as airlines transferred their operations to Glasgow Abbotsinch. Ryanair commenced services in 1994 and in 2002 passenger numbers were 1.5 million of which Ryanair accounted for 89 per cent. As in the case of Stansted, this was an airport which full service airlines were reluctant to serve and where new entrant airlines were required in order to exploit the potential of the airport.

Charleroi airport had 20,000 passengers in 1997. Ryanair commenced services there in 1998 in competition with Brussels National airport at Zaventem. In 2002 there were 1.27 million passengers at Charleroi of which 29,505, or 2.3 per cent, were non-Ryanair passengers. This airport was the subject of an adverse EU decision in 2004 which is currently under appeal and is examined later in the chapter.

Frankfurt Hahn airport had 20,000 passengers in 1997. Ryanair commenced services in 1998 and in 2002 there were 1.5 million passengers, of whom 35,000, or 2.4 per cent, were non-Ryanair passengers. There were several legal actions by Lufthansa against the name Frankfurt Hahn on the grounds that it is too remote from Frankfurt.

Airport competition in Europe has evoked a surprisingly positive consumer response. It appears likely to continue because of Europe's large supply of underused secondary airports. Airport competition is a consumer benefit from airline deregulation. The high cost base of the traditional airlines combined with their need to concentrate on hubs for the purposes of interlining and coordination resulted in a large market opportunity for new market entrants at Europe's secondary airports and a very positive consumer response to new airlines serving new airports (Barrett, 2000).

The Ryanair low cost base

The average Ryanair fare in 2004/5 is expected to be €38 and the net margin is expected to be 18 per cent. The ability to earn a large margin on these low fares requires a low cost base. Part of the Ryanair low cost base has been explained in the preceding sections. Many product features of traditional airlines have been unbundled out of the Ryanair product such as food and drink service and seat allocation. The point-to-point product is less expensive to provide than the interline at hubs product.

The use of secondary airports brings the scope for reduced airport charges and shorter turnaround times. The shorter turnaround times permit more journeys per day per plane which, coupled with the higher seat density of Ryanair planes, generate lower seat mile costs.

Other cost savings by Ryanair include lower aircraft capital costs achieved by negotiation with Boeing soon after the events of 9/11 when many other airlines were cancelling their orders. Internet ticketing, used by 98 per cent of Ryanair passengers, generates travel documents downloaded on the passenger's computer whereas traditional airline tickets required expensive high-security printing. Internet sales have also reduced costs by eliminating travel agents and expensive high street company sales offices. Marketing costs are reduced because low fares sell themselves and the airline has been successful in generating news coverage arising from legal and policy disputes with both national and European regulatory authorities.

The most significant contribution to the Ryanair low cost base however comes from its labour productivity. In its recruitment and deployment of labour Ryanair has chosen a balance between providing inputs from within the airline and outsourcing which is quite different from the traditional airline in the use of outsourcing. This is illustrated in Table 5.3, which shows the number of passenger flown per staff member in a number of European airlines in 2003.

Outsourcing brings a flexibility to an airline in choosing between different suppliers of services such as aircraft maintenance, handling at airports, catering and in-flight magazines. Outsourcing brings flexibility to the company in choosing whether or not to renew contracts as they expire. In inflexible labour markets securing efficiency gains from an inhouse labour force is likely to be more difficult and involve compensation for change.

The inherited corporate culture of Europe's legacy airlines was based on non-competing airlines determining market size in advance, price coordination and revenue sharing. This created considerable scope for rent-seeking by employees. Doganis (2001) described 'distressed state airline syndrome' in European aviation as shown in Table 5.4. The Ryanair product is contrasted in the table's second column with the difficulties encountered by the legacy carriers.

Ryanair staff hold shares in the airline. The share value and staff promotion prospects depend on the profitable expansion of the airline. Few Ryanair staff are over 35 years of age. The corporate culture of the staff is illustrated in

Table 5.3 Passengers per staff member, European airlines, 2003

Ryanair	10,050
easyJet	6,293
Aer Lingus	1,540
Lufthansa	1,281
German Wings	1,000
Iberia	978
Alitalia	959
SAS	898
British Airways	758

Table 5.4 State airlines and Ryanair contrasted

'Distressed state airline syndrome'	Ryanair
Substantial losses	High profit margin
Overpoliticisation	Independent
Strong unions	Minimal unionisation
Overstaffing	High productivity, outsourcing
No clear development strategy	Cost reduction strategy
Bureaucratic management	Low management costs
Poor service quality	Eliminating expensive services

Source: Doganis (2001) for column 1 above. Column 2 is author's assessment
of Ryanair under each element of the syndrome.

the Flynn–McAuley report to the Irish government on a general strike which closed Dublin airport on 7 March 1998. The object of the strike was to secure the unionisation of Ryanair. The report states that in authors' interviews with Ryanair staff 'the majority of those who met with the Enquiry appear to have a negative attitude to trade union recognition within the Company. Some are not even very tolerant of the right of a minority to join a union.' The report states that 'it is clear that most employees in Ryanair identify strongly with the Company and its management. They are proud of its achievements and success. They are confident that the Company will continue to grow and this will provide additional career opportunities for them.' The report also found that 'one of the principal advantages of working for Ryanair was stated to be the prospect of promotion which is regarded as being considerably better in Ryanair than in other airport companies. The Company's policy of promotion from within is highly regarded by employees'. According to the report, 'most employee groups consider that they work hard for the Company, harder and more effectively than workers in other airport-based companies' (Flynn and McAuley, 1998: 14). The Flynn–McAuley report shows that the corporate culture of Ryanair is strongly supported by the staff. Ryanair seeks to outperform other airlines and airport companies and the strong management style in the airline is highly regarded by the employees. The ratio of passengers to staff members has doubled from 4800 in 1998 to over 10,000 in 2004 and the staff numbers have also doubled to 2,500. This indicates that the workplace culture in the airline has strengthened since Flynn and McAuley reported. The Irish labour market has moved from 1.1 million in employment in 1986 to 1.9 million in 2004 and unemployment has fallen from 17.4 to 4.8 per cent in the same period. The workplace culture of Ryanair has underpinned its rapid growth in a full employment economy in contrast with a view that its labour costs required the high unemployment levels of Ireland in the airline's early years.

The sustainability of Ryanair

This section addresses four key issues influencing the sustainability of Ryanair, namely, the Ryanair product, the Ryanair airport policy, the low cost base of the airline and external factors. These issues are examined in this section.

The Ryanair airline product

Will passengers continue to seek the Ryanair product? The airline has increased from 4 million passengers in 1998 to 24 million in 2004. On its longest served route, Dublin–London, its March 2004 market share of 46 per cent is 1.5 times that of Aer Lingus, the dominant airline on the route, Europe's busiest, for some 60 years. The Ryanair market share on Dublin–London rose by 17 points between 2002 and March 2004. Passengers on this route have known the Ryanair product since 1986 and have chosen its tradeoff between price and service and between the Heathrow hub and the secondary London airports to an increasing degree as the market has matured. Two full service competitors on the route, Aer Lingus and British Midland, have relaunched themselves as low-cost airlines on the route, emulating the Ryanair model. British Midland had previously offered its Diamond Class service to all passengers and its withdrawal reflects both the cost of the service and the preference of passengers for price rather than service competition. Cityjet, previously an independent Irish airline and now a lower-cost part of Air France, offered a premium service from Dublin to London City airport but was unable to command a premium price for the product which included superior in-flight service, including champagne and leather seats, plus fastest access to the financial centre of London. Its market share was 5 per cent in 1998 and 3.1 per cent in the first half of 2004.

On the Dublin–London route prior to deregulation the alternative to air travel by Aer Lingus and British Airways was a nine-hour boat and train journey. Claims that the pre-deregulation air fares represented payment for a premium service were not widely believed and passenger numbers on the route stagnated for eight years before deregulation in 1986. The Aer Lingus low-cost model on Dublin–London is the same product as Ryanair except for Heathrow access and allocated seating. Research by Loddenberg (2004) indicates that Aer Lingus earns a premium of only €10 over Ryanair on the route.

There is also evidence of the ability of the Ryanair low-cost airline and secondary airport product to transfer to other markets as shown in Table 5.2. Ryanair dominates SAS and British Airways on London–Stockholm; BA, Alitalia and easyJet on London–Rome and London–Milan and BA and Lufthansa on London–Hamburg. In less than two years Ryanair achieved a 34 per cent share of London–Berlin and a 27 per cent share of London–Barcelona. The Ryanair product has therefore achieved market acceptance both in mature deregulated markets such as Dublin–London and newly entered routes such as London–Berlin and London–Barcelona.

The average Ryanair fare has fallen from €52 in 2001/2, to €46 in 2002/3 and €40 in 2003/4. The net margin has fallen from 24 to 21 per cent over the period, having peaked at 28 per cent in 2002/3. Ryanair has attracted an extra 12 million passengers in a period in which average fares were reduced by 23 per cent. Ryanair has been able to reduce costs by means such as internet sales, good aircraft procurement deals, attractive deals at low-cost airports and high staff productivity. The airline's current proposals to further reduce its cost base include abolition of checked baggage thus eliminating the baggage handling charge at airports and allowing passengers to check-in at departure gates; the replacement of reclining seats by cheaper fixed seats requiring less maintenance; pay-per-view movies on seat backs; developing in-flight and online ancillary sales of car hire, hotel rooms, train and bus tickets, travel insurance, phonecards, and so on, and the development of the airline's own credit card. Ryanair is also seeking to reduce its cost base at its Dublin hub by leading a campaign for competing terminals at the airport. Continuous declines in yields not accompanied by cost reductions would place Ryanair at risk even with its high net margin and its cash holdings of €1.2 billion in March 2004.

Downward pressure on yields may moderate as loss-making start-up airlines leave the market and full service airlines refocus on long haul routes rather than compete against low-cost airlines on shorthaul routes. EU rules forbidding state subsidies to national airlines are vital to airlines such as Ryanair since they impose a bankruptcy constraint on high-cost airlines which reduce their fares without reducing costs.

Therefore while the rate of price reduction in air fares charged by low-cost airlines is likely to be moderate, the passenger demand for the Ryanair product is likely to remain high. Like any business, Ryanair might lose focus and engage in prestigious projects such as a new corporate headquarters or new company logo or might otherwise 'lose the plot', but the signs are that it has defined a very definite product and sticks rigidly to that model over 180 routes and 17 bases.

Changes on consumer taste might turn away from the Ryanair product. There is little evidence of this to date. Markets, which did not generate a return, were quickly dropped and the planes transferred to better routes. The routes dropped include London to Reims, Clermont Ferrand, Maastricht, Groningen and Ostend; Frankfurt Hahn–Malmo; and Stockholm Skavsta to Oslo Torp, Aarhus and Tampere.

Ryanair obviously meets the market tests of attracting passengers who use the airline in rapidly increasing numbers. Perceptions of Ryanair are published in attitude surveys published both by the airline and in the Skytrax series. The surveys show both the positive and negative features of the airline. The survey responses published by Ryanair are positive and the airline claims to have a low ratio of complaints to passengers. The Skytrax surveys cover 23 responses between May and July 2004 when the airline carried over 6 million passengers, a response rate of under 4 per million passengers. The survey opinions about the Ryanair product are shown in Appendix A. Ten of the responses include favourable comment, usually referring to low prices, and early arrival at destination airports. Some responses mix praise and criticism such as a passenger who paid £0.49 from Stansted to Malmo and Gothenberg, liked the low fares but complained that there was no assigned seating. Thirteen responses were critical and four said they would never fly Ryanair again. The Skytrax airline ratings give Ryanair two stars – the same as, for example, Southwest and Air France economy class.

In its original market, Ireland, there is acceptance, after a learning curve experience, that budget airlines do not offer free meals and hotels to passengers on delayed flights. In other markets it may still be necessary to explain the

Ryanair product so that passengers may tradeoff price savings against service reductions. The market success of Ryanair to date indicates that the product/price tradeoff is broadly in line with customer requirements. Some passengers may return to full-service airlines after an unhappy experience with Ryanair but the airline continues to attract net additional passengers. When Ryanair withdrew from services on the London–Strasbourg route following objections from Air France, passenger numbers on the route immediately reverted to pre-Ryanair levels. Ryanair transferred its services to the rival Baden–Karlsruhe airport in Germany and its passengers followed.

The Ryanair airport product

The consumer response to secondary airports has been strongly positive. It appears unlikely that passengers on point-to-point flights to and from secondary airports would wish to revert to hub airports. The benefits of secondary airports within the airports include less walking time within terminals, less waiting time for baggage retrieval and cheaper car parking.

The summer 2004 British Airways (BA) marketing campaign echoes an earlier theme from inter-airport competition at Luton and Beauvais, that BA airports are closer to the main centres of population than secondary airports. On the other hand the time between touchdown and exiting the airport is likely to be significantly less at a secondary airport.

The hub airport system routed very large number of passengers through a small number of airports while leaving hundreds of airports in Europe underused. When hubs dominated, passengers using Stansted and Luton, for example, had long surface travel times to Heathrow. Each new secondary airport service has a local catchment area which is served far better in terms of access than when passengers were routed through hubs. Claims that Heathrow is closer to central London than Luton or Stansted may be irrelevant to most passengers. The British Airports Authority (2002) found that the high-speed rail route from the airport to central London was used by 8.4 per cent of passengers and virtually none of the staff employed at Heathrow. The origins and destinations of air passengers have diversified away from central business districts served by fixed links such as the Heathrow express rail connection to the centre of London. Civil Aviation Authority (CAP 703, 1999) data on passenger surface travel for Heathrow, Gatwick and Manchester airports confirm that the proportion of passengers accessing the three airports by car, hire car and taxi increased as shown in Table 5.5. For the majority of passengers, therefore, a slightly longer car journey to a secondary airport with lower parking charges and lower air fares is likely to be an attractive alternative. With a more dispersed pattern of location of both houses and businesses away from concentration in the central business district cars become the dominant mode of access to airports and secondary airports may actually have a competitive advantage for this category. The faster growth of leisure travel than the growth of air travel as a whole also increases the car share of airport surface access. Holiday trips to airports may involve several passengers and luggage for a number of

Table 5.5 Mode of access to major UK Airports, 1972–98 by market share

	Gatwick		Heathrow		Manchester	
	1972	*1998*	*1972*	*1998*	*1972*	*1998*
Car/car hire/taxi	52	70	59	67	83	90
Bus	9	10	32	14	16	4
Rail	37	20	0	17	0	6
Terminal passengers (million)	5.0	22.9	14.3	40.6	1.7	16.5

Source: Civil Aviation Authority (1999).

weeks on holiday. The door-to-door convenience of cars for people with luggage compared to having to access bus and train stations from home, change of mode at bus and train stations en route, and access airports from bus and train stations, also reduces the competitive advantage of hub over secondary airports. The development of secondary airports on lower-priced land further away from city centres is thus similar to the development of out-of-town shopping centres. Where the development of secondary airports involves the development of underused runways and termini with little incremental investment there are obvious gains to society as a whole. There is ample evidence therefore that Ryanair's policy of serving secondary airports is popular with passengers and that consumer and access transport factors will continue to favour their growing market share (Barrett, 2003).

The threat to the sustainability of Ryanair's secondary airports policy may come from regulators rather than from passengers, airlines or airport authorities. The threat comes from the EU Commission against the arrangements between Ryanair and Charleroi airport in Belgium. In February 2004 the EU Commission disallowed the airport arrangements between Charleroi and Ryanair on the grounds of lack of transparency, infringement of the private market investor principle, discriminatory exclusivity to Ryanair and the length of the agreement between the airport and Ryanair. The Commission's view is that the Charleroi arrangements constitute a public subsidy.

Ryanair has appealed the decision. The grounds for the appeal are that the Charleroi charges to Ryanair

1 were widely publicised;
2 are not exclusive but on offer to other airlines;
3 are higher than those on offer at private airports which operate according to the private market investor principle and
4 that private airports also enter into agreements with airlines for longer than the 15-year agreement between Charleroi and Ryanair.

A verdict in favour of Ryanair was handed down by the Court of First Instance in December 2008 and it is discussed in Chapter 10 below. The case has wide implications for the EU's many underused airports and for low-cost airlines excluded from hub airports by the current slot allocation system.

Charleroi was virtually empty for many decades before Ryanair entered the Dublin route in 1997 in competition with the Brussels National airport at Zaventem and the airlines, Aer Lingus and Sabena. Fares were extremely high at IR£650 (€825) return and there were frequent complaints about the lack of availability of Apex tickets on the route. Ryanair quickly became the market leader on the route. The Ryanair case is that its Dublin service brought Charleroi airport into profitability and that its 12 Charleroi routes are therefore an entrepreneurial commercial development.

The owners of Europe's large number of underused secondary airports face a number of market choices including shutting down. The land then becomes available for agricultural, industrial or housing. Should the airport remain open the lowest cost option is likely to be based on flying clubs, private flying and emergency services. The airport might next seek turboprop services but the high seat-mile costs will restrict their growth and public subsidies may be required. In moving to the next stage of development the airport's choice is between full-service legacy airlines and low-cost airlines.

No airline at Brussels National wanted to transfer flights to Charleroi, some 50 km from Brussels. Low-cost airlines on the other hand have been willing to take the entrepreneurial risks in serving secondary airports. The investment risk by both Ryanair and the airport at Charleroi put on the market an airport and airline product which no other competing airline or airport had previously undertaken.

In a private sector airport the market price of the airport reflects the expected profit stream of the airport in the hands of an efficient investor and airport operator. The development of the airport through the various traffic types as illustrated above requires that price should cover the marginal costs incurred. An airport scale of charges dating from when the airport was largely empty is irrelevant. A market test for the opinion that Ryanair has an unfair advantage over other airlines would be the existence of a scarcity value for the Ryanair slots at Charleroi. On the other hand, slots at Europe's hub airports command a premium for airlines with grandfather rights, and are a barrier to new market entrants.

Loddenberg (2004) speculates that the then Ryanair network of 161 routes over 17 countries may include too many 'nowhere' routes. The 'nowhere' routes may have either one remote airport (a 'somewhere to nowhere' route) or two remote airports (a 'nowhere to nowhere route'). Such routes endanger the sustainability of the airline, according to the 'nowhere' thesis.

In response, it must be said that all entrepreneurial activity involves risk. In the Ryanair case there has been no reluctance to cull unprofitable routes as illustrated in this chapter. Secondary airports are attractive to both Ryanair and its passengers because of their low costs and convenience to passengers in regions largely without service because of the legacy airlines focus on hubs. Two examples from the Loddenberg list of 'nowhere to nowhere' routes illustrate their attractiveness to passengers. Glasgow Prestwick to Bournemouth has two flights per day. The competing train service involves a journey time of over eight hours on average and an advance purchase fare of £44 (€66) return. The air product is thus attractive to passengers with even a low value of time savings. The Kerry–Frankfurt Hahn route sustains a year-round service to a major tourist area in the southwest of Ireland. Visitor numbers to Ireland have grown from a static 2 million for 20 years before access deregulation in 1986 to over 7 million, and Dublin and Kerry are the main growth centres. The airport is close to Killarney and there is a strong record of German investment in the area since the 1960s. The airport management offered an attractive cost base. The direct service to Kerry saves time compared with using the Frankfurt–Dublin or Frankfurt–Heathrow routings with the latter requiring a road or rail journey to Kerry from Cork. What may appear to be 'nowhere to nowhere' routes may therefore have a strong economic rationale in a deregulated market of low-cost airlines and airports.

The Ryanair cost base

Ryanair is a post-deregulation airline with a young labour force and a strong message on costs and productivity, Ryanair has not experienced the industrial relations problems encountered by, for example, Aer Lingus. Due to the latter's inherited workplace culture and monopolistic past, it is proving difficult to raise the Aer Lingus passengers per staff member from 1,000 to 2,000 without industrial unrest. In contrast Ryanair has raised its number of passengers per staff member from 4,800 in 1998 to 10,000 currently. Whilst it is recognised that this measure is not appropriate to comparisons between full service and low-cost airlines or between long- and short-haul operators, over time the series shows that the productivity of Ryanair staff has increased rapidly. Combined with the data on the Ryanair margin, it indicates that the balance between outsourcing and inhouse provision of services has been correct.

Ryanair staff currently hold over €130 million of shares in the company and the 2004 share option scheme offers staff share options up to 20 per cent of pay. The workplace culture described above remains strong compared to legacy airlines and airports seeking to adjust traditional organisations to a deregulated market.

Management culture change is also important in projecting an organisation's future. Ryanair's own checklist against a loss of focus on cutting costs includes moving to a new corporate headquarters, designing a new corporate logo, acquiring a company helicopter, joining representative bodies and quangos, serving on government commissions and appearing in the social columns of glossy magazines. The danger signals appeared to be well understood by management during the period of research for this chapter.

External factors

The winter of 2004/5 was predicted as a period of intense competition in European aviation. It was expected that there would be market exit by undercapitalised new entrants and intensified pressure for rescue packages for national airlines such as Alitalia. The July 2004 decision by the EU Commission to permit the Italian government to provide Alitalia with a €400 million loan following €1.4 billion in both 1997 and 2002 obviously created competitive problems for unsubsidised airlines such as Ryanair.

Fixed-sum compensation rules for denied boardings, delays and cancellations impose disproportionate costs on low-fare airlines. The imposition of departure taxes by governments similarly has a greater impact on low-fare than on high-fare airlines.

The Charleroi case verdict has important potential benefits for low-cost airlines. The benefits from airlines using previously under-utilised or empty airports rather than congested hubs is the vital economic consideration for the regions and airport managers concerned and a market opportunity for low-cost airlines. Legal decisions affecting legacy airline subsidies, passenger compensation, and secondary airport charges have big implications for Ryanair and other low-cost airlines.

Ryanair decided not to impose fuel surcharges during 2004. In the half year to September 2004 passenger numbers rose by 24 per cent, revenue by 21 per cent, and net margin increased to 28 per cent. Unit costs fell by 4 per cent. The yield decline was 5 per cent. The reduced rate of decline in yield and buoyant passenger growth indicate that fuel surcharges by other airlines encounter consumer resistance and some transfer to low-cost airlines.

Conclusion

This chapter examined the growth of Ryanair, its definition of the airline product and the response of passengers, the airline's low cost base and its use of secondary airports. Passengers have responded to the low fares and accept the tradeoff between these fares and the loss of many of the bundled services provided by legacy airlines. New secondary airports have been, somewhat surprisingly, successful. Their increasing use reflects an interest in low fares, point-to-point travel and a dislike of the congestion, confusion, and long walking times and waiting times at hub airports. The low cost base of Ryanair is a function of a simple product, high productivity of the airline staff and a policy of strict cost control over airports, aircraft suppliers and distribution costs. The product, the productivity and low cost base including the use of secondary airports and Ryanair's cost reducing corporate culture also appear to have a positive future even in the predicted short term difficulties facing European aviation.

References

Barrett, S.D. (1999) Peripheral market entry product differentiation, supplier rents and sustainability – a case study, *Journal of Air Transport Management* 5: 21–30.

Barrett, S.D. (2000) Airport competition in the deregulated European aviation market, *Journal of Air Transport Management* 6:13–27.

Barrett, S.D. (2003) Airports as multimodal interchange nodes, presented at Round Table 126, European Conference of Ministers of Transport, Paris.

Civil Aviation Authority (1999) Passengers at Gatwick, Heathrow, and Manchester Airports in 1998, CAP 703, Table 28.

Court of First Instance of the European Communities (2008) Judgement of the Court in Case T-196/04, Ryanair v Commission, Luxembourg, 17 December.

Doganis, R. (2001) *The Airline Business in the 21st Century*. Berlin: Routledge.

Fewings, R. (1999) Provision of European airport infrastructure, *Avmark Aviation Economist* 7: 18–20.

Flynn, P. and McAuley, D. (1998) *Report of Enquiry into the Industrial Dispute at Dublin Airport*. Dublin: Government Publications.

Loddenberg, A. (2004) *Report on Ryanair*. London: ABN-AMRO.

O'Leary, M. (1994) The challenge of replicating Southwest Airlines in Europe, presented at the 2nd International Aviation Conference, Institute of Economic Affairs, London.

Further reading

European Commission (2002) Benefits accorded by the Walloon region and Brussels South Charleroi Airport to the Irish airline Ryanair on its arrival and establishment at Charleroi, C(2002) 4832fin. Brussels: European Commission.

Appendix A: Ryanair Passenger Opinions, May–July 2004

Favourable

'Little to complain about with Ryanair-they were about 1/10th of the fares charged by premium airlines.'

'Ryanair offers a better option than BA or Lufthansa.'

'Overall they do what they say, cheap fares, no frills.'

'As a no frills airline there is no complaint on board.'

'Lack of frills aside, I have never been disappointed.'

'My travel allowance is 2 scheduled flights to England with Lufthansa and, hard as I try, I am not going to achieve this allowance with the 12 flights with Ryanair.'

'Both flights left on time and arrived early.'

'The only company that delivered me to my destination on average 10/20 minutes before scheduled arrival time.'

Critical

Six complaints regarding charges for overweight baggage

Four complaints regarding no seat allocation

Individual complaints were:

'Closure of departure gates too early'

'No compensation for delayed flights'

'Remote airport', 'Connecting bus failed to appear' (Both refer to Beauvais)
'No Dutch-speaking staff at airport' (Charleroi)
'Premium rate phone charges. This should be freephone.'
'Uncomfortable seats.'
'Weak customer service'
'Refused to accept wife's pre-marriage name on passport'
'No sick bag'
'They try to sell you too much on board.'

Source: Skytrax Passenger Opinions, 22 July 2004.

6 The new-entrant full-service airline

Market entry to the full-service airline market – a case study from the deregulated European aviation sector

Introduction

This chapter is a case study of Cityjet, a full-service airline serving Ireland, the United Kingdom, France, Spain, Italy, Germany and Belgium, founded in 1992. Cityjet was acquired by Air France early in 2000 and now operates as a lower-cost arm of that airline. The Cityjet case study illustrates the difficulties faced by a full-service airline seeking to serve the deregulated European aviation market. These difficulties include airport access, the frequent-flyer programmes and predatory responses of incumbents and ticket retailing. The experiences of market entry on Dublin–London and Dublin–Brussels are examined. The responses of Cityjet and Ryanair to the post-deregulation barriers to contestability in European aviation are contrasted and the implications for full-service and low-cost airlines are examined. The continuing role of Cityjet as a lower-cost subsidiary of Air France and its value to that group is discussed.

The development of Cityjet

In the seven and a half years from foundation to acquisition by Air France, Cityjet lost IR£22 million. At acquisition by Air France it had nine aircraft and 320 staff. Its route network is Paris–Florence (six daily), Paris–London City (six daily), Dublin–London City (four daily), Dublin–Paris (four daily), Dublin–Malaga (three weekly), and several French domestic services on behalf of Air France. The case study of Cityjet covers both the commercial decisions of Cityjet and the regulatory obstacles to new entrant airlines in Europe in the 1990s. This was a period of market liberalisation but with significant remaining obstacles to contestability.

The commercial aspects of the Cityjet case study are the choices of full service rather than budget as the target market; service rather than price competition; the critical choice of airport in London to counter slot shortage at Heathrow; and the issues of retail distribution and frequent-flyer programmes. The regulatory aspects of the Cityjet case study concern the post-deregulation barriers to new airlines in Europe and the appropriate policy responses.

Cityjet commenced services between Dublin and London City in January 1994 under the brand Virgin Cityjet. The Virgin brand cost Cityjet 4 per cent of receipts plus CRS fees. The target market was business travellers on the route, the busiest international scheduled route in Europe with over 2 million passengers in 1992 and over 4 million in 1998. The route was deregulated in 1986, well ahead of deregulation in Europe as a whole. British Airways in 1991 withdrew from all its services between Britain and the Republic of Ireland because intense competition had reduced its yields.

In 1994 Cityjet's major business class competitors were Aer Lingus and British Midland serving the Dublin–Heathrow route. The main budget airline competitor was Ryanair at Stansted and Luton. While Cityjet did not initially seek to serve the budget market, the Ryanair presence on Dublin–London attracted business passengers from the small and medium enterprise sector. Ryanair's aggressive publicity for its low fares may also have set a psychological limit to the fares that full service airlines could charge. The Civil Aviation Authority noted the increase in flights per weekday between December 1992 and 1997 as in Table 6.1.

Cityjet chose to serve London City because Heathrow, the main business airport, was effectively closed to new entrants. Cityjet also believed that there was a business market potential at London City due to its proximity to the financial services sector in the City of London. It was also hoped that, due the sheer size of Heathrow and its then relatively poor access to the centre and east of London, London City would attract significant numbers of passengers from Heathrow. The initial pricing policy of Cityjet was to match the Aer Lingus business fare of IR£270 return and to seek business traffic on the basis of better in-flight service and a more attractive and convenient airport in London. The in-flight service was well received and won an Airline of the Year Award in 1996 from the Air Transport Committee of the Chambers of Commerce of Ireland in a poll of the chief executives of the top 1,000 companies in Ireland.

These policies pursued by Cityjet did not succeed. Business traffic did not divert from Heathrow to London City as hoped. The full service airline concept was recognised in user surveys but did not divert a sufficient number of passengers from business class on either British Midland or Aer Lingus. In order to

Table 6.1 Typical number of services per weekday on Dublin–London route (December 1992–7)[a]

	1992	1997
Aer Lingus	15	17
Ryanair	9	18
British Midland	8	8
BA Cityflyer	–	4
Cityjet	–	7

[a] Source Civil Aviation (1998).

respond to the intense competition on the Dublin route Cityjet sought to attract budget travellers and at one point had as many as 40 fares seeking to attract passengers both from full-service airlines such as British Midland Diamond Service and Aer Lingus executive class, and from Ryanair's low-cost no-frills service.

Virgin opposed the partitioning of Virgin Cityjet aircraft between full-service and budget passengers and this led to further losses. Cityjet did not find the Virgin brand a worthwhile expense in promoting the service in the United Kingdom and in July 1996 ended the agreement. Virgin had no other services at London City, thus limiting the scope for business cooperation between the partner companies. The service was later switched to a joint Aer Lingus/Cityjet code and later to a joint Air UK Cityjet code while remaining a Cityjet operation (Civil Aviation Authority, 1998).

An additional problem to the poor response of the full-fare market to changing from Heathrow to London City was the aircraft type required to serve London City because of its short runway. The BAe 146 involved extra costs per seat, more than twice the costs of the 767-200, as shown in Table 6.2. London City was also an expensive airport for customer airlines. Cityjet estimated that London City landing charges in early 2000 were 1.8 times Heathrow, 2.5 times Gatwick, 3 times Stansted and 4 times those at Dublin.

Ticket distribution costs for Cityjet were expensive with override travel agent commission of up to 17 per cent, more than double the commission paid by its competitors. The problems faced by Cityjet on the Dublin–London route may be summarised as follows:

- It catered for a business class market in which British Midland Diamond Class and Aer Lingus Executive Class services had greater loyalty from their passengers than Cityjet envisaged. The inducements used by the then market leader Aer Lingus to retain passengers included frequent-flyer points and a London Business Bonus scheme which offered the choice of a free hotel night or car hire to business class passengers. Hanlon (1999) notes that 90 per cent of world business air travellers are members of a frequent-flyer programme (FFP) and US evidence that 57 per cent of business travellers choose flights in order to build up mileage points 'always or almost always'. A further 24 per cent do

Table 6.2 Operating cost disadvantage of BAe 146 as required at London City airport compared to 737-600, 1998[a]

	Seats	*Cost per seat-mile (US cents)*	*Index*
767-200	180	3.92	100
BAe 146	90	8.94	228

[a]Source: Database, Jet Operating Costs, *Avmark Aviation Economist* (1999), December 22.

so 'more than half the time' and 9 per cent less than half the time with only 2 per cent 'rarely if ever' and 3 per cent 'other'.

- Cityjet served London City airport which did not prove to be the attraction that Cityjet expected.
- London City was an expensive airport in charges to the airlines serving it.
- The choice of London City brought high aircraft costs because runway restrictions precluded the use of aircraft with low seat-mile costs such as the 767-200.
- Cityjet had high in-flight service costs.
- It was difficult to attract budget passengers because the Dublin–London route had in Ryanair the most successful low-cost new entrant airline in Europe. Ryanair also promoted the view that full-service air travel on short-haul routes was expensive to provide and of little utility to the passenger.
- Retailing of Cityjet tickets was expensive with commissions sought more than double the industry average.
- The use of the Virgin brand was unsatisfactory to Cityjet in terms of traffic generated in the United Kingdom. The airlines also differed over the provision of full service to budget passengers, a policy favoured by Virgin but resisted by Cityjet.
- In September 1999 Aer Lingus entered the Dublin–London City route shadowing the Cityjet timetable. Cityjet estimated its immediate losses at £0.2 million per month and estimated Aer Lingus losses at £0.35 million per month because of the latter's higher cost base and the use of hired aircraft to operate the service. Cityjet brought a case to the Irish Competition Authority complaining of predation but has not secured a response. Cityjet has also formed the opinion that the European Commission is not prepared to defend new entrants to the sector against predatory behaviour by incumbent airlines.
- The Cityjet market share of traffic on Dublin–London ranged in most years between 4 per cent and 5 per cent. This contrasts with the market share of Ryanair, the earlier challenger to the former national airlines, which attained market shares of over 40 per cent. The two airlines are contrasted below. Table 6.3 shows the number of routes and flights per Irish airline in December 1992 and 1997.

Table 6.3 Routes served and flights operated by Irish airlines (December 1992–7)[a]

	Routes		Flights	
	December 92	*December 97*	*December 92*	*December 97*
Aer Lingus	25	26	1,897	2,228
Ryanair	6	15	446	1,474
Cityjet	–	2	–	259

[a] Source: Civil Aviation Authority (1998).

Cityjet on the Dublin–Brussels route, 1995–7

In June 1995 Virgin Cityjet began a Dublin–Brussels service. The fare charged was £450 return compared to the Aer Lingus–Sabena fare of £650. The incumbent airlines immediately matched the Cityjet fare. The route is dominated by travel connected with public service and diplomatic travel by both Irish and EU institutions. No public service business transferred to the new service and Cityjet requested from the Irish government the reasons for this unwillingness to avail itself of the benefits of competition.

The Irish government without reference to EU procurement rules awarded the contract for public service air travel to a Dublin travel agency which negotiated a 27 per cent commission from Sabena with a rebate to the government departments. Cityjet lodged a claim for IR£2.5 million in November 1998 to cover losses on the route between June 1995 and March 1997. No defence was entered by the State at the time. A defence was later allowed by the High Court. Cityjet did not pursue the case due to its financial difficulties.

Cityjet also found it difficult to attract passengers away from Aer Lingus/Sabena flights on the Dublin–Brussels service. In this case, Cityjet used the same airports as its competitors at both ends of the journey and the ability of frequent-flyer programmes to retain passengers was notable. Aer Lingus also operated a Brussels Business Bonus offer of a free hotel night or car hire as in London. The Cityjet Dublin–Brussels service was operated initially under the Virgin brand 'before again codes were switched, with some flights operating under a joint Aer Lingus/Sabena code, others under Cityjet's own code' (Civil Aviation Authority, 1998).

In both its Brussels and London City cases the experience of Cityjet has been that the legal redress under EU and national competition policy is slow, cumbersome and expensive. This has also been the experience in the application of competition policy in other areas of transport. A system of protection against predation which imposes large costs on small companies and is incapable of delivering quick adjudications and redress offers little support to new market entrants and does not promote contestability.

After the end of the agreement with Virgin, Cityjet needed new funds. Malmo Aviation of Sweden and several institutional investors took the airline out of examinership in late 1996. Early in 1997 Cityjet won an Air France contract to operate the Paris–London City route. This form of 'big brother contract flying' was to prove important in protecting Cityjet from the abuse of dominance by rival airlines. The Swedish partners then sought to take over the airline but the Irish investors bought them out in August 1997. In 1998, the financial problems of the airline became severe again. The fleet of BA 146 and Saab aircraft was expensive to operate. National Jet Systems of Australia expressed a strong interest and Speedwing Consultants examined the airline. Air Foyle of Luton took a 50 per cent stake with Air France taking 25 per cent. Air Foyle rented the Cityjet licence and it was used by easyJet on some of their Luton services. In April 1999, the shares of Air Foyle and Air France were increased to 66 and 33 per cent, respectively. Air France bought out Air Foyle in early 2000.

Cityjet as an Air France subsidiary

In 1997, Cityjet began service on Dublin–Paris (CDG) in a code share with Air France. The arrangement brought benefits to Air France in lowering its costs on the route while retaining a feed to its Paris hub. The relationship with Air France became the vital one in securing the future of Cityjet. The current role of Cityjet as an Irish-based company wholly owned by Air France is to provide a low-cost full-service branch within the Air France group. The savings are derived from lower wage costs, lower social insurance and higher productivity than in the rest of the Air France group. The trade unions within Air France allow aircraft with fewer than 100 seats to be operated by partners or other airlines. The licensing policies of the Irish Aviation Authority allow for productivity some 15 per cent higher than in France. The overall savings to Air France from having an Irish-based wholly owned subsidiary are estimated at 40 per cent.

Ireland has the most highly deregulated aviation market in the EU with Ryanair the first new entrant airline to exceed the passenger numbers of the incumbent national airline. The Air France acquisition of Cityjet allows it to bring some of the benefits of deregulation in Ireland to the French market which is among the less deregulated aviation markets in Europe. In the summer of 2000, the Dublin–Paris route had 13 flights per day, five to Charles de Gaulle by Aer Lingus and four by Cityjet/Air France with four to Beauvais by Ryanair.

The absorption of Cityjet into Air France might therefore be seen as a second-best solution. The structure of the European aviation market makes it difficult for Cityjet to sell its product to the open market but as part of Air France it has a continuing role because of its lower cost base than its owner airline.

The ability of Cityjet to achieve for Air France significant cost reductions on the unit cost of that group indicates that Cityjet has a continuing commercial role in European aviation. The Cityjet management is critical of market regulators in Europe because of their failure to design a regulatory environment to promote and sustain contestability. The absence of transparent tendering for the public service travel market between Dublin and Brussels was a huge obstacle to the Cityjet service between the cities. The failure of regulators to examine alleged predation on the Dublin–London City route was also a serious blow to the airline. The end of Cityjet as an independent airline left its promoters convinced that in Europe aviation is a rigged market dominated by alliances in which consumers and small airlines have little influence on either national or EU regulators.

Distribution was a major difficulty for Cityjet. The airline believes that there is little protection for either passengers or new entrant airlines because travel agents function as an agent of the incumbent airlines and not on behalf of the passenger or as an 'honest broker'. The development of the Internet in recent years came too late for Cityjet to market its services directly to passengers.

Access to Heathrow was denied to Cityjet because of a shortage of slots at the airport. The slot shortage has become a barrier to new market entry because slots have been allocated to incumbent airlines in order of seniority under so-called 'grandfather rights'. The EU has failed to produce a pro-contestability policy on slots. The scarcity value of slots has become an important item in the asset base of Europe's national airlines in particular. No European government supports ending the grandfather rights allocation of slots.

Cityjet and Ryanair – new entrants contrasted

In addition to the barriers to contestability faced by all new entrant airlines, Cityjet can be seen, with the benefit of hindsight, to have erred in concentrating on service rather than price, and in serving London City airport rather than, for example Gatwick. London City was an expensive airport and its runway length required a more expensive aircraft, the BAe 146.

Ryanair chose to compete on price and to eliminate services such as free food and drink, reserved seating, newspapers, airport lounges, seat allocation and downtown sales offices. Ryanair chose secondary low-cost airports with discounted low charges to airlines. Ryanair also bypassed travel agents through telemarketing and Internet sales. Ryanair cut its costs so low that the incumbent airlines could not profitably match its fares. Its entry to a route typically caused the market to expand by more than the Ryanair number of passengers but yields presumably fell as the incumbent airlines responded to the new entrant. Cityjet on the other hand sought to attract their high yield passengers from the incumbent airlines serving the same airports. The typical Ryanair scale of entry was larger than Cityjet. The rapid market expansion following the entry of Ryanair to a market made a predatory response by the incumbents more difficult than the smaller market entry by Cityjet (Barrett, 1999).

Table 6.4 summarises the experiences of both Ryanair and Cityjet as new market entrants in a deregulated aviation sector. The list of obstacles to contestability

Table 6.4 Comparative impact of post-deregulation barriers to contestability on Cityjet and Ryanair[a]

Barrier	Impact on Cityjet	Impact on Ryanair
Hub airport dominance	High costs at London City	Use low-cost airports
CRS bias	High fees to travel agents	Internet sales; 5 per cent agent and CRS companies commission
FFPs	Difficult to attract	Abolished FFP/cut fares business travellers
Predation	Not protected	Protected during Aer Lingus rescue
State aids	Cityjet and Ryanair faced Aer Lingus which received IR£175 m in state aid	

[a] Source: Based on Levine (1987).

in the deregulated European aviation market is based on Levine (1987). The policy of Ryanair was to drive costs and fares down so that Europe's full-service airlines could not match Ryanair fares. Cityjet competed on service and found it difficult to attract business travellers to London City airport and away from frequent-flyer programmes by established airlines. Ryanair's service to small airports brought a ready response from passengers with spectacular success at Prestwick, Bournemouth, Beauvais, Charleroi, Torp, Skavsta, Treviso, Genoa, and at its Stansted hub (Barrett, 2000).

Cityjet relied on travel agents with large overrides to retail their products. For Ryanair the development of the Internet and the growth of telemarketing came at the right time and the airline now bypasses agents and CRS for 80 per cent of its passengers. Ryanair abolished its frequent-flyer programme to secure a least-cost operation. Its target market was those paying for their own flights including small businesses. Cityjet tried a variety of frequent-flyer programmes but failed to induce transfer from the established business class airlines.

The EU has made progress in ground handling but there are still barriers to full competition between airlines and other handlers. Having been protected during the Aer Lingus rescue period Ryanair is now sufficiently large to be protected from predation by established European airlines. Cityjet did not have that size but is now available to promote competition and lower costs within the Air France group. This Demsetz competition allows Cityjet to take its product to the market within the Air France group as an alternative to the many post-deregulation barriers to contestability experienced by the airline as an independent entity (Demsetz, 1968).

Neither airline has gained significantly from EU competition policy apart from a dawn raid on Aer Lingus in relation to price reductions on UK provincial routes, following a complaint by Ryanair. Both saw their major rival Aer Lingus receive £175 million in government assistance. The adverse impact on Cityjet was probably greater than on Ryanair which has subsequently extended its network far beyond routes where it competes with Aer Lingus.

Conclusions

The Cityjet case study indicates that full-service airlines face many difficulties in the deregulated market. Incumbents exercise hub airport control and have effective frequent-flyer programmes. New entrants incur extra retailing costs in order to secure travel agent support. New full service airlines also face competition from budget airlines whose message is that in-flight service is not worth the expense on short-haul routes. EU policy on predation is weak according to both the new entrant airlines examined.

References

Barrett, S.D. (1999) Peripheral market entry, product differentiation, supplier rents and sustainability in the deregulated European aviation market – a case study, *Journal of Air Transport Management* 5: 21–30.

Barrett, S.D. (2000) Airport competition in the deregulated European aviation market, *Journal of Air Transport Management* 6: 13–27.

Civil Aviation Authority (1998) *The Single European Aviation Market: The First Five Years*. London: Civil Aviation Authority.

Demsetz, H. (1968) Why regulate utilities?, *Journal of Law and Economics* 11: 55–65.

Hanlon, P. (1999) *Global Airlines*. Oxford: Butterworth.

Levine, M. (1987) Airline competition in deregulated markets; theory, firm strategy and public policy, *Yale Journal on Regulation* 4: 393–494.

7 Commercialising a national airline

The Aer Lingus case study

Introduction

In 2004 Goldman Sachs, in a study for the government of Ireland on the future of Aer Lingus, found that of 18 European countries examined only five retained 100 per cent state ownership of the national airline. The states were Malta, Czech Republic, Hungary, Greece and Portugal. This chapter examines the decline of the once-dominant national airline model in European aviation policy using Aer Lingus as a case study.

The concept of a 'national airline'

The assertion of national property rights to airspace dates from 1919, 16 years after the first aircraft journey. The assertion of national property rights was further increased by the defeat of US proposals for open skies at the Chicago Aviation Conference of 1944 by European countries afraid that under free trade, the US would dominate post-war aviation. Aviation was organised instead on a bilateral 'Noah's Ark' basis. No international flights could take place without the agreement of two governments and two national airlines. Bilateral international aviation agreements typically determined market size and market shares in advance and the fare to be charged. New market entrants, price competition and capacity competition were precluded. National airlines colluded in regard to matters such as the restraint of service competition, revenue pooling, and interlining through IATA, the International Air Transport Association.

Aer Lingus was established by the government of Ireland in 1936 at a time of strong protectionist emphasis in Irish economic policy. Public policy protected Aer Lingus even before it commenced operations. The Air Navigation (International Lines) Order of 1935 gave the Minister for Industry and Commerce control over air services 'with a view to the limitation or regulation of competition as may be considered necessary in the public interest'. In 1935, Crilly Airways sought to operate air services between Ireland and Britain but was informed that the Minister was unable to consider the proposals. The reason given was the government intention to set up a national airline at the earliest possible date.

Share's history of Aer Lingus records many further examples of regulatory capture by the airline. In 1949 a proposal for a service from Cork to Britain by Cambrian was refused 'on the grounds that air transport policy did not contemplate that airlines other than Aer Lingus would operate a scheduled service between the two countries'. In 1960 a proposal from Silver City for a car-carrying service from Liverpool to Dublin was refused because Aer Lingus 'was considering the opening of a similar service on the route'. Share (1986) records that 'other airlines were in this period equally unsuccessful in their intentions to serve Ireland' and that proposed Rome–Paris–Dublin and Milan–Paris–Dublin services were successfully opposed by the Aer Lingus board.

Share states that the thinking behind the Bill establishing Aer Lingus 'which enshrined the position of the State as the sole international carrier, had been influenced by European developments. KLM had been set up in 1919, Lufthansa in April 1926 and Air France in 1933: all State entities benefiting from official restriction of competition.' Share recalls that such was the strength of protectionist opinion within the Irish government that the Minister explained that 'though he wished to minimise competition on economic grounds, he recognised that no one country could hope to reserve for its own nationals the whole of air transport between its own territory and that of another country.'

FitzGerald (1961), an economist at Aer Lingus, and later Taoiseach (Prime Minister), in a wide-ranging examination of Irish state companies offered two main reasons for their establishment. These were 'a desire to maintain in existence a bankrupt, or virtually bankrupt, undertaking, whose preservation is believed to be in the national interest', and 'a desire to initiate an economic activity deemed necessary in the national interest – but one which for one reason or another – private enterprise has failed to inaugurate or to operate in a sufficiently extensive scale'. He included Aer Lingus in the second category of filling a role where private enterprise did not exist. The evidence from Share is that, far from filling a void left by the private sector, Aer Lingus successfully lobbied governments to keep other airlines out of the market. It achieved regulatory capture of its parent government department.

National pride in owning a national airline was also a factor influencing public policy in the area. 'You saw for the first time an Irish plane with a shamrock. There was a great deal of emotional pride in the thing.' This account by a member of the airline's publicity department of the opening of the New York route in 1960 is taken from Share (1986).

The national airline saw itself as a leader in Irish representation abroad. Share's account of the opening of the New York service also contains a statement by the airline's publicity department member that 'the tourist board and the people in the consulate worked with us like they were all members of Aer Lingus'. National airlines were also seen as a focus for citizens living abroad.

In tourism promotion the factors considered important were the use of a national symbol, the shamrock, to promote both Ireland and the airline, the presence of the airline sales offices in prestigious major downtown areas of important cities abroad and projecting a positive image of Ireland in the circumstances of the time.

A national airline was seen as proof on an entrepreneurial spirit and nationalism combined. 'From the beginning Aer Lingus demanded and achieved the highest standards from the women. They were expected to be typical of the very best of Irish womanhood' (Weldon, 2002). The journey to Ireland by the national airline had therefore a strong national flavour from the Aer Lingus booking office onwards. The Irish holiday experience began not on arrival in Ireland but on boarding an Aer Lingus flight.

The benefits from a national airline

The Economists Advisory Group conducted a cost–benefit analysis of Aer Lingus which was published by O'Donoghue (1969). The findings were as follows.

- Aer Lingus provides employment opportunities for people, some of whom would either be otherwise unemployed or would have to work in less productive and therefore less well-paid jobs. Aer Lingus operations earn foreign exchange which could otherwise only be earned at significantly greater cost in real resources. The primary increase in income generated by Aer Lingus provides additional spending and so generates further income through multiplier effects.
- The operations of Aer Lingus and the advertising which goes through them have significant effects in encouraging tourism and promoting trade. The existence of good air services enhances the attractiveness of Ireland for industrial firms, especially those with headquarters overseas.
- Our attempts to quantify these and other benefits indicate that the true social rate of return on the capital employed by Aer Lingus is probably between 11 per cent and 26 per cent, compared with the return actually accruing to the firm and shown in the accounts of 4 per cent. These estimates are conservative in that they do not fully take account of the social benefits from commercially unprofitable routes (Weldon, 2002).

The key elements in the Aer Lingus cost–benefit analysis were therefore the then high level of unemployment in Ireland, the country's inability or unwillingness to use flexible exchange rates and the ability of a relatively closed economy with spare capacity to generate multiplier effects. In addition the airline's services promoted tourism and trade. Shadow pricing for these factors increased the airline's return on capital from 4 per cent to between 11 and 26 per cent.

The non-competing national airlines might thus use cost–benefit analysis to claim that they were of benefit to society as a whole. The airline defended the anti-competitive market structure of the sector with claims that this brought lower rather than higher fares. FitzGerald described the fares charged in 1948 as 'one of the rare cases where a monopoly led to cheaper fares' (Share, 1986). This optimistic view was echoed by Bristow (1984) in a report for Aer Lingus entitled 'Aspects of the regulation of air fares in Ireland'. 'There is no evidence that regulation has allowed the efficiency and costs of Aer Lingus to get out of line with those of other comparable European airlines. Nor are Irish fares generally higher than

Table 7.1 The benefits sought and actual result of the national airline policy in Ireland

Benefits sought	Results
A national airline	Ban on new entrants
Serving the national interest	Serving the national airline interest
	Regulatory capture
National pride	Excess access costs
Irish representation abroad	Very high fares for emigrants returning for short notice reasons and emergencies
Tourism promotion	Tourism restricted by high access fares and controlled capacity
Employment	A low productivity airline
Foreign exchange	Reduced tourism due to high access costs
11–26% social return	Negative impact on economy due to high access costs and loss of national competitiveness. 'Multiplier effect' overstated benefits since other projects also could have these impacts on the same estimation methods
An efficient monopoly	Excess costs and fares compared to the denied market alternative

fares elsewhere in Europe. Indeed, the average fare per mile paid by Aer Lingus passengers is lower than that paid on Major European airlines.'

Table 7.1 lists in column 1 the benefits sought from having an Irish national airline. Column 2 summarises the actual results compared with each of the benefits sought. By the 1980s there was a widespread view that the time had come to deregulate access transport. Column 2 in its marked divergence from the policy aspirations in column 1 illustrates the factors which motivated the policy changes from 1984 in the Oireachtas (parliament) and from 1986 in the marketplace. With the benefit of hindsight since deregulation the points made in column 2 can be seen to have been far stronger than even the critics of the national airline policy argued before deregulation.

The case against national airlines

Share (1986) states that 'as consumerist and monetarist attitudes became fashionable in the early and mid-1980s, the social role of Aer Lingus came increasingly under scrutiny' including from the present author, who was 'conducting a sustained campaign in favour of de-regulation of air fares with particular reference to Irish Sea routes'. The alleged high fares charged by Aer Lingus came under public scrutiny and by 1986 Ireland became the first European country to allow a new market entrant to compete with its national airline on its major route. This was some 11 years before the deregulation of European Union (EU) aviation in 1997.

Ireland was the first EU country in which the new entrant airline exceeded in passenger numbers the national airline and went on to become more than four times bigger. It might be said that national airlines worked neither in theory or practice and that the Irish case study was hugely influential in the later move by the EU to a contestable market in aviation. Table 7.1 contrasts the goals of national airline policy as discussed above with the results with the shift in public opinion which saw the parliamentary revolt against the Air Transport Bill in 1984 and the licensing of Ryanair in 1986.

Nine types of benefit sought from having an Irish national airline are listed in Table 7.1. The table also shows the results of the policy in regard to each of the benefits sought. The contrast between the benefits sought and the result is contrasted in each category. Having a national airline led to the regulatory capture of the Department of Transport and the banning of new entrants in decade after decade. It is unrealistic to have the department responsible for regulating a sector also being responsible for a state company in the sector. The inevitability of a state company in a sector achieving regulatory capture over its parent department leads to the national interest being identified, in this case, with the national airline interest.

While there may be an element of national pride in owning a national airline the risk taken is that the ability of a national airline to have government act on its behalf by excluding new market entrants will lead to higher access transport costs which are not in the national interest. Similarly, while having national airline offices abroad and a presence at foreign airports may have raised Ireland's profile and the standing and the morale of Irish emigrants, the very high fares charged by national airlines seriously penalised emigrants returning on short-notice trips. Irish communities in Britain were major advocates of airline deregulation as a response to high fares.

While Aer Lingus offices and airline advertising abroad raised the image of Ireland this was not sufficient to offset the high fares charged. The White Paper on Tourism Policy in 1985 (Government of Ireland, 1985) found that the number of tourists by air from Britain to Ireland declined by 50 per cent between 1975 and 1983. The supply restrictions and quantity controls in bilateral air agreements meant that passengers were pushed into higher fare categories at times of peak demand.

The use of a national airline as a means of generating employment runs the risk of over-manning in the airline, high access transport costs leading to lower national competitiveness and lower national employment in sectors which depend on air access such as tourism and internationally traded goods and services. Table 7.2 contrasts employment in the protected sector of Irish airlines in 1985 and in 2004. In 2004 the Irish labour market was working far better than in 1985. In 2004 there were 1.9 million people at work and 4.3 per cent unemployment in contrast to 1.1 million at work and 17 per cent unemployment in 1985. In a full-employment economy there is no divergence between the price of labour and its opportunity cost and a policy of deliberately over-manning a national airline in order to reduce unemployment is harmful both to the airline and the national economy. The economy in which the Economists Advisory Group shadow-priced labour below the market price in 1965 was not the full employment economy of 2005.

Table 7.2 Passengers and staff employed, Irish airlines, 1985/6 and 2004

	Passengers (million)	*Staff*
1985/6 Aer Lingus	2.3	6500
2004 Ryanair	30.0	2500
Aer Lingus	7.0	4200
Cityjet	1.0	500
Aer Arann	0.6	300
2004 Total	38.6	7500

The case that foreign exchange earnings in Ireland in the 1960s should be shadow priced at a premium compared with the same amount of home market earnings applied in an economy experiencing a deficit in its balance of payments and being unable or unwilling to devalue. This was not the case in 2004 with a positive trade balance in goods and services.

The inclusion by the Economists Advisory Group of multiplier impacts even in an economy with idle resources such as Ireland in the 1960s is open to question since all projects in an economy with idle resources will have multiplier effects. The inclusion of multiplier effects for public sector investments gives each project a higher rate of return but does not change their rankings. Since the multiplier effects of private sector investments were not included in their assessments, the inclusion of these effects in the assessment of public sector projects only raises their relative rate of return and thus distorts the ratio of public to private investment.

Deregulation – the evidence

The hope that Aer Lingus might be an efficient monopoly became forlorn in an era of deregulation. Many studies showed that air fares in market where governments excluded new entrants were significantly in excess of those with new entrants. Before US airline deregulation in 1970, Jordan estimated that air fares in California where the state did not exclude new market entrants were only 47 per cent of those on interstate routes on which the federal government excluded new entrants after 1938 (Jordan, 1970). Kahn (2004) estimates that US airline deregulation saved passengers $440 million a year after deregulation in 1978. In Europe, the Cascade studies (European Community, 1981) found that fares charged by charter airlines to sun-destination countries which had liberal market entry arrangements in order to promote tourism were between 32 per cent and 37 per cent of the fares charged on routes operated by national airlines from which new entrants were excluded.

Table 7.3 shows the estimated savings from moving from the state airline to charter airline model. The expectation that fares would fall in a more competitive regime was a major factor in the parliamentary debates on the failed Air Transport Bill in 1984. There was little public confidence at the time that Ireland had in fact developed an efficient monopoly in air transport. This was supported by a

Table 7.3 The cascade study of lower fares by
charter airlines in Europe, 1981

Scheduled airline cost per passenger index	100
1. Deduct commission	92
2. Tourist class	84
3. Seating density	80
4. Load factor	59
5. Peak/trough ratio	62
6. Utilisation	60
7. Standards	51
8. Not applicable	37
Derived charter	37
Actual charter	32

Source: European Community (1981).

Note
The differences between the fares charged on charter and
scheduled airlines is attributed to factors such as higher load
factors, seat density and utilisation by the charter airlines
in addition to lower selling costs for charters, single class
operation, and alleged lower standards on charters in respect
of items such as in-flight service.

Table 7.4 Fares and passenger growth on the
London–Dublin route and major short-haul routes
compared, 1980–5

London to ...	Fare increase (%)	Passenger increase (%)
Glasgow	31.9	40.4
Edinburgh	31.9	58.3
Belfast	40.9	30.7
Manchester	45.5	41.9
Aberdeen	29.2	34.5
Newcastle	38.8	18.4
Paris	63.2	17.1
Amsterdam	38.5	24.1
Dublin	72.6	2.8
Frankfurt	43.2	40.1
Brussels	43.6	20.4
Average	43.7	29.9

Source: Civil Aviation Authority (1987).

comparison of air fares on 11 major short-haul routes from London in the 1980s
conducted by the Civil Aviation Authority (1987) and shown in Table 7.4.

Table 7.3 indicates that Europe's scheduled airlines could have produced a
charter-type product for 37 per cent of their costs of producing their scheduled
product. While this would still exceed the 32 per cent of scheduled fare actually

charged by the charter airlines the exercise raises the question why the scheduled airlines did not test the market for their charter product costing only 37 per cent of the scheduled airline product they were already selling. The Cascade Studies, commissioned in defence of Europe's national airlines, in the event found that scheduled airlines could reduce their costs by almost two-thirds and that charter airlines in Europe were already doing so. The fare reductions achieved by the Ireland/UK deregulation in 1986 came as no surprise therefore in the wake of the Cascade studies.

Table 7.4 shows that of 11 major short-haul routes from London between 1980 and 1985, Dublin–London had by far the lowest traffic growth at 2.8 per cent compared to an average of 29.9 per cent. The fare increase of 72.6 per cent on Dublin–London was the largest by a margin of over 27 points and compared with an average of 43.7 per cent for the 11 routes. The contrast between the Dublin and Belfast routes was notable. The Belfast volumes rose by 30.7 per cent or 11 times the Dublin growth rate. The Belfast fare increase of 40.9 per cent was 56 per cent of the increase in fares between Dublin and London.

The poor Aer Lingus performance on its major route, Dublin–London, between 1980 and 1985, was an emphatic version of a problem which was Europe-wide. Doganis (2001), writing from the unique perspective of holding consecutively the chair of aviation economics at Cranfield University and chief executive of Olympic Airways, described 'distressed state airline syndrome' which had the following elements:

- substantial losses;
- overpoliticisation;
- strong unions;
- overstaffing;
- no clear development strategy;
- bureaucratic management; and
- poor service quality.

The strong political and trade union opposition which led to the resignation of the three most senior Aer Lingus managers in November 2004 is the most recent example of distressed state airline syndrome in Ireland. The other elements of the Doganis list of problems were present also in the Aer Lingus case.

1   The history of loss making is recorded in Weldon (2002) with 28 loss-making years in Aer Lingus between its establishment in 1936/7 and 2001 when it lost €140 million and had 6.6 million passengers.
2   Overpoliticisation is indicated by the political appointment of directors and the travel concessions involved which made the directorships popular to political supporters of the parties in power. In parliament on successive days the Taoiseach (Prime Minister) opposed the MBO (management buyout) proposal for the airline and supported trade criticism of management at the airline (Parliamantary Debates, November 16/17, 2004). A further example

of overpoliticisation was the success of Aer Lingus in achieving regulatory capture over the state aviation licensing body.

3   Strong unions exert pressure on Aer Lingus management through the Prime Minister and through the Irish social partnership system. The Prime Minister stated in parliament that unions opposed the low-cost model chosen by Aer Lingus since 2001. 'The unions are not convinced that this business model is necessarily the best … There has been a difficult IR position. The workers and the unions are concerned that the very people they were dealing with as management wanted to make themselves extremely rich. That was the underlying position of the trade union movement to which I have been listening all year … They are determined not to yield up savings to a management team concerned with its own position rather than the company's future' (Parliamantary Debates, 16 November 2004). The Aer Lingus senior management team resigned on that date. The resignations were intended to take effect in May 2005 but further political pressure caused them to be brought forward to January 2005.

4   Overstaffing is indicated in Aer Lingus employment of over 6,000 staff to carry 2.0 million passengers in 1977/8. This indicated a serious productivity problem which was confirmed by a series of survival plans when the airline later faced competition.

5   The lack of a clear development strategy for the airline is illustrated by the Aer Lingus policy of developing instead some 40 non-airline businesses (Share, 1986). These were intended to assist the airline to generate funds to counteract cyclical declines in air transport profitability but in the event made little contribution.

6   The bureaucratic management of Aer Lingus is illustrated by the cost inefficiencies of the airline, its stagnation in the years before deregulation and the diversion of management attention to the non-airline businesses.

7   The service quality problem is illustrated on Aer Lingus short-haul routes when in-flight service was unbundled from high unrestricted fares. Most passengers opted for fully flexible tickets without business class in-flight service. The service did not therefore satisfy the market test. On only two routes, Dublin–London and Dublin–Brussels, were a sufficient number of passengers willing to pay for executive class to make it a viable proposition.

Deregulation – the experience 1986–2004

The immediate impact of the deregulation of the Dublin–London route in 1986 was the reduction in the unrestricted return fare of 57 per cent. Initially Ryanair, the new entrant airline, was restricted in the capacity it was permitted to offer on the route based on turboprop aircraft. It acquired jet aircraft with much lower seat-mile costs and was in time allowed to sell the extra seats. By August 1987, the first full year of deregulation, passenger numbers on Dublin–London were running 92 per cent ahead of August 1985, the last full year of pre-deregulation policies on the route. From its pre-deregulation position as the fifth busiest route of those shown in Table 7.4, Dublin–London became the busiest international route in Europe and in some years exceeded Tokyo–Taipei to become the busiest international air route in the world. As new market entrants availed of deregulation to open new routes at Cork, Shannon, Knock, Kerry, Waterford and Galway, the deregulated Ireland–UK air market grew bigger than the markets serving far larger populations than Ireland such as the UK routes to Germany, France, Italy, Belgium and the Netherlands. The most notable knock-on impact of these large increases in supply and reductions in price of access transport was in tourism to Ireland where a sector stagnant for 20 years at some 2 million visitors became the fastest growing tourism sector in the Organisation for Economic Cooperation and Development (OECD). The success of airline deregulation in Ireland had a major impact on public opinion in favour of deregulation in other sectors (Organisation for Economic Cooperation and Development, 2001).

The deregulated airline product

Airline deregulation, in addition to allowing new market entry and price and capacity competition, allowed the product to be redefined. In the cartel of national airlines the product was rigidly defined. Table 7.5 shows some 17 product differences between those sold under the previous agreements between national airlines and the deregulated product now available.

The production of the deregulated airline product, in addition to the cost-reducing measures in Table 7.5, involves much higher productivity than attained by national airlines. The higher productivity is achieved by reducing the cost base, simplifying the product, using a single aircraft type in order to maximise pilot productivity, reducing aircraft turnaround time at airports to 25 minutes compared

Table 7.5 The 'national airline' and deregulated airline products contrasted

Customer service items deleted

Deregulated airlines have deleted sweets, newspapers, free food and beverages, seat allocation and business class. There are now more seats per aircraft and the load factors (proportion of seats sold) are higher

Airport service items

Deregulated airlines use secondary airports. No interlining or connecting journey tickets are sold. Passengers and baggage must be checked in at each airport on a multi-stage journey. There is no airport business lounge service

Ticket restrictions

Tickets are not sold through travel agents and there are no airline ticket sales offices. There is no frequent flyer programme. There are strict penalties for 'no-show' passengers

Some service improvements

While significant fare savings have been the main consumer gain from deregulation of European aviation there have been service improvements such as avoiding congested hub airports, better punctuality at uncongested secondary airports and less walking distances and baggage waiting times, fewer bags lost because of the simple point-to-point product and no risk of denied boarding on overbooked flights compared to traditional airlines whose overbooking policy imposed the cost of no-show passengers on overbooked passengers rather than on the no-shows to an hour to 75 minutes by traditional airlines, and outsourcing services such as passenger and baggage handling, maintenance and catering.

Irish airlines under deregulation

Table 7.2 shows the structure of Irish airlines before deregulation in 1986 and in 2004. Total passenger numbers carried have increased from 2.3 million in 1985/6 to almost 39 million in 2004. Staff employed increased from 6,500 to 7,500. Productivity increased from 354 passengers per staff member per year to 5,147; that is, 14.5 times the pre-deregulation level. The responses to deregulation are examined below for three new entrants, Ryanair, Cityjet and Aer Arann, and then for the incumbent national airline, Aer Lingus.

Ryanair had a headstart in benefiting from European deregulation because the Irish government was first to deregulate the main route of its national airline. It has the lowest cost and highest profitability model in Europe with profits of €201 million in the half year to 30 September 2004 and the highest profit margin in world aviation at 28 per cent. Goldman Sachs notes that Ryanair is the only European airline that has outperformed the FTSE Eurotop 300 index over the past 10 years. It has been an innovator in dispensing with the services of travel agents and downtown sales offices by use of the Internet, and in the promotion of low-cost secondary airports. Ryanair extended its low-cost model to the UK regions in the early 1990s, to UK internal routes in the mid-1990s and to mainland Europe routes after EU deregulation in 1997. Its low-cost model has been successfully transferred from Irish Sea routes to Italy, Germany, Scandinavia, and France. It has been able to attract market share from national airlines with high costs, such as SAS and Lufthansa, and those which emphasise their hub airports at the expense of regional services, such as Alitalia, Iberia and Air France. With an estimated 30 million passengers in 2004, Ryanair is the third ranking international passenger airline in the EU, after Air France/KLM and Lufthansa. High productivity within the airline and outsourcing give Ryanair an estimated 12,000 passengers per staff member per year, almost three times that attained by Southwest, the airline on which Ryanair is modelled. It has surmounted two major post-deregulation barriers to contestability in aviation. It avoids hub airports where legacy airlines control market access by grandfather rights to the slots. Ryanair uses instead empty non-hub airports with lower costs and quicker turnaround times. These airports typically achieve a 25 per cent market share early after deregulation and on a mature deregulated route such as Dublin–London more than half the passengers now do not use Heathrow. Both Internet booking and non-hub airports are very popular (Barrett, 1999, 2000; Civil Aviation Authority, 2004; Williams *et al.*, 2003).

Cityjet is a full-service lower-cost section of Air France based in Dublin. In the year ended March 2004 its profits were €7 million. It employs 500 people and carries 1 million passengers per year on six routes.

Aer Arann has grown from the Aran Island public service obligation route to a network of 25 routes of which five are PSO (public service obligation) services from Dublin to Kerry, Galway, Knock, Sligo and Donegal. It has 650,000 passengers per year and 300 employees. It took over internal routes left by Aer Lingus as part of its restructuring programme. Its largest volume route is Dublin–Cork which it has developed to a frequency of 11 weekday services. Aer Arann has also developed regional services from Waterford, Galway, Cork, Kerry and Derry to Britain to points not served by Aer Lingus and Ryanair and has a service from Lorient in France to Galway and Waterford. Aer Arann had profits of €2.6 million in 2003 on turnover of €43.7 million. Unsubsidised routes and commercial receipts on subsidised routes in 2003 accounted for 60 per cent of its revenue.

Aer Lingus in 2003 reported a profit of €69.2 million, an increase of 96 per cent on 2002. Its costs were reduced by 30 per cent from the 2001 level and the operating margin was 9.3 per cent. The projected profit for 2004 is €95 million. In October 2004 the airline announced that 1,600 employees had applied for its voluntary redundancy programme. Whereas the overall passenger increase in 2003 for the airline was 6.2 per cent, the increase on the North Atlantic was 19.4 per cent, to 1.1 million, and on the continental European routes the increase was 27.6 per cent to 2.1 million. Irish Sea route traffic declined on Aer Lingus from 3.7 to 3.4 million with Ryanair the market leader on all routes where the two airlines competed.

The Aer Lingus strategy has been to reduce costs and fares. The average European fare was reduced by 30 per cent on traditional routes between 2001 and 2004. Restrictions on fares have been removed and all fares are sold on a one-way basis. The low-cost model has been adopted. A total of 50 per cent of bookings are made over the Internet. Food service has been unbundled from the issue of unrestricted tickets and only on two European routes, Dublin–London and Dublin–Brussels, do more than ten passengers per flight seek to purchase the business class product with food and beverage service included. Expensive downtown sales offices have been closed and the airline's low productivity problem tackled with 1,600 applications for voluntary redundancy in late 2004. The airline's frequent-flyer programme is being scaled back to some 7,000 regular high-yield passengers.

Aer Lingus has left all domestic routes in Ireland with the exception of Dublin–Shannon. Dublin–Cork, which Aer Lingus served for 40 years, now has a far more frequent service by Aer Arann. Snacks, beverages and newspapers are now sold rather than distributed free on Aer Lingus flights. Seat allocation, travel agent ticket sales for half the passengers and a slimmed-down frequent-flyer programme remain from the previous Aer Lingus product but most of the changes made by the low-cost airlines, and shown in Table 7.5, have been made by Aer Lingus also. The airline has been reinvented to deliver low air fares with seat allocation. It has opened 37 new routes serving new mainland Europe secondary destinations from Dublin and Cork at lower fares with 25-minute turnaround services and substituting direct service for long waiting times at hub airports such as Heathrow, Frankfurt, Paris and Madrid.

Aer Lingus remains a member of the One World alliance of 'quality airlines' serving 570 destinations worldwide. The other members are American Airlines, British Airways, Cathay Pacific, Finnair, Iberia, Lan Chile and Qantas. Interlining traffic is low yield business for short-route feeder airlines such as Aer Lingus at

Heathrow, but costly to provide at a level of service similar to that provided by the long-haul partner airlines. Two-thirds of Ireland–London traffic is carried by Ryanair, British Midland and other rival airlines. Of the Aer Lingus one-third share, some 30 per cent are interlining at Heathrow and are thus low yield to the feeder airline. Loddenberg (2004) indicates that for point-to-point traffic Aer Lingus commands a premium at Heathrow of only €10 over Ryanair at Luton and Stansted. The opportunity cost to Aer Lingus of using its valuable Heathrow slots for such low-yield traffic should be examined.

The point-to-point product provided by low-cost airlines is simpler and less expensive to provide and Aer Lingus is now emulating this model. At New York the Aer Lingus estimate is that only 7 per cent of its passengers interline with its One World partner, American Airlines. The union view is that far more Aer Lingus passengers at JFK New York travel onward with Jet Blue whose terminal is beside the Aer Lingus building. The onward bookings are made by passengers themselves on the Internet. No interlining agreement between Aer Lingus and Jet Blue is required. The benefit to Aer Lingus from membership of One World at either Heathrow or JFK is therefore doubtful. By leaving the One World Alliance Aer Lingus could emulate the Ryanair model and serve the wider European market. This offers more market opportunities than being a small member of an airline alliance. Goldman Sachs (2004) 'notes that the European Commission actively promotes the idea of a consolidated European airline sector, based around British Airways, Lufthansa, and Air France'. Goldman Sachs regards this vision as 'unrealistic' and 'based on the political aspiration of creating European champions as global leaders in the sector'. The value of consolidation and alliances to a reinvented low-cost Aer Lingus is questionable.

The Aer Lingus case study indicates that the national airline model is expensive and is deserted quickly by passengers when a competing low-cost model becomes available. For example, Byrne (2004) notes that in 1995 when his airline Cityjet entered the Dublin–Brussels route in competition with Aer Lingus, the fare was €762 or over €1000 at 2004/5 prices. This contrasts with an average Aer Lingus fare of €82.52 one-way, including charges on mainland Europe routes and the average Ryanair fare of €38 plus €12 in taxes and charges. The 1995 national airline product on Dublin–Brussels was not sustainable in a deregulated market.

Two national airlines, Swissair and Sabena, have left the market. KLM has been taken over by Air France and Alitalia required a further rescue tranche in 2004. Norway, Sweden and Denmark avoided the national airline concept from the outset and ran SAS as a joint venture. Aer Lingus as a badge of Irish nationality may now actually restrict the airline's horizons. It has not developed any hubs or routes outside the Irish market unlike Ryanair which has become a much larger airline serving the single European market. 'Ryanair now carries the Irish harp to regions that had little acquaintance with it in the past,' is part of the Goldman Sachs (2004) assessment of whether a 'national airline' promotion value might be lost if the airline ceased to be fully state owned. Goldman Sachs state that 'most governments no longer view ownership of airlines as an important element of public policy and use other means to achieve their objectives as airline stakeholders'.

The economic rents generated by 50 years of protectionist policies for Aer Lingus brought low productivity rather than high wages. A 'quiet life' is a form of monopoly rent. The Flynn and McAuley (1998) report on the 1998 strike by the staffs of Aer Lingus and Aer Rianta at Dublin Airport found that 'it is clear that most employees in Ryanair identify strongly with the Company and its management. They are proud of its achievements and successes. They are confident that the Company will continue to grow and this will provide additional career opportunities for them.' The Ryanair staff interviewed 'consider that they work hard for the Company, harder and more effectively than workers at other airport-based companies'. The evidence over the entire period of protectionism in European aviation is that the protected airlines employ large numbers of staff in support services such as administration, ticketing, sales and promotion, catering, and handling, thus reducing average earnings in the airlines compared to high productivity airlines with fewer support staff and performance-related pay.

In recent years Aer Lingus has overcome many of the problems of distressed state airline syndrome as shown in Table 7.4. There are few, if any, remaining benefits to the airline from state ownership. Table 7.6 shows that full state ownership of national airlines in Europe is now confined to a handful of small airlines in smaller countries.

Table 7.6 Ownership structure of European national airlines, 2004 (% share)

	State	*Employees*	*Private*
Adria	–	6	94
Aer Lingus	85	15	–
Air Baltic	53	–	47
Air Frnace	44	11	45
Air Malta	100	–	–
Alitalia	62	12	27
Austrian	40	–	60
British Airways	–	10	90
Czech Airlines	100	–	–
Finnair	65	–	35
Iberia	–	9	91
KLM	25	–	75
Lufthansa	–	1	99
Luxair	21	–	79
Malev	100	–	–
Olympic	100	–	–
SAS	54	–	46
TAP	100	–	–

Source: Goldman Sachs (2004).

Note
The French government announced in December 2004 its planned reduction in its holding in Air France–KLM from 44 to 18 per cent.

Table 7.7 The declining role of commercial state enterprises (CSE) in Irish employment, 1980–2003

	CSE employment	National employment	CSE share (%)
1980	90,375	1,163,000	7.8
1990	71,013	1,100,000	6.5
2003	48,000	1,811,000	2.7

Source: Irish Statistical Bulletin, ESRI Quarterly Economic Commentary, Chubb B., The Government and Politics of Ireland (third edition).

Table 7.7 shows the state commercial company model in rapid decline in Ireland. Employment in commercial state enterprises has fallen by half since 1980 and their share of total national employment has fallen by almost two-thirds. Being a state commercial company may be a double disadvantage for Aer Lingus. If government intervenes to help it the commercial airlines will object to the EU. If the government imposes roles or duties on the airline as owner it will probably succeed through a politically appointed board, but harm the airline. Megginson and Netter (2001), in a review of some 224 privatisation studies worldwide, state that 'research now supports the proposition that privately owned firms are more efficient and more profitable than otherwise-comparable state-owned firms'. They state that 'we know that privatisation works in the sense that divested firms almost always become more efficient, more profitable and financially healthier'.

Given the success of the former management in transforming the airline there was merit in the MBO proposal submitted by Aer Lingus management. The proposal was withdrawn and the management resigned in November 2004. Management with a proven record in negotiating the low-cost model with staff, airports, suppliers and passengers and good recent profitability might have had an advantage in financial markets over the replacement management team.

A trade sale runs the risk of reduced competition if a competitor bought Aer Lingus or destruction of the low-cost profitable model if another legacy airline bought the company and restored a high-cost corporate culture. A share issue would allow the airline to raise the €300 million currently needed to make initial payments on a €1.2 billion long-haul fleet investment programme.

Conclusion

The view of this study is that the concept of a national airline is rooted in a protectionist era long gone from Irish economic policy. The policy had serious anti-competitive impacts from the beginning and imposed large costs rather than generating benefits to the economy. The traditional national airline model of Aer Lingus was undermined by competition but it has reinvented itself since 2001 to become a profitable low-cost airline. That success indicates a future with private investment in the reformed low-cost Aer Lingus. The resignation with effect from January 2005 of the management team which had accomplished the transformation of the airline illustrates the political and trade union obstacles which still confront managements seeking to transform Europe's legacy airlines.

References

Barrett, S.D. (1999) Peripheral market entry, product differentiation, supplier rents and sustainability in the deregulated European aviation market – a case study, *Journal of Air Transport Management* 5: 21–30.

Barrett, S.D. (2000) Airport competition in the deregulated European aviation market, *Journal of Air Transport Management* 6: 13–27.

Bristow, J. (1984) Aspects of the regulation of air fares in Ireland, Dublin, in Share, B. (ed.) *The Flight of the Iolar, The Aer Lingus Experience, 1936–1986*. Dublin: Gill and Macmillan.

Byrne, P. (2004) *Fuelled by Belief, The Cityjet Story*. Dublin: Liffey Press.

Civil Aviation Authority (1987) Competition on the main domestic trunk routes. CAA Paper 87005, London.

Civil Aviation Authority (2004) Civil aviation authority, the effect of liberalisation on aviation employment. CAP 749, London.

Doganis, R. (2001) *The Airline Business in the 21st Century*. London: Routledge.

European Community (1981) *Report on Scheduled Passenger Air Fares in the EC*. Brussels: European Community.

FitzGerald, G. (1961) *State Sponsored Bodies*. Dublin: Institute of Public Administration.

Flynn, P. and McAuley, D. (1998) *Report of the Enquiry into Strike at Dublin Airport*. Dublin: Government Publications.

Goldman Sachs International (2004) *Evaluation of Ownership Options Regarding Aer Lingus plc*. Dublin: Government Publications.

Government of Ireland (1985) *White Paper on Tourism Policy*. Dublin: Government Publications.

Jordan, W. (1970) *Airline Regulation in America*. Baltimore, MD: Johns Hopkins University Press.

Kahn, A. (2004) *Lessons from Deregulation*. Washington, DC: American Enterprise Institute – Brookings.

Loddenberg, A. (2004) *Report on Ryanair*. London: ABN-AMRO.

Megginson, W. and Netter, J. (2001) From state to market; study of empirical studies on privatization, *Journal of Economic Literature* 39: 321–89.

O'Donoghue, M. (1969) A cost–benefit evaluation of Irish airlines, *Journal of the Statistical and Social Inquiry Society of Ireland* 22: 155–80.

Organisation for Economic Cooperation and Development (2001) *Regulatory Reform in Ireland*. Paris: OECD.

Share, B. (1986) *The Flight of the Iolar, The Aer Lingus Experience, 1936–1986*. Dublin: Gill and Macmillan.

Weldon, N.G. (2002) *Pioneers in Flight, Aer Lingus and the Story of Aviation in Ireland*. Dublin: Liffey Press.

Williams, G., Mason, K. and Turner, S. (2003) *Market Analysis of Europe's Low Cost Airlines*. Research Report 9, Cranfield Air Transport Group, Cranfield.

8 Airport competition

Low-cost airlines and low-cost airports

(I) Airport competition in the deregulated European aviation market

The first part of this chapter examines the economics of competition between airports in Europe in the context of airline deregulation. It examines the history of airports in Europe not engaging in competition and the reasons proffered for non-competing airports before airline deregulation in Europe. The economics of low-cost airlines and the implications for airports are examined. Case studies are presented of airport competition in the UK, France, Belgium, Norway, Sweden, Italy and Germany. The scope for further airport competition in Europe is examined. The Ryanair case study is used to illustrate the user impacts of the combination of both airline and airport competition. The scope for further airport competition in Europe and its sustainability are examined.

European airports in the era of non-competing airlines

After the Chicago conference in 1944 aviation was organised on a bilateral basis in which a route was typically served by only one airline per country. These airlines did not compete on price, agreed capacity on routes in advance and pooled revenues. Compared to a contestable system with freedom of entry and exit the European aviation system after Chicago was criticised for high fares, high costs, low productivity, and rent seeking by airline staff and management as well as by suppliers of services to airlines such as booking systems and services at airports. By contrast in Europe's most successful airline market deregulation, on routes between Ireland and the UK, fares have fallen by as much as 70 per cent. Airline staff productivity in terms of passenger numbers per staff member in the Ryanair case in 1998 was 4,800 compared with an average of 752 for 14 member airlines in the Association of European Airlines (Barrett, 1999). Deregulation has also put pressure on external airline costs such as reservation systems, ground handling and airport charges. Ryanair reduced travel agent commission from 9 to 7.5 per cent and sells over one-third of its tickets through its telemarketing service, Ryanair Direct. It does not operate its own downtown ticket sales offices. The deregulated market for airport handling in Europe allows new airlines the option of either itself engaging in handling or using specialist handling companies, a choice not available to earlier new entrants such as British Midland at London Heathrow. The elimination of in-flight catering removed another airline service supplier with returns on capital in excess of the return on capital in the airline sector (Borgo and Bull Larsen, 1998).

New entrant airlines engaging in the promotion of competition between airports has also been a recent feature of airline deregulation in Europe. This did not happen before deregulation of airlines. Airlines then colluded to increase fares in line with costs. There was little competitive pressure on the cost base. The world of non-competing airlines was mirrored in non-competing airports. Collusion between airlines restricted innovation such as the development of new airports and routes. Any new development required the agreement of two colluding national airlines and governments, and the sharing of revenues and capacity. The more conservative or high-cost airline in a bilateral agreement was thus able to veto innovation by the more dynamic airline. An airline seeking to develop new routes might face a reduction in its share on busy established routes in order to restore balance between countries in a bilateral agreement. Europe's national airlines achieved control over hub airports through the grandfather rights system of slot allocation. The earning of supernormal revenues at slot-constrained hub airports became a feature of European aviation. The high cost base of European aviation prevented the low fares, which might have promoted the development of low-cost airports. The requirement to engage in price collusion prevented any passing on to the passenger of the savings from developing low-cost services at low-cost airports.

Airport management at hub airports in a system of non-competing airlines was able to pass on costs without incurring the resistance from airlines that price competition between airlines would have generated. The ease with which cost increases could be passed on to non-competing airlines made life easier for airport managers. The ease with which the established airlines gained control of hub airports through the slot system reflects a lethargy in airport management combined with a view that high-cost airlines were a more secure source of airport revenues than a world of competing airlines and airports. In the world of non-competing airlines airports were also seen by their managers as a minor branch of the public service rather than as a major business which the sector was to become.

In 1976 the UK Department of Trade described the closed world of non-competing airports and airlines and proposed a monopoly. While 'there is no doubt, and understandably in some cases, a degree of local pride in the ownership and operation of regional airports', common ownership would have the advantages outlined in Table 8.1.

In the context of a deregulated aviation market in Europe since 1 April 1997 and the steady liberalisation of the market in earlier years the perspective of the Department of Trade is dated. It fails to recognise the rents earned in non-contested markets and the gains from competition. The Airport Strategy for Great Britain document did not secure ownership of the British airports system for the British Airports Authority (BAA). Local authority airports continued to

Table 8.1 Obstacles to European airport competition post the Chicago convention

Obstacles	Consequences
Pertaining to airline collusion	
Ban on new airlines	Lack of innovation in route development; lack of low-cost non-colluding airlines.
Ban on price competition	Low-cost airports unable to offer lower fares.
Market sharing	Interchangeable tickets led to concentration of airlines at hub airports; airlines at new airports were required to reduce capacity at hubs.
Airline control of hub airports	
Grandfather rights to slots	Airlines with slots at hub airports concentrated on hubs thus raising the asset value of slots; airport management was weakened by ceding property rights to airlines.
Airport structure and management	
Lack of independent corporate structure	Weak airport management structure; lack of interest in efficiency and competition.

operate independently. The document is, however, a useful summary of airport policy in the era before competition in European aviation.

The argument against independent airports was made again in the preparation for the privatisation of the BAA in 1986. The BAA management did not want a competitive airport sector after privatisation and successfully persuaded the government to privatise the BAA as a single entity rather than as competing airports.

Successful opposition to competitive airport privatisation in Britain in the 1980s

Several of the obstacles to airport competition shown in Table 8.1 might have been tackled by the competitive privatisation of the BAA in 1987. However, the BAA argued successfully against competitive privatisation. The UK Department of Transport (1985) decided to privatise the BAA as a single entity. Each BAA airport was formed as a separate company under a single holding company. The reasons advanced for single entity privatisation were that 'the volume of business switching from one airport to another within a group to enjoy lower landing charges or better service standards is, on past experience, very small; the effect of airport charges on airline costs is relatively unimportant; and separate ownership would introduce undesirable rigidity into the administration of Government policy for route licensing'. As a substitute for a more competitive privatisation the Monopolies and Mergers Commission was required to monitor the BAA's affairs in order to prevent abuse of its dominant market position under single entity privatisation.

Each of the points made in the White Paper was debatable at the time and can be questioned in the light of subsequent developments in aviation. The opening of a second airport in Belfast in 1983 had already provided a case study of airlines moving from Belfast International to Belfast City. Citing 'past experience' as the basis for the statements that airlines would not change airports in order to save costs or improve service missed the point that pressure for regulatory change was already undermining the Chicago system. The Anglo–Dutch liberalisation took effect in 1984 and the more dramatic Anglo–Irish liberalisation of 1986 was imminent. The share of airport charges in airline costs was dismissed as 'relatively unimportant' by the White Paper. The point was contentious in 1985. When air fares fell by as much as 70 per cent following the Anglo–Irish liberalisation of 1986 airport charges rose proportionately in their share of the ticket price.

The claim that separate ownership of airports 'would introduce undesirable rigidity into the administration of Government policy for route licensing' was unproven then. The subsequent liberalisation in Europe abolished Government controls over route licensing.

The successful arguments in opposing competitive airport privatisation in Britain were made by Boyfield (1984) and Foster (1984). Boyfield stated that 'Government planning restrictions affecting capacity and the number of air transport movements preclude the establishment of a totally free market. ... The practical difficulties of gaining official approval to build a new airport, and the long lead time before the substantial capital required begins to show returns, virtually rule out the competitive threat which would be posed by new entrants.'

Foster argued against the competitive privatisation of the BAA on the grounds of product diversity, the minuscule share of airport charges in airline costs, economies of scale in airport operation and the risk of underinvestment in airports. He wrote that 'the product is diverse, varying by time as well as place. Different consumers want different attributes not readily provided at each of these airports.' He also claimed that 'it is difficult for airports to compete on price since airport charges are only a small proportion of airline costs – rarely more than 5 per cent.' On economies of scale he claimed that 'only a small number of airports can be viable, given economies of scale in operation.' He also argued that 'the long-run planning of an airport system almost inherently requires agreement on an overall strategy for investment or entails the risk of underinvestment.'

The Boyfield argument presents planning restrictions as obstacles to a 'totally free market'. Quality controls on social costs such as noise, pollution, congestion, and environmental spillovers are implemented with the target of improving the overall welfare of society. They are thus quite different from quantity controls which are welfare reducing by creating rents for incumbents.

Contestability theory emphasises that the efficiency of incumbents can be achieved by competition among a small number of firms combined with the possibility of potential new entrants (Baumol, 1982). The unitary privatisation of the BAA reduced the potential gain from competitive privatisation. In the London area, for example, only Luton and London City are outside the now privatised BAA system and have only 5 per cent of passenger numbers at airports in the area. In central Scotland the unitary privatisation of Glasgow, Edinburgh and Prestwick gave one company some 95 per cent of passengers in the area. Competitive options were available in privatising the BAA group of seven airports.

The traditional view that airport investment is inevitably large, requires long-run planning and must be part of an overall strategy contrasts with the experience of London City airport in the 1980s. The cost of the project was £7 million and the construction time was forty weeks.

The Foster arguments in relation to product diversity, airport price competition, economies of scale and the risk of underinvestment without an overall investment strategy are each contestable. While it would be difficult to replicate Heathrow at a new airport because of its large network of services worldwide there may be categories of passengers for whom the agglomeration of services at Heathrow is of little importance or even a negative factor. Other airports in the London area are unlikely to be substitutes for Heathrow in the case of intercontinental passengers changing from feeder services at Heathrow. For passengers interested in cheap point-to-point travel to London, the prospect of a range of airports with lower fares may be attractive and avoiding Heathrow seen as a benefit.

The argument that it is difficult for airports to compete on price because airport charges are rarely more than 5 per cent can be assessed in the light of the circumstances of European aviation in the mid-1980s and subsequent developments. Airport charges are a higher proportion of airline costs on shorter routes. As Table 8.2 shows, their proportion in Europe in 1984 was significantly above 5 per cent. In addition to airport charges proper, airports are a major cost centre for airlines as shown in Table 8.2. The non-competing airlines used non-competing airports, which in turn did not ensure competition for the services provided at airports such as handling and navigation charges. The scope for competition between providers of services at airports is examined later as this section deals with competition between rather than within airports.

Foster's third point against competitive privatisation of airports is economies of scale. He maintains that because of economies of scale only a few airports can be viable. The evidence for this assertion was not convincing at the time it was made. In 1982/3, for example, in the larger airport category, Manchester with 5 million passengers made a profit of £7.3 million while Gatwick with 11 million passengers made a profit of only £775,000. In the medium airport category, Edinburgh lost

Table 8.2 Airport and related charges as a proportion of airline costs in Europe

Aircraft and passenger handling	12.22
Aircraft passenger charges	5.15
Landing charges	4.07
En-route navigation	3.61
Airport navigation	0.85
Total	25.90

Source: Commission of the European Communities (1984).

£1.3 million on 1.2 million passengers while East Midlands made a profit of £1.1 million on 900,000 passengers. The largest loss-making airport, Stansted, had an income 14 times greater than Gloucester-Cheltenham, which made a profit of £50,000 on an income of £166,000 compared with Stansted's loss of £4.55 million.

Foster's final point is that without an overall strategy for airport development there is a risk of substantial underinvestment. Economics provides no reasons why the market would under-invest in airports. On the contrary, the evidence is that monopoly restricts output below the competitive level. This causes price to rise and monopolistic rents to be generated. The congestion at many of Europe's hub airports indicates that the traditional non-competitive organisation of the airport industry has led to under-investment, notwithstanding Foster's claim that competitive privatisation would lead to under-investment. The Boyfield/Foster arguments against competitive airport privatisation are summarised in Table 8.3.

While the Boyfield/Foster arguments were reflected in the government choice of single entity privatisation of the BAA there were opposing views. Starkie and Thomson (1985) stated that it was 'doubtful that there are economies of scale to be realised by multi-airport ownership'. Starkie and Thomson state that 'overall, we do not find BAA's case in favour of maintaining the unity of the present organisation very convincing'. They saw benefits from a competitive airport system. 'If BAA was to act as a profit maximiser, divided ownership by introducing more competition into the system, would have the effect of tempering the power that BAA would otherwise have to push up prices and restrict output.' Barrett asserted that 'the obstacle to applying contestable markets to airports is administrative rather than economic. There should be full competition between separate independently managed airports'.

The impact of airline deregulation on airport competition in the 1990s

In the world of non-competing airlines prices increased compared with the competitive model. Costs also increased so that supernormal profits did not result from the high fares charged. The economic rents earned are shown in high wage costs and low productivity in European aviation. In the model of non-competing airlines airports did not compete either and there was no competition among service providers at airports.

Table 8.3 The Foster/Boyfield case against competitive airport privatisation, 1984

---

1. Planning controls and long lead times preclude new entrants.
2. Product diversity.
3. Small share of airport charges in airline costs makes airport competition difficult.
4. Only a small number of airports can be viable given economies of scale in airport operation.
5. Market provision of airports risk under-investment.

Source: Public Money (1984), General Series 4.

In the model of competing airlines price competition leads to concern over costs both within airlines and service providers to airlines, including airports and services at airports. Competition between airlines also covers service competition. Airlines choosing to compete on price seek to achieve cost reductions through the elimination of in-flight catering, seat reservations, newspapers on board, expensive downtown sales offices, airport lounges, frequent-flyer clubs and airport costs. The latter costs may be tackled within airports by seeking discount schemes for new traffic and declining the use of facilities such as airbridges. Low-cost airlines may also seek to transfer services to low-cost airports.

Airline deregulation progressed slowly in Europe but was a major factor in stimulating airport competition. Falling fares in deregulated markets raised the pre-deregulation airport charge automatically as a proportion of ticket prices. The stimulatory impact of low fares increased demand hugely. Airport managers with excess capacity began to see low-cost airlines as a means of filling that spare capacity.

In the world of non-competing airlines fares were agreed by national airlines and typically rubber-stamped by government departments. The new entrant competing airlines did not have the economic rents to share with either their own staff in the form of high wage costs and low productivity, or with suppliers of services such as airports, handlers, CRS suppliers or travel agents. It was inevitable that airline competition would lead to airport competition. For airport managers the new competitive airline market meant that pricing policy for their airline customers could no longer be based on a set of prescribed prices presented on a 'take it or leave it' approach. For new entrant airlines the opening bid was frequently to seek zero airport charges or discounts as high as 90 per cent.

Previously, the incumbent airlines tended to serve the same airports thereby facilitating interlining and other forms of collusion. Through the grandfather rights system they acquired control over the allocation of capacity at hub airports. Scarce slots at hub airports became a major asset for the incumbent airlines at Europe's major airports.

The new entrant airlines did not typically issue interlined tickets but specialised in cheap point-to-point travel. Their preference for different airports was a function of reducing airport costs, establishing a separate identity in the marketplace, and serving markets and catchment areas inadequately served by existing airports. The search for new airports led the new airlines to examine alternatives such as airports no longer required for military use; airports with reduced passenger numbers due to market changes and airports established with goals such as the promotion of regional or local development.

The existence of significantly underused airports close to the catchment areas of slot-constrained airports may be attributed to a lack of competition in both the airline and airport sectors, lack of new entrant airlines and a lack of commercial focus at the airports. The Association of European Airlines (AEA) which represents national airlines serving the traditional airports points out that many of the low-cost airlines have based their operations at low-cost airports. 'About 45 per cent of their operations are at airports with no or little service by the mainline carriers' (Association of European Airlines, 1999).

The corporatisation and privatisation of airports has increased rapidly since the privatisation of the BAA in 1986. Nichols *et al.* (1999) report that there were 60 privatised airports in 1999 and expect 120 more in the following five years. They found the process most advanced in Europe and Latin America, virtually complete in the UK, in full swing in Germany and Italy, and underway in Spain, Portugal, India, Thailand, Australia, the Caribbean and South Africa. Clinch (1999) notes the commercialisation of four local authority airports in England when the government freed Manchester, Newcastle, Leeds/Bradford and Newcastle airport from local authority borrowing controls thus allowing them to raise private finance. In 1998, Luton signed a 30-year agreement with a consortium of Barclays Bank, Airport Group International and Bechtel Enterprises to invest £100 million in the airport.

The commercialisation and privatisation of airports together with the deregulation of aviation open up the possibilities for competition between airports seeking to attract airlines. Privatisation makes explicit the profitability of airports. Borgo and Bull Larsen (1998) note that the profitability of privatised airports such as BAA, at 17 per cent, is almost three times the return on investment in airlines. Privatisation and competition among both airports and airlines is likely to erode the traditional rents earned both by airline staff and the suppliers of services to airlines, including airports.

In 1993 Aer Rianta, the Irish Airports Authority, formalised its earlier rebates and marketing supports into a discount scheme. The object was to promote volume growth at its airports at Dublin, Cork and Shannon. The results of airline deregulation between Dublin and London had been so spectacular that the government of Ireland sought to use the combination of both airline competition and reduced airport charges in order to promote greater overall national competitiveness.

The elements in the 1993 Irish airports discount scheme were

1   a discount for new routes and traffic growth of up to 90 per cent;
2   a 25 per cent discount on low-fare routes to Britain;
3   a 50 per cent winter landing charge discount; and
4   a £1.50 discount for use of a low-cost pier.

The schemes were worth £9 million to Ryanair in 1998. This was almost a quarter of its profits of £37 million in the year ended 31 March 1998 (DKM, 1999). The major beneficiaries of the discounts in the four years to 1997 were Ryanair who received £23 million and Aer Lingus who received £21 million. Dublin Airport doubled its passenger numbers between 1993 and 1998. Table 8.4 illustrates the discount schemes for new routes and traffic growth from 1993. In a world of non-competing airlines the above airport savings would not have been passed on to passengers in lower fares. Competition has ensured that the savings have been significant. The future of the scheme depends on the appointment of an independent airport regulator in 2000.

Table 8.4 Dublin airport discount schemes for new routes and traffic growth (% discount)

	1994/3	1995/4	1996/5	1997/6
1	70	80	–	90
2	70	80	–	90
3	50	60	–	90
4	40	50	–	70
5	30	40	–	50
6				50
7				50

Source: DKM (1999).

The impact of airport competition on ticket prices

Research by the Institute du Transport Aerien (ITA) examined airport charges at 37 European airports and compared these with ticket prices in May 1996 in order to estimate the share of airport charges in the price of an airline ticket (Wrobel, 1997). The average turnaround for a B737-500 was 1,488 ECU (£1,211). The most expensive airport was Vienna at 2,026 ECU in terms of charges and charge-like taxes. In terms of total taxes the most expensive was Glasgow at 2,981 ECU. The highest share of airport charges in a return airline ticket was found by Wrobel to be 16.7 per cent in the case of a Frankfurt–Munich ticket. In the intra-EU category the highest airport shares in the ticket price is 9.3 per cent for both Paris–Heathrow and Dublin–Heathrow. The ticket prices cited by Wrobel are the highest paid in economy class. He acknowledges that the choice of this fare has the effect of reducing the share of airport costs in the ticket price. 'A more precise approach would have involved the calculation on the yield for each of the routes instead of on the price on an economy class airline ticket. If this were done the percentages would probably be double those indicated above, considering that the fares actually charged are often lower' (Wrobel, 1997).

The understatement of airport charges as a proportion of airline ticket price by Wrobel by as much as 100 per cent as in his statement cited above may be even greater. This can be seen by reference to routes from Glasgow and Dublin to London, which we examine later. The fares used by Wrobel are the equivalent of £241 return on Glasgow–London and IR£345 on Dublin–London. Wrobel estimates that 11.4 and 9.3 per cent, respectively, of these fares are incurred on airport charges; that is, £27.47 on Glasgow–London and £32.09 on Dublin–London. Both these routes are served by Ryanair with a yield of £70 return. The Glasgow–London airport charge used by Wrobel is therefore 39 per cent of the Ryanair yield on Glasgow–London and 46 per cent of the yield on Dublin–London. These costs are 3.4 times the share found by Wrobel on Glasgow–London and 4.9 times the share found by him on Dublin–London.

The Italy–UK service cited by Wrobel is Rome–London with a fare of £662 and airport charges of 2.8 per cent estimated as a proportion of this fare. On the six

Ryanair routes to Italy the average fare is £80. The airport charges cited by Wrobel would amount to 23 per cent of the £80 fares. That is 8.28 times the Wrobel figure.

The key to the impact of competition on the Italian, Glasgow and Dublin routes to London in reducing costs and fares to much below the levels cited by Wrobel is both the entry of new airlines such as Ryanair, and new and discounting airports such as Prestwick, Stansted, Luton, Dublin, Rimini, Treviso, Genoa, Ancona, Turin and Pisa. Airlines seeking to compete in the deregulated market will seek to reduce airport charges. The cost of airport charges to Ryanair in 1997/8 was 12.6 per cent of total operating costs, significantly lower than the Wrobel airport data would lead one to expect when applied to the airline's low fares. This indicates that the airline had pushed down airport costs as part of its general cost and fare reduction policies.

Passenger and airline non-price advantages of low-cost airports

In addition to the lower fares available from low-cost airlines and airports other advantages for passengers may result from airport competition. Passengers may experience less congestion at airport terminals, car parks and access transport. There is likely to be less walking time within the airport. The market entry of new airports also increases the number of people within the catchment areas of airports. New airports have also sought to attract passengers by low-cost bus and train fares and cheap car parking.

The airline advantages of low-cost airports include easy availability of slots and quick turnaround times. Since capacity is limited at Europe's hub airports and controlled by the incumbent airlines the scale of entry required by a new entrant low-cost airline may only be possible at a new airport.

Passenger choice of airport

The UK Civil Aviation Authority (1997a, b) surveyed passengers at the five London airports, Manchester and Birmingham in 1996. While the CAA did not ask a direct question about the role of low-cost airlines in influencing airport choice the exercise is nonetheless a useful examination of airport choice in England.

Heathrow was chosen by 57.8 per cent of total passengers at the seven airports. It was chosen by 29.4 per cent of its passengers because of the flights and packages available, by 23.4 per cent because of its connecting flights and by 15.8 per cent because it was the airport closest to home. Gatwick was chosen by 22 per cent of passengers at the seven airports: 38.9 per cent chose it because of the flights and packages available. 24.1 per cent chose it because it was close to home and 10.15 per cent because it was cheaper. London City had a market share of under 1 per cent in the sample of airports and 35.1 per cent chose it because it was near their place of business.

The airports in the sample that have taken the greatest interest in low-cost airlines are Luton and Stansted. They cater for strong local markets with 43.4 and

35.9 per cent, respectively, citing 'near home' as their reason for choice of the airport. Both attracted passengers because of their low cost, at 26.7 per cent for Luton and 18.5 per cent for Stansted. London City and Stansted were the leading examples of airport choice because passengers preferred the airport in the case of 9.6 and 9.0 per cent of passengers, respectively. By contrast Birmingham, Manchester and Heathrow were the preferred airport choices of 2.4, 3.2 and 3.2 per cent of their respective passenger numbers. Surface access was cited by a maximum of only 0.5 per cent as a reason for choosing an airport. This was the case at Stansted and Birmingham. Airline choice influenced 0.7 per cent of passengers at Gatwick, 0.6 per cent at Heathrow, 0.3 per cent at Luton and zero at Stansted, Birmingham and Manchester. The latter two are shown as strong regional airports with over half their passengers living nearby.

The CAA studies of airport use in Scotland (1997a) found that about 45 per cent of passengers at Edinburgh, Aberdeen and Glasgow chose airports because they were closest to home. In the case of Glasgow, which is examined further in the case studies of airport competition, 1.8 per cent of passengers chose it because they preferred the airport and 1.8 per cent because they found it cheaper. The CAA study of airport use in the east of England in 1994/5 found that up to 74 per cent of leisure passengers chose their local airport with Newcastle chosen most for that reason (UK Civil Aviation Authority, 1995a). However, Teesside attracted 8 per cent of its leisure passengers because they preferred the airport, compared to 2 per cent at Humberside and Norwich, and 1 per cent at Newcastle. This choice is examined further in the case studies of airport competition.

The CAA 1994/5 study of airport use in Wales and the south and southwest of England found that the proportion of passengers indicating airport preference in their choice between Bristol, Cardiff and Exeter never exceeded 2 per cent (UK Civil Aviation Authority, 1995b).

The potential for airport competition in Europe

Studies by Cranfield University Air Transport Group indicate that there is considerable scope for airport competition in Europe (Fewings, 1999). For example the Cranfield studies found that in France, the UK and Germany, there were, respectively, 32, 34 and 28 airports within one hour's surface access of another airport. In the ten countries studied there are 131 airports within one hour's surface travel and 369 within one to two hours' surface travel journey time. A wider Cranfield study of airports covered 13 countries and 431 airports. Table 8.5 shows the division of airports into runway lengths of 1,600 m or more. For example, in Norway there are 23 airports of 1,600 m runway length or more, 5.3 per million population. There are 28 airports with runways under 1,600 m, 6.5 per million population. All the airports studied in Austria and Finland have runways in excess of 1,600 m. In France, airports with runways in excess of 1,600 m outnumber the shorter runway airports by ten to one, in Germany by three to one and in the UK by over two to one. In Spain the ratio of runways over 1,600 m to shorter runways is nine to one and in Sweden over six to one.

Table 8.5 Level of airport and runway provision in Europe (1998)

| | Number of airports per million inhabitants | |
| | Runway length | |
	Over 1,600 m	Under 1,600 m
Austria	0.8	0.0
Denmark	1.9	0.4
Finland	4.1	0.0
France	1.0	0.1
Germany	0.3	0.1
Greece	2.5	1.2
Iceland	22.5	26.2
Ireland	1.1	2.5
Italy	0.6	0.1
Norway	5.3	6.5
Scotland	1.6	2.1
Sweden	4.3	0.7
UK[a]	0.7	0.3

Source: Fewings (1998).

Note
[a] Includes Scotland.

The large number of relatively little-used airports in Europe illustrates the concentration of the established high-cost airlines at hub airports which the incumbent airlines controlled through the slot allocation system. The high fares charged restrained the development of non-hub airports. The large supply of airport capacity now available in new locations reflects the civilianisation of military airports and the construction of airports by both local and national governments as a means to promote local and regional development.

The Cranfield research shows the availability of significant airport numbers in Europe. The CAA passenger surveys indicate a significant preference for local airports. The combination of these factors with the availability of service by new low-cost airlines, more commercial operation of airports and downward pressure on fares and costs set the economic background to the case studies examined in the next section.

The potential gains from the more competitive environment at airports are as high as 90 per cent of airport charges, based on the discounts in the Dublin example, and 50 per cent in the case of handling charges, based on the British Midland case for competitive handling at Heathrow (UK Monopolies and Mergers Commission, 1985). The savings are significant in the context of the earlier Cascade studies. These showed that by producing a charter-type product, Europe's scheduled airlines could price air travel at between 32 and 37 per cent of the scheduled airline fare (Commission of the European Communities, 1981). We next examine 17 case studies of airport competition in Europe in 1999.

Case studies in European airport competition

The Dublin–London deregulation of 1986 – Luton in competition with Heathrow

This case study covers airport competition on what became the busiest international scheduled air service route in the world with over 4 million passengers in 1998 with service to five London airports. Prior to deregulation the route had experienced little growth in the previous ten years and was concentrated at London Heathrow with a minimal service to Gatwick. Table 8.6 shows growth on the route from 1985, the last full year of pre-deregulation policies, to 1998 and the market share of each of the London airports on the Dublin route.

The initial airport competition with Heathrow came from Luton. In 1987, the first full year of deregulation, Luton took 20 per cent of the market which had expanded by 65 per cent on the pre-deregulation passenger numbers. The Luton share was therefore 33 per cent of the pre-deregulation market in 1985.

The main asset of Luton in reducing Heathrow's market share was a Ryanair fare of IR£95 compared with the incumbent airlines' fare of IR£208. There was also in the catchment area of North London a sizeable Irish ethnic population, which had objected strongly to the pre-deregulation fares. The disadvantage of Luton was slow surface access to central London. The airport was negatively portrayed in an advertising campaign in Ireland between Air Lingus and Ryanair. Luton also lost market share due to below-cost selling by Air Lingus on the Heathrow route. A combination of increased capacity and reduced fares on Dublin–Heathrow undermined Luton's ability to compete. By 1993 Aer Lingus was insolvent and EU approval for a IR£175 million rescue was required. The airline admitted to losing IR£20 million on its London services. It reduced its frequency on Dublin–Heathrow and withdrew from Gatwick.

Luton was vital to the success of the Dublin–London deregulation. Slot constraints at Heathrow and Gatwick prevented the size of the impact on the market, which Ryanair made by using Luton. The 20 per cent market share of

Table 8.6 Impact of airline and airport competition on the Dublin–London route (1985–98)

	Market (000s)	Index	Market shares (%)				
			LHR	LGW	LTN	STN	LCY
1985	994	100	100	–	–	–	–
1987	1,636	165	80	–	20	–	–
1990	2,383	240	76	10	12	2	–
1993	2,415	243	69	2	6	23	–
1996	3,343	336	51	13	6	26	4
1998	4,078	410	46	14	7	27	5

Source: UK Civil Aviation Authority.

Dublin–London traffic held by Luton in 1987 has never been exceeded by Gatwick which in terms of passenger numbers overall is the second airport in the London area. The transfer of most Ryanair services from Luton to Stansted in 1991 sharply reduced Luton's share of the growing Dublin–London market. There remained, however, a strong local market in the Luton area. Ryanair increased its capacity at Luton in 1998 and 1999 with the airport's 6 per cent market share rising to 8 per cent in 1999/2000. In 1998 Luton–Dublin traffic volumes were back to the 1990 levels. Luton has recently attracted low-cost airlines such as easyJet and Debonair. However, Bonnassies (1999) estimates that airport charges for a 737-300 are 52 per cent higher at Luton than at Stansted.

Stansted in competition with Heathrow

Stansted became the focus of Ryanair operations in 1991 when most of its Luton services were transferred. The initial impact was small with 0.2 million passengers in 1991 when Stansted had 1.7 million passengers. By 1999 Ryanair had 3.2 million passengers at Stansted, on 20 routes. Stansted had 27 per cent of the Dublin–London route of over 4 million passengers in 1998. Ryanair also has three Stansted services to Irish provincial airports at Cork, Kerry and Knock and two internal UK routes, to Prestwick and City of Derry in Northern Ireland. Ryanair also had six Stansted routes to Italy, four to France, two routes to Sweden and one each to Germany and Norway. These routes present interesting case studies of airport competition at both ends of the routes served. In addition to the low fares charged from Stansted by Ryanair the airport has the advantages of fast surface access to London and its own catchment area northeast of London.

Table 8.7 shows the growth of both Ryanair traffic and total traffic at Stansted during the 1990s. Table 8.8 shows the new services to mainland Europe started between 1997 and 1999. Table 8.9 compares the passenger numbers on eight of these routes in 1998 and the numbers on the established services from Heathrow

Table 8.7 Ryanair and total traffic at Stansted (1990/9)

	Total passengers (millions)	Ryanair (millions)	Ryanair share (%)
1990	1.2	–	–
1991	1.7	0.2	17
1992	2.3	0.6	26
1993	2.7	0.7	26
1994	3.3	0.8	24
1995	3.9	1.0	26
1996	4.5	1.3	29
1997	5.4	1.5	28
1998	6.8	2.1	31
1999	7.7	3.2	42

Table 8.8 Ryanair services Stansted to mainland Europe (1997/9)

Startup	Route
1997	Oslo (Torp), Stockholm (Skavsta)
1998	Kristianstad (Malmo), Treviso (Venice), Rimini, Pisa, St Etienne, Carcassonne
1999	Frankfurt (Hahn), Biarritz, Brittany (Dinard) Genoa, Turin, Ancona

Table 8.9 Passenger numbers on new Stansted routes compared with Heathrow alternative (1998)

Stansted route	Passengers	Share[c] (%)	1997 (%)
1 Carcassonne	38,481[a]	37	–
2 St Etienne	41,641[b]	14	–
3 Pisa	78,392[b]	28	–
4 Rimini	38,504[b]	29	–
5 Treviso	80,420[a]	36	2,876 (2)
6 Skavsta	189,691	23	89,776 (11)
7 Kristianstad	54,708[a]	20	–
8 Torp	109,489	17	16,494 (3)
Heathrow alternative routes			
1 Toulouse	103,456	98,226	
2 Lyons	288,472	245,806	
3 Pisa (LGW)	276,971	239,669	
4 Bologna	134,613	118,709	
5 Venice	225,578	151,594	
6 Stockholm	809,406	793,290	
7 Malmo	268,195	259,956	
8 Oslo	645,994	602,949	

Source: UK Civil Aviation Authority.

Note
[a] Commenced May 1998.
[b] Commenced June 1998.
[c] Share of Stansted to Heathrow traffic.

to the major mainland Europe airport in competition with the new airports served. Table 8.9 covers a full year's operation of two routes involving airport competition both in the London area and in mainland Europe. These are Stansted to Oslo with Torp competing with Oslo and Stansted with Heathrow and Stansted to Skavsta which competes with Heathrow–Stockholm.

The services started in May and June 1998 (to Carcassonne in competition with Toulouse, St Etienne in competition with Lyons, Pisa in competition with a Gatwick service, Rimini in competition with Bologna, Treviso in competition with Venice, and Kristianstad in competition with Malmo) are shown in Table 8.9

Table 8.10 Access and capacity of airports in competition in Europe, Summer 1999

Dominant airport			Competing airport		
	Accessibility (k)	*Gates*		*Accessibility (k)*	*Gates*
Bologna	6	n.s	Rimini	4	n.s.
Brussels	12	40	Charleroi	50	2
Florence	14	5	Pisa	2	8
Frankfurt	12	154	Hahn	95	20
Glasgow	14	33	Prestwick	48	8
London LHR	24	181	Gatwick	45	n.s.
			Stansted	51	59
			Luton	45	n.s.
			City	10	10
Lyons	25	53	St Etienne	56	n.s.
Malmo	30	16	Kristianstad	64	3
Manchester	14	59	Liverpool	10	1
			Leeds/Brad	13	n.a.
Oslo	50		Torp	103	5
Paris	23	169	Beauvais	75	4
Stockholm	40	50	Skavsta	87	10
Toulouse	8	14	Carcassonne	68	n.s.
Venice	13	20	Treviso	16	n.s.

Source: Janes airports and handling agents, World Airline ABC.

compared with a full year's operation of the competing Heathrow service. Table 8.10 shows the indicators of minor airport access and capacity compared with the major airports served from Heathrow. The data in Table 8.9 indicate that a service from Stansted to a minor airport on the European mainland is likely, even in its early days, to be seen as a good alternative by over a fifth and as much as a third of passengers using routes from major airports in mainland Europe to Heathrow.

Stansted–Torp/Heathrow–Oslo

The Stansted–Torp route was started in 1997. In 1998, the first full year of operation, the Stansted–Torp service has 109,000 passengers or 17 per cent of the Heathrow–Oslo route. This share has reportedly held in the first-half of 1999. Torp has a separate catchment area south of Oslo in addition to attracting budget-sensitive passengers not catered for by the tradition of high fares from Scandinavia to Britain.

Stansted–Skavsta/Heathrow–Stockholm

The Stansted–Skavsta service started in 1997. In its first full year of service, 1998, it carried 190,000 passengers or 23 per cent of the Heathrow–Stockholm service.

Nielsen (1999) states that 'half of the route's passengers are Stockholm citizens, proving the local catchment area's acceptance of this fledgling airport'.

Stansted–Kristianstad/Heathrow–Malmo

This service started in May 1998 and in its first 12 months of operation it carried 82,000 passengers compared with 268,000 on the Heathrow–Malmo service. Stansted–Kristianstad will also compete with Heathrow–Copenhagen from 2000 when surface connections will be improved by the road and rail bridge connecting Sweden and Denmark.

Stansted–St Etienne/Heathrow–Lyons

This service from Stansted commenced in May 1998. In its first 12 months it carried 57,000 passengers or 21 per cent of the Heathrow–Lyons traffic. Bonnassies (1998) estimated that in 2000, St Etienne will have 300,000 passengers compared with 100,000 in 1997.

Stansted–Carcassonne/Heathrow–Toulouse

The Stansted–Carcassonne service commenced in June 1998 and in its first 12 months carried 65,000 passengers, or 63 per cent of the passengers on the Heathrow–Toulouse route.

Stansted–Pisa/Gatwick–Pisa

The Stansted–Pisa service commenced in June 1998. In its first 12 months it carried 128,000 passengers or 46 per cent of the numbers on the Gatwick–Pisa service in the calendar year 1998.

Stansted–Treviso/Heathrow–Venice

The Stansted–Treviso service commenced in May 1998 in competition with the Heathrow–Venice service, which had 226,000 passengers in the calendar year 1998. In the first 12 months of the Stansted–Treviso service 117,000 passengers were carried. This is 52 per cent of the Heathrow–Venice traffic. The combination of a new low-fare airline and new airports at both ends of the journey has proved attractive. Venice and Treviso airports are almost the same distance from Venice city centre.

Stansted–Rimini/Heathrow–Bologna

The Stansted–Rimini service commenced in June 1998 in competition with Heathrow–Bologna, which had 135,000 passengers in the calendar year 1998.

The Stansted–Rimini route had 63,000 passengers in its first 12 months, or 47 per cent of the Heathrow–Bologna passenger numbers.

The Stansted startup services in 1999

The 1999 startup services to mainland Europe comprised the first German route to Frankfurt (Hahn), three further Italian routes to Genoa, Turin and Ancona, and two further French routes to Biarritz and Dinard. Rowe (1995) stated that Genoa then had 850,000 passengers at an airport with a capacity of two million and that better surface access would make Genoa a competitor with Milan and Nice. The services started in the summer of 1999 and data are not sufficiently available to estimate market shares at the time of writing. However, load factors of over 75 per cent in the early months indicate that these markets also welcome airport and airline competition.

Prestwick

In terms of the growth of passenger numbers at an almost empty airport the Prestwick case study is dramatic. Prestwick was the designated airport for transatlantic services from Scotland. There were 650,000 passengers at the airport in 1976/7. There was a decline to 255,000 in 1982 and a partial recovery to 317,000 in 1989, the last full year of Prestwick's transatlantic gateway status. The end of that status was announced on March 6, 1990. Northwest and Air Canada transferred to Glasgow in May 1990 and British Airways in August. Traffic fell from 93,000 in 1990 to a low of 10,000 in 1993. Ryanair started a Prestwick–Dublin service in 1994 and in 1995 the route was the market leader over the long-established Glasgow–Dublin service as shown in Table 8.11. The total market in 1998 was four times the market in 1993 when Glasgow–Dublin was both a monopoly airline and airport route. As a monopoly the route contracted by 17 per cent between 1990 and 1993.

Table 8.11 Impact of airline and airport competition on Dublin–Glasgow route, 1990–8

	Market (000s)	Index	Market shares (%)	
			Glasgow	Prestwick
1990	120	100	100	–
1993	99	83	100	–
1994	197	164	59	41
1995	274	228	44	56
1996	320	267	44	56
1997	365	304	44	56
1998	395	329	47	53

The second route established at Prestwick by Ryanair was the Prestwick–Stansted service, which commenced in late 1995 almost a year and a half before the EU deregulation of cabotage services in April 1997. In 1998 there were 233,000 passengers on Prestwick–Stansted in a total market of 2.4 million passengers between Glasgow and Prestwick and Heathrow, Gatwick, Luton and Stansted. Glasgow–Heathrow is the dominant route with 73 per cent of passengers. However, some 650,000 passengers use the other airports at the London end of the journey and 233,000 use Prestwick rather than Glasgow.

The third route established at Prestwick by Ryanair is the Prestwick–Beauvais service started in 1998 and serving a new airport at each end of the journey. The 1999 projection is that the total Glasgow–Paris market will be 150,000 and that 90,000 will use the Paris–Beauvais route. The balance will use indirect routes, changing planes en route, mostly at Heathrow and Birmingham.

Prestwick is 38 miles from Glasgow compared with 8 miles for the city airport. Prestwick does not have a significant catchment area and is required to attract passengers from other parts of Scotland. It is owned by the Stagecoach Bus Company and offers low-cost access by road and rail. The 1999 projection is for 700,000 passengers, about 85 per cent of them on Ryanair flights. This is a remarkable transformation from the low of 10,000 passengers in 1993 and far more passengers than in the airport's former heyday as a compulsory airport for transatlantic services. It is an interesting result of airport competition in this case that the result is the opposite of the previous administrative distribution of traffic. In a market system of airport competition transatlantic traffic has chosen Glasgow but Prestwick has attracted a larger number of passengers to low-cost short-haul services.

Paris CDG/Beauvais

Beauvais is served by Ryanair from Prestwick and from Dublin. The projected traffic of 90,000 on the Prestwick–Beauvais service is greater than the total traffic on all routes at both these airports in 1993. In 1996 Beauvais had only 60,000 passengers and the 1999 projection is for 360,000. The Dublin–Beauvais service will carry 230,000 and the total Ryanair traffic of 320,000 will account for 89 per cent of traffic at Beauvais.

In 1996 there were 307,000 passengers on the Dublin–CDG route. The 1998 market was 348,000 on Dublin–CDG and 190,000 on Dublin–Beauvais. The total market grew by 75 per cent and the Beauvais share from zero to 35 per cent. The airport attractions of Beauvais are its small size and less crowding and confusion than at CDG. Access time to Paris city is 1 hour compared with 45 minutes from CDG. Beauvais also offers a large reduction in fares from the pre-deregulation level of over IR£600 in the early 1990s and £425 when Cityjet, an Irish independent airline serving the business passenger, entered the route in 1995. The Ryanair average fare is £80. Cityjet and Air France have sought to promote CDG as a hub for traffic from Ireland to the Air France worldwide network and that will limit the market share of Beauvais in competition with CDG.

Brussels South (Charleroi)/ Brussels Zavantem

In 1998 traffic at Charleroi was 210,000 passengers with the Ryanair Dublin service accounting for 155,000 or 74 per cent. The Charleroi share of traffic to Dublin was zero before the Ryanair service commenced in May 1997 and exceeded 50 per cent for the first time in November 1997. The average market share for 1997 was 38 per cent and for 1998 it was 48 per cent.

Charleroi's success as an airport may be attributed to its own catchment area south of Brussels and ease of access in 40 minutes to the city centre. It is also a far less crowded airport than Zavantem. On the airline side the low Ryanair fares contrast with the high traditional fares from Ireland to mainland Europe, a factor noted in the Beauvais case study also. On the Brussels–Dublin route there was considerable irritation at the high fares previously charged among both the Irish employees of the European institutions and Irish visitors to Brussels. Sabena is a relatively passive partner of Aer Lingus on the Dublin–Zaventem route and has not sought to develop hubbing traffic from Ireland. For point-to-point traffic from Dublin, Charleroi has been a very successful competitor with Zaventem.

Airport competition in Northern England

The competing airports in this case study are Manchester, Liverpool and Leeds/Bradford. Liverpool and Leeds/Bradford are, respectively, 18 and 38 miles from Manchester, which is the market leader in the area. The case study of competition between these three airports has a longer time span than most of the case studies examined above. This case study includes periods of relative fast growth by each of the competing airports, changes in market share and changes in airport attitudes to low-cost airlines. Table 8.12 shows the development of the total market from Dublin to the three northern English airports from 1990 to 1999.

Table 8.12 Impact of airline and airport competition on Dublin routes to the north of England (1990–9)

	Market (000s)	*Index*	*Market shares (%)*		
			Leeds/Bradford	*Liverpool*	*Manchester*
1990	428	100	17	26	57
1993	500	117	9	41	50
1994	611	143	9	31	59
1995	737	172	10	23	67
1996	860	201	15	18	67
1997	950	222	19	18	63
1998	990	231	19	17	64
1999[a]	950	222	23	23	54

Note
[a] Estimate.

In the initial phase Liverpool dominated the low-fare market in the region with fares which were significantly lower than those to Dublin from Manchester and Leeds/Bradford. In 1993 it had a market share of 41 per cent of traffic between Dublin and northern England.

The second stage of this case study brought the entry of Ryanair to Manchester in 1994. The Dublin–Manchester route had stagnated for 15 years and contrasted with the large growth on Dublin–London after deregulation in 1986. Traffic on Dublin–Manchester in 1995, the first full year of deregulation on the route, was double that in 1993, the last full year of pre-deregulation policies. The availability of low fares to Dublin both at Manchester and Liverpool saw Liverpool's share of Manchester passenger numbers to Dublin fall from 82 per cent in 1993 to 27 per cent in 1996. Liverpool–Dublin, in competition with a high-fare high-cost policy at Manchester in 1993, had 205,000 passengers. This declined to 154,000 in 1996 in competition with a low-fare low-cost policy at Manchester.

The third stage of the case study of airport competition in northern England for Dublin traffic was the entry of Leeds/Bradford to low-fare low-cost service to Dublin in 1997. Traffic between Leeds/Bradford and Dublin increased four-fold after the market entry of Ryanair and its market share doubled in 1997 compared with 1993.

The fourth stage in this case study occurred in the summer of 1999 when Manchester lost interest in discounting airport charges to low-cost airlines. Ryanair reduced its frequency on Dublin–Manchester from five to two per day and added an extra rotation to both Liverpool and Leeds–Bradford. Since full fare airlines have not replaced the Ryanair seats preliminary estimates are that Manchester–Dublin passenger numbers will fall by perhaps 120,000 in 1999 and that two-thirds of this will transfer to Liverpool and Leeds/Bradford with slightly more growth at Liverpool because of its greater proximity to Manchester. The Manchester change of policy in 1999 towards low-cost airlines has interesting implications for the sustainability of low-cost airport policies. In 1994 extra low-yield traffic on the important and long stagnant Dublin route was a priority and the success of the change of policy was rapid and dramatic. By 1999, however, the airport had a different assessment of its development with less spare capacity and a target of developing long-haul services. It will be interesting to see if Manchester changes policy again, perhaps on completion of investment programmes to further increase capacity. Other possibilities are that Liverpool and Leeds/Bradford might seek extra growth or other airports might seek to enter the market. It is ironic that due to Manchester's change of policy in the summer of 1999 the Ryanair yield on Dublin–Manchester increased. The airline therefore had greater resources at its disposal in seeking out further new airports for its network.

Teesside/Newcastle

This market to Dublin was dominated by Newcastle. The new entrant, Teesside, is 28 miles from Newcastle. It entered the Dublin route in 1997, took almost half the market in 1998, and became market leader in the first quarter of 1999.

Table 8.13 Impact of airline and airport competition on Dublin routes to northeastern England (1990–9)

| | Market (000s) | Index | Market share (%) | |
			Newcastle	Teesside
1990	30	100	100	–
1997	79	263	88	12
1998	129	431	51	49
1999 (Q1)			46	54

Table 8.13 shows the data for these routes from 1990 to 1999. Unlike other UK provincial routes to Dublin, Newcastle airport traffic did not stagnate in the years before competition. Nonetheless traffic growth in 1998 was greater than in the total period 1990–7. All of the 1998 growth occurred at Teesside, which attracted in 1998 more than twice the traffic at Newcastle at the beginning of the decade. In the CAA studies cited previously Teesside was found attractive by leisure passengers in influencing their airport choice. The availability of low fares at Teesside was also a factor in increasing its share of this market in a short period of airport competition.

City of Derry

Service to City of Derry from Stansted commenced in July 1999. The projection was for 130,000 in a full year compared with only 49,000 passengers at the airport in 1998. The competing airports are Belfast International and Belfast City which are, respectively, 65 and 77 miles away. Belfast International has 2.6 million passengers per year and Belfast City about half that number. The three competing Northern Ireland airports illustrate three diverse sources of market entry to airport competition. Belfast International was previously an exclusively military airport. It is now owned by TBI which also owns Skavsta and Cardiff. Belfast City was previously a test base for the adjacent aircraft factory. City of Derry serves both the western counties of Northern Ireland and the adjoining region of the Republic of Ireland and is promoted by both governments as a means of stimulating regional development through reduced access transport costs. The initial load factors on the Derry–Stansted service exceeded expectations. The strong competition between the two Belfast airports, both privately owned, was joined, on the London route initially, by a new competitor in the west.

The sustainability of airport competition

Competition between airports was restricted in the past because competition between airlines was minimal in Europe. Airline deregulation and the entry to the market of low-cost new airlines have created new opportunities for airports wishing to increase their business. Many of the results in the case studies examined above have been spectacular in the increased number of passengers generated by smaller airports making special deals with low-cost airlines in order to attract market share from the dominant airport in the region.

In examining the sustainability of airport competition and cost and price reductions to attract low-cost airlines there may be a difference over the short and long term. An airport may at a stage in its development have spare capacity. It may merely want to fill this spare capacity until the airport resumes a perceived normal growth path. The longest established low-cost airline, Ryanair, has a proven record in generating extra passenger numbers virtually from the startup date and becoming the market leader in as little as six months.

Before addressing the question of whether airports would wish to sustain a discounting regime in the long term the sustainability of low-cost airlines in terms of passenger support and profitability are examined. Many previous low-cost airlines have enjoyed a popular public image but went broke. Ryanair, on the other hand, is one of the most profitable airlines in the world with a net margin of 16.5 per cent (Borgo and Bull Larsen, 1998). Profits in the first quarter of 1999 were £14.2 million on a turnover of £66.2 million. The product of a low-cost airline, minimal in-flight service, no interlining, seat allocation or frequent-flyer programme, low travel agent commission and low-cost airports has been both attractive to passengers and shareholders. Passengers accept that the large savings in fares are financed in part by reductions in service compared to a full service airline. Residual nostalgia for a once-eulogised standard of service by national airlines occasionally leads to criticism of the low-cost airlines but there is little nostalgia for pre-deregulation air fares. It is Ryanair policy to seek discounts at all the airports it serves in return for the passenger numbers its record indicates that it will generate. In addition it currently proposes that the airport passenger charge should be capped for a 737 at 100 passengers. As the airline moves to a fleet of 737-800 aircraft while capping airport charges this would reduce airport charges per passenger by a further 31 per cent.

Airlines are not immune from making mistakes but the present indications are that the low-cost airline is sustainable and can continue to meet the needs of both passengers and shareholders. On the staff side there is an acceptance that productivity far higher than the tradition in European national airlines is required to sustain the low fares and high profitability of Ryanair. Pay at the airline is above that of competitors and performance and attendance premiums are paid. The traditional low productivity of Europe's national airlines was a product of non-competing airlines. Staff and management at Ryanair accept that the traditional low productivity of Europe's national airlines could not be replicated in a new entrant low-cost airline in a competitive market. The majority of the staff at Ryanair are below 30 years of age and may regard the low-productivity European national airline as neither attainable nor desirable in a deregulated market.

The alacrity with which the passengers in the case studies used new low-cost airports raises questions for traditional airport management. While the airport industry might see the new airports in the case studies above as hugely inferior to

Heathrow, Manchester, Glasgow, Stockholm, Brussels, Oslo, Venice and CDG, passengers have been readily willing to change airports. Many of the benefits which the leading airports saw themselves bestowing on passengers appear in the case studies to be pretty worthless when compared with a low-fare low-cost airport without congestion, confusion and long walking times. Incremental construction at busy airports seems invariably to lead to longer time spent by passengers within terminals and on occasion a bus journey from terminal to plane. Airports appear not to include these passenger costs in their assessment of what passengers require. The prospect of a virtual greenfield site empty airport has attracted many passengers in the 17 case studies above.

As with other industries where competitive forces have been weak, airports in a competitive world will have to serve better their customers, both airlines and passengers. While airlines in Europe have taken steps to change from the old days of non-competing airlines and rent-seeking staff and management, until recently there has been little evidence of a similar urge to reform Europe's airports. The productivity of staff and investments at Europe's airports will require evaluation in a more competitive environment. Regulation by governments of air fares in Europe was highly inefficient as reflected in the margin by which regulated fares substantially exceed those now available from low-cost airlines using low-cost airports. Regulatory formulae such as RPI-X, allowing airports to increase their charges by the retail price index minus 3 per cent in the case of the BAA at Heathrow and Gatwick, yield far lower savings to airlines and passengers than the discounts at new airports negotiated by low-cost airlines. In a competitive airport environment airport managers will have to engage in price negotiations with airlines rather than present a fixed set of charges on a 'take it or leave it' basis. Functions traditionally performed in-house will have to be subject to competitive tendering. Productivity comparisons will have to be made with airports which find it profitable to discount airport charges by as much as 90 per cent, or to remit them entirely, in the case of new business generated by low-cost airlines. Extraction of economic rents from non-competing airports and airlines is at the core of transforming European aviation from collusion to competition. These permanent increases in efficiency are the foundation for airline and airport efficiency and competition rather then temporary price reductions to utilise short-term spare capacity.

Two airports in the case studies above have changed their policies during the period under review. The Manchester case study described the policy change by the airport, which will end in 1999 the very rapid growth of Dublin–Manchester traffic since 1994 and increase the market share of both Liverpool and Leeds/Bradford. The availability of low-cost substitute airports limits the ability of Manchester to pass on increased airport charges, over the discount levels, to passengers.

Dublin airport's discount programme has been associated with rapid increases in the number of passengers and increased profits at the airport. The airport has experienced capacity problems both in its terminals and car parks. The airport has proposed ending the 25 per cent discount on low-fare routes to Britain and scrapping the 50 per cent winter discount while winding down the growth discounts on passenger and landing charges. Ryanair proposed a further discount scheme on routes to mainland Europe and to build its own terminal at Dublin airport. Having secured a better deal at Stansted, the airline has shifted its emphasis to new routes to the European mainland at Stansted rather than Dublin, as shown in Table 8.8. The Irish government has renewed the discounts for a further year and promised to establish an independent airport regulator late in 1999. The state airport body, Aer Rianta, has over 95 per cent of air passengers in the Republic of Ireland. Only two independent airports, Kerry and Knock, take jet aircraft and their competitive impact is limited to taking some traffic from Cork and Shannon. Some passengers in the northwest might divert to the new Derry services described in final case study. In the past some Dublin airport passengers diverted to Belfast because of high fares ex Dublin before deregulation in 1986.

Dublin is a vital hub for Ryanair notwithstanding its transfer of emphasis on new routes to Stansted since 1997. In 1999 the airport proposed a slot system for Dublin, the antithesis of the low-cost airport model. As Aer Lingus and Ryanair are about the same size at Dublin it is not clear which airline would chair the slot allocation committee. The slot system has been strongly opposed by Ryanair because low-cost airlines need to expand their output rapidly to cater for the large increases in demand which typically follow their market entry.

Stansted is the major point of expansion of new Ryanair services to mainland Europe since 1997. Major increases in traffic to Ireland have occurred since Ryanair began to serve Stansted in 1991. Full-fare airlines were reluctant to serve Stansted and the airport lost money. The discounts for low-fare airlines at Stansted have brought benefits to passengers, airlines and the airport and have generated overall efficiency gains reflected in lower fares. The present policy of discounts at Stansted brings benefits to the BAA also. The policy change against discounts at Manchester and contemplated at Dublin is not proposed either at Stansted or any of the other airports in the 17 case studies considered above. The airport sector in Europe is developing low-cost airports discounting their charges heavily in order to attract low-cost airlines.

Conclusions

This section has examined the impact on the demand side for airports of airline deregulation, and the emergence of low-cost airlines. On the supply side the chapter examined the impact of privatisation, commercialisation, and market entry of new airports because of factors such as the reduced military requirement for airports and the availability of airports seeking to promote local and regional development. Seventeen case studies were presented based on the experience of Ryanair, the longest-established low-cost airline in Europe and the most experienced in developing passenger volumes at airports competing with the main hub airports. The case studies covered airports in Ireland, the UK, France, Italy, Sweden, Norway, Belgium and Germany. The case studies included both mature and recent cases of airport competition. Airport competition was essential both to start and sustain Europe's most dramatic deregulation on the continent's busiest international route, Dublin–London. The gains to passengers in terms of reduced fares and service from five instead of one London airport have been large. The North of England case study of airport competition covers a decade in which there were several changes of policy by the airports concerned and may thus have implications for projecting forward the newer case studies above.

The quick success of the combination of both new-entrant low-cost airlines and airports has been remarkable in several of the case studies such as Prestwick, Lyons, Charleroi, Kristainstad, Skavska, Treviso, Teesside, Leeds/Bradford, Beauvais and Carcassone. The list of successful case studies in airport competition is not completed. The Cranfield studies cited in the text indicate a large potential number of new airports, which could be served by Europe's new low-cost airlines. The realised gains from airport competition have been impressive in the case studies and the lower fares have been financed both by more efficient airlines and airports. The role of airport management in the new environment will be quite different to the uncompetitive undynamic past.

(II) How do the demands for airport services differ between full-service carriers and low-cost carriers?

The low-cost carrier segment of the industry has grown rapidly in the last decade and this growth has been coincident with the reform of the airport business. Although carriers like Southwest have been in business in the US for over 30 years it is only recently that the low-cost carrier sector in Europe has emerged as such a fast growing segment of the industry. This growth is a combination of external factors such as the economic downturn but also due to institutional reform in Europe with deregulation and market integration. The airport business has also been transformed from a public utility to one of the modern business and this shift has contributed to the success of the low-cost carrier growth. However, this growth has created some tension since airports that previously serviced only network carriers were now servicing the low-cost carriers with their simpler network and emphasis on connectivity. Having airports specialize in servicing one type of carrier rather than another could in some cases relieve this tension. Indeed, this was a usual outcome of the strategic positioning of low-cost carriers as secondary and reliever airports were a natural part of their business strategy.

Many airports in different parts of the world do not have the option of choosing among clients. This seemingly places different business demands on the airport for service and capital investment. The natural question to ask is how these demands might differ and are there substantive differences between full-service and low-cost carriers?

The impact of airline deregulation

The question raised regarding differences in demand for airport services among carrier types shows how much European aviation has changed since the first scheduled low-cost airline in Europe, Ryanair, commenced on the Dublin–London route in 1986. In the days of non-competing airlines there was no price competition, markets were determined in advance both in terms of total market size and market shares, and new market entrants were banned.

European air fares were repeatedly shown in the annual International Civil Aviation Organization (ICAO) surveys to be the highest in the world. Airlines regulated non-price competition in areas such as food service through the airlines cartel, the International Air Transport Association (IATA). The airlines also achieved regulatory capture over their supervisory government departments. Fares were set far in excess of the European charter airlines which carried over 40 per cent of air passengers within geographical Europe at fares of about a third of those charged by scheduled national carriers between the cities of northern Europe.

In the non-competing airline scenario there was inadequate attention paid to the costs of airlines, either internal or external. Airports were part of a system where the absence of price competition reduced efficiency incentives. Since no airlines competed on price, increases in costs were passed on to passengers by airlines acting jointly. Airports were part of the airline cost base but in the world of non-competing airlines without a choice of competing airports, increases in airport costs were easily passed on also.

Airlines accepted each other's tickets and concentrated services at a few hub airports which they served jointly in order, *inter alia*, to engage in interlining. Airports were managed as minor public sector bodies. Hub airports abdicated control over their vital runway capacity to airline scheduling committees chaired by the national airline. The allocations were made on the grandfather rights principle and few slots were available at hub airports.

Europe's high-cost national airlines enjoyed both regulatory capture over governments and de facto control over the major airports. Since the profitability of the sector was marginal the case was made that the economic rents from the protectionism afforded by European governments to their national airlines were overwhelmingly enjoyed by the staff in a combination of high ratios of wages to GDP per head and low productivity by comparison with, for example, North American airlines. Airline management also gained from the system that gave them probably the best economic rent of all, a quiet life because new entrants and price and capacity competition were banned.

As the Organisation for Economic Cooperation and Development (2001) has documented, the movement to airline deregulation in Ireland, the first such policy movement in Europe, happened by accident. Legislation to imprison and fine heavily travel agents convicted of discounting airline tickets below ministerial approved prices provoked a unique parliamentary revolt in 1984. In response to the parliamentary revolt against the penalties for selling cheap airline tickets, the government licensed Ryanair to operate a Dublin–London (Luton) service from May 1986.[1]

In August 1987, the first full year of deregulation on the Dublin–London route, passenger numbers were 92 per cent greater than in August 1985, the last full year of pre-deregulation policies. By the late 1990s there were almost 4.5 million passengers on the route compared to under 1 million in a market that was static for seven years before deregulation. The route became the second busiest in the world after Tokyo–Taipei. Air travel between Britain and Ireland at more than 8 million passengers exceeded the passenger numbers between Britain and Germany, France and Italy, countries with populations far larger than Ireland's four million. In the 20 years before airline deregulation the number of foreign tourists to Ireland was unchanged at 2 million. In the period after deregulation the number rose to over 6 million.[2]

The results of airline deregulation for airports in Europe may be even more radical than for the airlines. From examples such as California and Texas, deregulated state aviation markets, from the US experience after 1978, and the European charter market, the successes of European airlines under deregulation were to some degree predictable. Since European air fares had further to fall than the world average, the fare reductions were predictable but have in fact been greater than the advocates of deregulation had expected. The fare reductions have been as high as 80 per cent off the standard scheduled fares of the incumbent airlines.

Airports as a contestable market

Perhaps more remarkable than the airline impact of airline deregulation in Europe has been the role of airports. The early examples of Luton as a competitor for Heathrow, Liverpool in competition with Manchester and Prestwick with Glasgow have been added to by examples such as Beauvais, Charleroi, Torp, Skavasta, Hahn, Stansted, Treviso, Orio al Serio, and Ciampino. Table 8.14 contains examples of airport competition in the deregulated European aviation market. The combination of low-cost airline and low-cost airports has been significant both in terms of gaining market share and expanding the size of the overall market.

Table 8.14 Case studies of airport competition in the deregulated European aviation market, 2002

Hub airport	New airport(s)	New share (%)	Route(s)
Heathrow	Stansted, Luton, Gatwick, City	52	Dublin/London
Glasgow	Prestwick	60	Dublin/Glasgow
Manchester	Liverpool/ Leeds/Bradford	33	Dublin/North West England
Brussels	Charleroi	66	Ireland/Belgium
Stockholm	Skavsta/Vasteras	31	London/Stockholm
Oslo	Torp	23	London/Oslo
Venice	Treviso	50	London/Venice
Milan	Orio/Serio	21	London/Milan
Franfurt	Hahn	22	London/Frankfurt
Hamburg	Lubeck	27	London/Hamburg
Rome	Ciampino	29	London/Rome
Paris	Beauvais	35	Dublin/Paris

Source: Barrett (2000) updated by Civil Aviation Authority and airline data.

The gains to the passenger from this combination of airline and airport competition may be summarised as follows:

* lower air fares;
* using smaller airports with shorter waiting times for baggage, shorter walking times at airports, less confusion at airports, and so on; and
* increased use of local airports reduces the need to travel long surface distances to hub airports.

The alacrity with which passengers have transferred to the new airports may also require airport managers at established airports to reflect on their loss of point-to-point passengers to the new airports. The disutility felt by passengers at Europe's hub airports may be said to include long walking distances at terminals, delays waiting for baggage, difficult transfer connections, congestion at airport terminals and on access routes, and boredom.[3]

The policy environment for new airport managers since airline deregulation may be summarised as follows:

* the regulatory barriers to new business have been removed;
* new airlines are seeking to serve new airports; and
* the passengers on the new airlines are willing to transfer to new airports.

Because of the lower air fares charged by the new airlines and the greater pressure they exert on total costs the airport revenues from the new airlines will have to be earned in highly competitive markets.

The business relationship between airports and low-cost airlines

Table 8.14 illustrates the important impact of new entrant airlines and airports on 14 European routes in 2002. The impacts are considerable. For example, the most mature route deregulation, Dublin–London, could not have happened at a Heathrow monopoly in 1986. The new market entrant, Ryanair, did not have access to slots there. Luton airport was thus an indispensable part of deregulation as was Stansted subsequently.

Luton's share of Dublin–London traffic peaked at 20 per cent in 1987. This share fell because of reduced fares available at Heathrow, difficulties of surface access to London because of the lack of a rail link from Luton airport, and some anti-Luton airport advertising by Aer Lingus. From 1991 Stansted became the major focus of airport competition with Heathrow.

Liverpool had a 41 per cent market share in 1993 of the 500,000 annual passengers between Dublin and the northwest of England. The other shares in this market were Manchester, 50 per cent, and Leeds–Bradford, 9 per cent. Ryanair in 1993 served Liverpool only in this market but subsequently served all three competing airports. The market doubled by the end of the decade. When Manchester sought to increase its charges to Ryanair in 1999 the airline transferred capacity to Leeds/Bradford thus raising its share of the market to 23 per cent. When Manchester and Ryanair agreed to restore reduced airport charges the return of capacity caused the Manchester share to increase again.

In the Charleroi case study of airport competition the factors involved were the wish of the local government of the region to promote economic development, and very strong resentment of the £650 Dublin–Brussels fare charged by Aer Lingus and Sabena. Charleroi now dominates the Irish routes from Dublin and Shannon and is a hub for nine routes serving Glasgow, Liverpool, London, Carcassone, Pisa, Venice and Rome, in addition to Dublin and Shannon. It has 22 per cent of London–Brussels traffic.

The other case studies indicate that there is a good supply in Europe of underused airports, which have proven to be an attractive option for deregulated airlines and their customers. Since the deregulated low-cost airlines operate on a point-to-point basis their passengers do not need the facilities for transfer passengers provided at hub airports and have readily transferred to the new smaller airports within an hour's journey from a hub city.

A further role for new airlines has been to link second city airports directly to the newly served airports in contrast to the traditional national airlines that concentrated on the national hubs. The traditional concentration of Alitalia on Milan and Rome has facilitated the entry of new airlines to regional city airports such as Bologna, Venice, Pisa, Turin and Genoa.

The low-cost airline entering into business talks with airport managers will have a record of developing new routes and products. The cost base of the new airlines is low because the low productivity and high-cost operation of the traditional non-competing airline has been replaced by far higher productivity. The number of passengers per staff member at Ryanair, for example, exceeds 8,000 compared with an average of 873 for the eight national airlines with which it most frequently competes; these are Aer Lingus, Air France, Alitalia, Austrian, British Airways, Lufthansa and SAS.

In addition the low-cost airline will have reduced service costs by abolishing in-flight service, business class, free newspapers, seat allocation, interlining, frequent-flyer clubs and business lounges. Retailing costs will have been reduced by abolishing expensive downtown sales offices, travel agents, 'bought-in' computer reservation systems, and the traditional book of airline tickets. The new airline will have a low marketing budget on the basis that low fares sell themselves. The fleets used will typically be 'one size fits all' in contrast with the variety of aircraft in the traditional airline fleet with consequent higher flying costs and maintenance costs than the new entrant. Airports negotiating with the new low-cost airlines will find a radical change therefore from the old world of non-competing airlines and airports.

Airport negotiations with low-cost airlines

Airports in negotiation with low-cost airlines will be immediately aware that there is no prospect of achieving the aeronautical revenues achieved by hub airports from full-service airlines. For airports close to capacity there is no attraction in having low-cost airlines except at off-peak periods. Since low-cost airlines require a 25-minute turnaround they may not want to serve busy airports even if the costs were reduced. Since their passengers are on simple point-to-point journeys, they require a simple airport product rather than the complexity of the busy hub with several terminals, interlining, long walking distances, and so on.

For an airport manager with excess capacity the low-cost airline may be a welcome business partner. The positive aspects of such a business partner include the following factors. The low-cost airlines have a strong track record in delivering business even to virtually empty airports. The low-cost airlines offer non-aeronautical revenue sources such as catering and shopping for services normally provided as in-flight services by full-fare airlines. Low-cost airlines generate a greater than average use of car hire where they serve smaller airports. In making deals with low-cost airlines the airports trade off a reduction in aeronautical revenues in return for extra non-aeronautical revenues. This has been a trend at all airports for some decades.

An empty airport is of little use to either commercial owners, such as Prestwick, or to airports with a mandate to promote regional development, such as Charleroi or Derry that was given such a role by the UK and Irish governments. Prestwick has obviously made a decision to utilise a largely empty airport with the passengers of low-cost airlines and has built a hub of six routes serving Dublin, Paris, London, Brussels and Oslo. Airports with a regional development mandate have found it difficult to attract full-cost airlines away from the hubs at which they concentrate their operations in order to interline with their 'partner' airlines. It requires something more dramatic to generate volumes at lesser-used airports and low-cost airlines have that track record. The other alternative to the low-cost airline is the public service obligation (PSO) option in which smaller operators are subsidised to feed national hub airports. The experience of these services has been that they are operated with expensive turboprop aircraft, charge high fares and require large public subsidies but do not generate significant volumes of passengers. The use of slots at hub airports for small aircraft is also unattractive to both airlines and hub airports. In seeking to develop commercial revenues for the airport itself and development in the adjoining region the low-cost airline may represent better value per unit of cost than either seeking a full-service airline or a PSO operator.

A parameter in business discussions between airports and low-cost airlines is that the penalty for non-agreement by the airport is likely to be the loss of the low-cost airline and its passengers to a competing airport. With the benefit of hindsight, we can now say that the established high-cost airlines neglected many fine airports in Europe in their focus on hubs. These airports now have a commercial mandate replacing a minor role in the public sector. In addition demilitarisation in Europe has freed military airports for possible civilian use (Fewings, 1998) has drawn attention to the many such airports in Europe with 32, 34 and 28 in France, the UK and Germany, respectively. His wider study of 10 EU countries found 131 airports within one hour's surface travel time of an existing airport. Even if all this available capacity at Europe's airports were to be taken up there is also the prospect of new airport investment. Barrett (1984, 2000) questions the assumptions of long lead times, high capital intensity and economies of scale in airport operation which were traditionally felt to rule out significant new market entry in the airport sector.

Low-cost airlines may be of interest to airport managers within a multi-airport company. Stansted and Hahn are examples of where the owners have major busy airports at Heathrow and Frankfurt but who use low-cost airlines to secure business for the lesser airports. The judgement call here is that Stansted and Hahn would not have been developed by relying on full-cost airlines to transfer part of their services from Heathrow and Frankfurt.

Low-cost airline negotiations with airport managers

Table 8.15 summarises the requirements of low-cost airlines in their negotiations with airports. The case for low airport charges is that the large declines in air fares since the market entry of low-cost carriers has raised the share of airport charges in the price of an airline ticket. The low-cost airlines have raised their productivity in terms of passengers carried per staff member to 8,000 in the case of Ryanair, based on 16 million passengers and 2,000 staff. Some part of the productivity difference is accounted for by better services and longer flights by the full-service airlines and by contracting out rather than performing services in-house. Nonetheless the productivity performance of the low-cost airlines supports their stance that having achieved very high productivity within the airlines they wish to extract similar productivity gains from all suppliers of services to the airlines.

Table 8.16 contrasts the aeronautical revenues of Europe's hub airports, as found by Warburg Dillon Read (1999) and the costs of the same services at the airports served by Ryanair. Only a small fraction of the traditional airport charges is likely to be paid by the low-cost airline. If the airport requires a higher yield the low-cost airline is likely to take its business elsewhere.

Here low-cost airlines will point out that if they cut an established airline fare by as much as 80 per cent the old airport charges, as a proportion of the ticket price, will rise dramatically. They will typically refuse to pay the old airport charges,

Table 8.15 The airport requirements of low-cost airlines

1. Low airport charges
2. Quick 25 min turnaround time
3. Single-storey airport terminals
4. Quick check-in
5. Good catering and shopping at airport
6. Good facilities for ground transport
7. No executive/business class lounges

Source: Interview with Michael O'Leary, Chief Executive, Ryanair by author, January 2003.

Table 8.16 Airport aeronautical revenues per WLU, Europe,
1998–2000 ($) and Ryanair charges at Dublin and UK airports

Hubs		Nonhubs	
MAN	11.1	Dublin	204
VIE	9.0	Gatwick	179
HAM	8.6	Birmingham	155
FRA	8.1	Manchester	122
BAA	7.1	Luton	119
ADP	5.7	Stansted	102
BRU	5.6	Leeds/Bradford	36
AMS	5.5	Cardiff	31
CPH	5.0	Bournemouth	>30
SEA	4.5	Liverpool	>30
AENA	4.0	Bristol	>30
ADR	3.8	Prestwick	>30
Aer Rianta	3.4	Teesside	>30
		Derry	>30

Source: Warburg Dillon Read (1999).

threaten to take their passengers elsewhere and seek low, zero or subsidised airport services. Table 8.16 shows the success of low-cost airlines in negotiating reduced charges by contrasting the University of Westminster (2000) study of charges actually paid by Ryanair with the charges at Europe's main airports analysed by Warburg Dillon Read (1999). Based on Table 8.16 the estimated aeronautical revenues per passenger of $9 at Vienna, $8.6 at Hamburg and $8.1 at Frankfurt are most unlikely to be achieved. Irish state airports through Aer Rianta receive only 40 per cent of Hamburg's revenues. Eight provincial UK airports receive about $1 or less in aeronautical revenues per passenger from Ryanair.

Many air fares in Europe have declined by as much as 80 per cent since the advent of low-cost airlines. Airport charges to the low-cost airlines will come under even more downward pressure. Some airports may even have to subsidise airlines to use them and seek the maximum passenger impact per unit of subsidy.

Quick turnaround times of 25 minutes are a core part of the low-cost airline product. Compared to an airline with a 1-hour turnaround time on a 1-hour stage length, an airline with a 25-minute turnaround time will be able to fly an extra two rotations per day thus achieving better fleet utilisation and staff productivity.

The single-storey terminal building requirement is intended to secure simplicity of operation with both arriving and departing passengers on the same level. It is also intended to reduce gold-plating of investment plans by non-competing airports. The low-cost airlines believe that gold-plating occurred in the past. Where airport facilities are separately priced, such as airbridges, the low-cost airlines decline to use them. They prefer steps, which are cheaper to use.

The quick check-in requirement is to reflect the lower costs of the new airlines in this area. Low-cost airlines have a simple point-to-point product in contrast with airlines where check-in is delayed by interlining and onward journeys on a single ticket, seat allocation, separate business and first class, and frequent-flyer points. These all slow down check-in compared with a low-cost carrier. Ryanair carries 25 per cent of passengers at Dublin but requires only 11 per cent of check-in desks. It checks in 130,000 passengers per year per check-in desk at Dublin compared with 48,000 for all other airlines. At Stansted the Ryanair throughput is 110,000 per desk and 70,000 for other airlines indicating that even where the traffic types are broadly similar the low-cost airline requires less infrastructure for check-in.

The need for good catering and shopping facilities at airports serving low-cost airlines arises because the low-cost airlines do not provide in-flight services such as catering and newspapers. There is both a scope and need for such services at airports for the passengers of low-cost airlines. There is also a business opportunity for airports to increase their non-aeronautical revenues.

Good facilities for ground transport at new airports catering for the passengers of low-cost airlines are important because many of the newly served airports are more remote from major cities than the hub airports. These facilities include bus services which connect to flights, car hire parks which are convenient to the terminal, and discounted rates for car parking. Passengers on low-cost airlines have a higher than average use of car hire. Promotion of low-cost car parks and good public transport has been part of the marketing of low-cost airports such as Prestwick and Charleroi, for example.

The opposition of low-cost airlines to airport lounges for business and executive passengers is based on a general opposition to high-cost facilities and gold-plating in general. These lounges have a reported cost of $1 million and raise the cost base of airports in a way which is opposed by low-cost airlines.

Future development of low-cost airports in Europe

The research of Fewings (1998) indicates that there is considerable scope for further development of low-cost airports in Europe. Table 8.17 summarises Fewings' study of 13 countries with 431 airports. The table shows that, for example, in Norway, there are 23 airports with runways of 1,600 m or over; that is, 5.3 per million population. There are 28 airports with runways shorter than 1,600 m; that is, 6.5 per million population.

The unweighted average number of airports per million population for 13 countries in Table 8.17 is 3.2. Excluding Iceland, which is shown to be a special case, and airports with runways under 1,600 m, there are on average two airports per million population with runways able to take the 737 and similar aircraft which are the core of the low-cost airline fleets.

Behind the list of airports in Table 8.17 is a further possibility of converting military airports and private sector investment as at London City. It is likely therefore that there will be further routes opened by low-cost airlines serving new airports and providing a product that combines both the low-cost airline and low-cost airports. The evidence is that passengers will continue to respond favourably to

Table 8.17 Level of airport provision in Europe, 1998, number of airports per million inhabitants

	Runway length over 1,600 m	Runway length under 1,600 m
Austria	0.80	0.0
Denmark	1.9	0.4
Finland	4.1	0.0
France	1.0	0.1
Germany	0.3	0.1
Greece	2.5	1.2
Iceland	22.5	26.2
Ireland	1.1	2.5
Italy	0.6	0.1
Norway	5.3	6.5
Scotland	1.6	2.1
Sweden	4.3	0.7
UK	0.7	0.3

Source: Fewings (1998).

these new products and the profitability of the low-cost airlines such as Southwest and Ryanair indicates that the supply side will continue. Airports therefore may have to deal with the low-cost airlines or risk losing market share and, indeed, total markets.

Summary

The impact of low-cost airlines on fares and passenger numbers in the deregulated European aviation market has been dramatic. Probably the most radical impact of European airline deregulation, in contrast with the North American precedent, has been the willingness of passengers to use new airports which are typically more distant from major cities than the traditional hubs. The low-fare airlines have also brought service to 'second city' airports bypassed by the concentration of national airlines on hubs. They have also delivered passenger numbers to airports with PSO or regional development goals much in excess of alternatives such as turboprop aircraft with low volumes, high costs and less passenger attractiveness.

A strong case can be made for airport managers negotiating with low-cost airlines. They have good growth records, prospects and the market rates, their profitability record is impressive. Their record in delivering the promised growth in passenger numbers is impressive. They are obviously tough negotiators with airport managers. The pricing policy of Ryanair, for example, has been to reduce fares by as much as 8 per cent per year, and to seek cost reductions from very high staff productivity growth and from all suppliers of services to the airline. Strategies to reduce the cost of bought-in supplies to the airline include; ending the use of travel agents and bought-in computer reservations systems (CRS); ending of in-flight services; and negotiation of large discounts from aircraft manufacturers. Airport managers are not exempt from their cost-cutting intentions.

By contrast, full-service airlines have low-growth prospects on their European routes. Two of these airlines, Sabena and Swissair, went bankrupt. Olympic exhibited in the words of former chairman and aviation economist, Rigas Doganis, distressed state airline syndrome (Doganis, 2001). The symptoms included substantial losses, over-politicisation, strong trade unions, low productivity, bureaucratic management, poor service quality and no clear development strategy. In 2003 British Airways lost its place in the FTSE 100 list of major companies. Many airlines will follow low-cost carriers most of the way down the cost-reduction path. For example, in the 2004 judicial review of the Commission on Aviation Regulation determination on Irish airport charges, Aer Lingus supported the views of Ryanair. Should Ryanair obtain government approval for its own low-cost terminal at Dublin, Aer Lingus has stated that it will seek to transfer some of its business there. If the government approves the Ryanair terminal there will then be competition between low-cost and full-service terminals within the one airport. This will exert pressures on the operators of the full-service terminal to reduce costs just as high-cost airlines have faced in the past. As we unbundled the traditional airline/airport product, relatively few passengers have been willing to purchase separately the extras previously included in the high prices previously charged. They opt instead for the low-cost product sending out the market signal that the traditional airline/airport product was not really a luxury after all.

Deregulation of airlines in Europe and the surprising success of airport competition as low-cost airlines and their passengers moved to new airports have changed the airline–airport interface. How should airports respond? Mostly, they should recognise that the old aviation order of Chicago in 1944 has gone. Chicago nowadays is more famous for the espousal of market economics than for the defence of non-competing airlines and their airports. Airports have to respond to the world of the low-cost carrier. They may not wish to follow the full agenda of the low-cost airlines but market forces will bring them most of the way.

Notes

1 For an outer offshore island the impact on Ireland of airline deregulation was dramatic. Fares fell by 54 per cent on the first day of deregulation from £208 to £94.99. The average Ryanair fare in 2000, at £38 per stage, was the equivalent of a day's average wage. The 1984 pre-deregulation fare of £208 was then a week and a half's wages in Ireland.

2 The startup airline Ryanair in 2002 carried 16 million passengers and the prediction for 2003 was 24 million including 2 million from the acquisition of Buzz from KLM. This made it the fourth largest airline in Europe in terms of passenger numbers. The 2002/3 winter timetable served 58 airports in 12 countries.

3 The Mintel International (2000) states that 33 per cent of airport users found airports 'boring'. The age group finding airports most boring was the 35–44 age group and the AB social group. Mintel found that the percentage of those finding the main UK airports boring ranged from 29 per cent at Heathrow to 32 per cent at Gatwick and 33 per cent at Manchester.

References

Association of European Airlines (1999) *Association of European Airlines Yearbook*, Vol. 7. Brussels: AEA.

Barrett, S.D. (1984) *Airports for Sale, the Case for Competition*. London: Adam Smith Institute.

Barrett S.D. (1999) Peripheral market entry, product differentiation, supplier rents and sustainability in the deregulated European airline market – a case study, *Journal of Air Transport Management* 5: 21–30.

Barrett, S.D. (2000) Product differentiation supplier rents and sustainability in the deregulated European airline market—a case study, *Journal of Air Transport Management* 5: 21–30.

Baumol, W.J. (1982) Contestable markets: an uprising in the theory of industrial structure, *American Economic Review* 72: 1–15.

Bonnassies, O. (1998) Stansted: the low-cost alternative airport?, *Avmark Aviation Economist* February/March: 2–6.

Bonnassies, O. (1999) Growth at regional airports, *Avmark Aviation Economist* January/February: 2–3.

Borgo, A. and Bull Larsen, T. (1998) Strategy losses, *Airline Business*. 14(8): 84–9.

Boyfield, K. (1984) Competition and regulation in privatising the British Airports Authority, *Public Money General Series* 4.

Clinch, S. (1999) UK airports in the black, *Airports International* April: 18–20.

Commission of the European Communities (1984) Civil Aviation Memorandum No. 2. Brussels: CEC.

DKM (1999) *Charges for Low-Fare Airlines at Dublin Airport*. Dublin: DKM.

Doganis, R. (2001) *The Airline Business in the 21st Century*. London: Routledge.

Fewings, R. (1998) Provision of European airport infrastructure, *Avmark Aviation Economist* 15 (6): 18–20.

Foster, C. (1984) Privatising British airports: what's to be gained?, *Public Money General Series* 4, 19–23.

Mintel International (2000) *Report on Airports*. London: Mintel.

Nichols, W.K., Koll, E. and Stevins, A. (1999) Airport privatisation, *Airports International* June: 16–20.

Nielsen, H. (1998) Skavsta takes giant leap, *Airports International*, January/February.

Organisation for Economic Cooperation and Development (2001) *Regulatory Reform in Ireland*. Paris: OECD.

Rowe, R. (1995) Aerporti di Genoa. *Airports International*, November/December:

Starkie, D. and Thomson, D. (1985) *Privatising London's Airports*. London: Institute of Fiscal Studies.

UK Civil Aviation Authority (1995a) *Passengers at Airports in the East of England in 1994/5*. London: HMSO.

UK Civil Aviation Authority (1995b) *Passengers at airports Wales, and South and South West of England in 1994/5*. London: HMSO.

UK Civil Aviation Authority (1997a). *Passengers at Aberdeen, Edinburg, Glasgow and Inverness Airports in 1996*. London: HMSO.

UK Civil Aviation Authority (1997b) *Passengers at Birmingham, Gatwick, Heathrow, London City, Luton, Manchester and Stanstead airports in 1996*. London: HMSO.

UK Department of Trade (1976) *An Airport Strategy for Great Britain*. London: HMSO.

UK Department of Transport (1985) *Airports Policy*. London: HMSO.

UK Monopolies and Mergers Commission (1985) *The British Airports Authority*. London: HMSO.

University of Westminster (2000) *Study of Ryanair Airport Charges*. London: University of Westminster.

Warburg Dillon Read (1999) *Review of Strategic Options for the Future of Aer Rianta*. Dublin: Warburg Dillon Read.

Wrobel, A. (1997) *Airport Charges in Europe*. Paris: Institut du Transport Aerien.

9 Regulating and dismantling a national airport monopoly
A case study

Introduction

Ireland has had a strongly pro-contestability policy for airlines since 1986 when Ryanair entered the Dublin–London route. It was the first country in Europe in which a new market entrant, Ryanair, carried more passengers than the previously protected national airline, Aer Lingus. The extension of competition between airlines to the airport sector has been more difficult however. The European airport market is characterised by multiple airport ownership by airport companies, which dominate the major city markets. This chapter examines three important policies to address the efficiency and contestability of airport markets in Ireland since 2001. These were (1) the establishment of an independent airport regulator, the Commission for Aviation Regulation, in 2001; (2) the dismantling of the national airport monopoly in stages starting in 2004; and (3) a policy of competing terminals at Dublin Airport, announced in 2002 but scrapped in 2005.

Airport dominance in Ireland

Table 9.1 shows the dominant position of Aer Rianta/Dublin Airport Authority in 2006 among airports in the Republic of Ireland. Its three airports at Dublin, Cork and Shannon accounted for 95 per cent of passengers at Irish airports and 72 per cent used its main airport at Dublin. Only two independent airports, Knock and Kerry, had runway capacity for jet aircraft. Both Knock and Kerry have unsubsidised routes to the United Kingdom and Kerry has one route to Germany. Both Knock and Kerry have a subsidised service to Dublin. Of the remaining four airports, Galway and Waterford have unsubsidised routes to the United Kingdom, France and the Netherlands. Sligo and Donegal have unsubsidised services to the United Kingdom. Galway, Sligo and Donegal have subsidised public service obligation routes to Dublin.

The background to legislation for airport regulation

In common with the rest of Europe Ireland experienced little interest in air-port competition in a regulatory world in which airlines did not compete.

Table 9.1 Passenger numbers and market shares at Irish airports, 2006

Airport	Passenger number	Market share (%)
Dublin	21,265,887	72.4
Shannon	3,690,889	12.6
Cork	3,023,527	10.2
Knock	608,296	2.1
Kerry	392,576	1.3
Galway	245,918	0.8
Waterford	80,792	0.3
Donegal	46,731	0.2
Sligo	34,292	0.1
Total	29,388,908	100

Source: Transport 2006, Central Statistics Office.

Airlines concentrated on hub airports where they interlined and exchanged tickets. As airline competition developed with the licensing of Ryanair on Dublin–Luton in 1986 the initial pressure on airport charges was alleviated by a phased discount scheme by Aer Rianta from 1993 to 1998. Up to 1998 Aer Rianta was an agent of the state. In 2001 it was established as a semi-state company. Ownership of the assets was then transferred to the company. The independent regulator for airports, the Commission for Aviation Regulation, was established in 2001 and ownership and control of airports were separated in that year. The Commission's deliberations on the cost structure at Dublin, Cork and Shannon brought into sharp focus the differences between Aer Rianta which argued that its charges were reasonable, and the airlines, especially Aer Lingus and Ryanair, which argued that charges were unacceptable due to low labour productivity and weak capital investment appraisal. The Commission's verdict favoured the complainant airlines and the statutory appeal panel supported the verdict. Aer Rianta then took legal action against the Commission for Aviation Regulation. Legal fees accounted for 56 per cent of expenditure by the Commission in 2002 and 36 per cent in 2003. The legal action, at the High Court and then at the Supreme Court, was dropped by the Dublin Airport Authority in October 2004 following the abolition of Aer Rianta. The criticisms of Aer Rianta by the Commission for Aviation Regulation covered both operating costs and investment expenditures. The Commission's research was conducted by US consultants Infrastructure Management Group (IMG).

The operating efficiency of Aer Rianta airports

IMG found that Dublin's cost per work-load unit (WLU) was 30 per cent higher than the average of the best of its peers, Brussels, Copenhagen, Glasgow and Stansted. In a wider sample of 11 European airports Dublin had total operating expenses per WLU in line with its peers. The additional airports in the wider sample were Birmingham, Düsseldorf, Manchester, Munich and Vienna. In its analysis

Table 9.2 Operating cost per WLU, Dublin and comparator airports, (€), 1999

Dublin	10.35
Brussels	5.53
Copenhagen	4.84
Glasgow	7.91
Oslo	9.98
Stansted	8.53

Source: IMG (2001) Benchmarking Report, Commission for Aviation Regulation, p. 21.

Table 9.3 Staff productivity at Dublin and comparator airports (WLU per staff member)

Dublin	10,248
Brussels	37,158
Copenhagen	14,697
Glasgow	14,349
Stansted	17,367
Oslo	n.a.

Source: IMG, op cit., p. 19.

Table 9.4 Operating cost per WLU at Cork, Shannon and comparator airports, (€), 1999

Cork	8.2
Shannon	20.6
Basel-Mulhouse	7.8
Cardiff	13.6
Leeds-Bradford	10.9
Luton	14.5

Source: IMG op cit., p. 45.

of this benchmarking exercise the Commission recommended that Dublin should halve the difference between its costs and the best of its peers over a five-year period by about half; that is, 15 per cent. Table 9.2 shows the cost per WLU at Dublin and the other benchmarked airports in the IMG study. Table 9.3 shows staff productivity at the same airports measured by WLU per staff member.

The comparator group for Cork and Shannon airports in the IMG benchmarking study was Basel-Mulhouse, Cardiff, Leeds-Bradford and Luton. IMG found that Cork was more efficient than its peers and Shannon was much less efficient than its peers. The cost data from the IMG report for this group of airports are shown in Table 9.4 and the labour efficiency data are shown in Table 9.5.

Cork's labour productivity was 15 per cent above the average of its UK peers of 9,669 WLU per staff member while Shannon's WLU per staff was only 37 per cent

Table 9.5 Staff productivity at Cork, Shannon and comparator
airports (WLU per staff member), 1999

Cork	10,452
Shannon	3,591
Basel	16,600
Bristol	11,220
Cardiff	13,658
Luton	7,472
Leeds/Bradford	6,324

Source: IMG, op. cit., p. 43.

of the average of its UK peers. Based on the IMG analysis the Commission
found that

> there is room for Dublin and Shannon Airport's operational efficiency to be
> improved. The scope for such improvement has been evaluated at 3.5 per cent
> per annum at Dublin and 4 per cent per annum at Shannon Airport ... The
> overall price cap does not assume any efficiency improvement at Cork Airport
> as the IMG Benchmarking Report found Cork Airport's efficiency to be
> comparable to that of its peer group.
>
> (Commission for Aviation Regulation, Determination 2001a: 28–9)

Capital expenditure efficiency of Aer Rianta

Table 9.6 shows the differences in the capital expenditures proposed by Aer Rianta
and accepted by the Commission. The differences are attributed by the Commission
to a failure to consult with airport users about the investments proposed and the
failure of Aer Rianta to adequately analyse the investment programme.

The sole member of the Commission for Aviation gave five reasons for the
refusal of some £726 million of capital expenditure; that is, a rejection rate of
73 per cent of the £998 million sought by Aer Rianta. The reasons were:

1   poor consultation with users of the airport;
2   lack of transparency in quality of information provided to users of the airport,
    particularly as to planned costs of proposed projects;

Table 9.6 Proposed and agreed capital investment programmes at
Irish state airports, 2001 (IR£ m)

Airport	*Aer Rianta proposal*	*Regulator's decision*
Dublin	757	160
Shannon	106	56
Cork	136	57
Total	998	272

3   construction (both past and planned) of facilities that are inefficient and/or do not meet the requirements of users of the airports in line with best international practice;
4   inadequate or non-existent cost benefit analysis or business cases undertaking to justify specific CAPEX programmes; and
5   internal inconsistencies in information supplied by the applicant (Aer Rianta) to the respondent (the Commission for Aviation Regulation) on the CAPEX programme (Prasifka, 2002).

In addition the Commission reduced the regulatory asset base of Aer Rianta in respect of three investments it judged to be built in excess of requirements. These were Pier C at Dublin which had an excess construction cost of 22.6 per cent compared with similar buildings in Dublin, a terminal at Shannon which exceeded by 21.2 per cent the required space for expansion during the study period, and the investment in extra stands at Dublin Airport surplus to requirements. Dublin in 2001 had 65 stands compared to the 59 required in 2005 (Commission for Aviation Regulation, CP8/2001b: Appendix 4).

Airline criticisms of airport monopoly in Ireland

Aer Lingus paid 48.9 per cent of Aer Rianta's aeronautical revenues in 2000 and accounted for 40 per cent of passengers through its three airports. The Aer Lingus complaint against Aer Rianta stated that

> charges were being made unilaterally by Aer Rianta without taking account of the views of, or impact on, airport users. Airport users had no alternative to Aer Rianta in respect of the services provided at the airports, and there was no means by which Aer Rianta could be compelled to provide its services in a cost-effective way and in a manner which was responsive to the commercial needs of airport users.
>
> (Walsh, 2002: 2, 35)

The proposed increases submitted by Aer Rianta to the Commission for Aviation Regulation in 2001 were estimated by Aer Lingus to increase its aeronautical charges by Aer Rianta from €26.5 million in 1998 to €44.9 million in 2002, an increase of 69 per cent (Walsh, 2002: 2, 4–5). This contrasted with a reduction of 40 per cent in real terms between 1994 and 1998 from €5.87 to €3.78. This was a contribution to a successful programme of tourism promotion when Air Rianta was a government agency. Between its establishment as a separate agency, in 1998, and 2000, real aeronautical revenues per passenger increased by 32 per cent in the interval before the establishment of the regulatory agency.

Ryanair, the second largest customer at Aer Rianta airports, contended that 'Aer Rianta has consistently abused its monopoly power in recent years, but especially since 1999, to dramatically increase costs and charges of operating at its airports' and 'has been profligate in its capital spending programmes and provided vastly over-specified facilities that do not meet the requirements of users' (Callaghan, 2002: 9). Other industry objectors to the Aer Rianta operating and capital costs included British Airways, British Midland, Cityjet, IATA, the Irish Exporters Association, the Irish Hotels Federation, and the Shannon Airport Marketing Consultative Committee.

Criticisms of low labour productivity and weak capital investment appraisal throughout the Irish public sector have been frequently made in sectors such as public transport, electricity, the state telephone company and the national airline (Barrett, 1998). Aer Rianta, as a public sector body serving non-competing airlines, mostly state-owned, showed many elements of distressed state airline syndrome (Doganis, 2001) such as over-politicisation, strong unions, overstaffing, bureaucratic management, poor service quality and no clear development strategy.

The Aer Rianta response

Aer Rianta strongly objected to the analysis of its operational and capital expenditures by the CAR in legal proceedings which commenced with the lodgement of a request for judicial review in the High Court in October 2001 and ended with the withdrawal of a Supreme Court action by the company in October 2004. The statement grounding the application for judicial review sought to quash the CAR determination of the level of charges because the CAR did not have power to decide the appropriate capital expenditure for Aer Rianta airports, or to disallow capital expenditure committed or incurred before the establishment of the CAR in 2001. Aer Rianta also submitted that CAR had attached excessive regard to the alleged non-consultation by Aer Rianta with airport users and submitted that CAR had exceeded its legal power and authority. Aer Rianta also submitted that CAR had unlawfully delegated its functions to the IMG consultants. Aer Rianta also submitted that the CAR decisions lacked transparency and objective justification and contained errors. Aer Rianta submitted also that CAR 'irrationally and incorrectly assumed that rental revenue streams correlated with passenger numbers' and 'erroneously assumed that it was correct to provide for general productivity growth in projecting operation expenditure'. It was claimed that the Commission for Aviation Regulation 'placed undue and disproportionate emphasis on cost benefit analysis as the principal means of determining the capital programme'. Aer Rianta also submitted that the CAR recommendations would result in a significant reduction in the number of passengers at Cork and Shannon contrary to duty to support balanced regional development (Aer Rianta, 2001).

Aer Rianta also expressed concerns about the criticisms of airport investments by airlines. 'In general, airline operators have a powerful incentive to oppose large scale expansions of airport facilities, given that such expansion will frequently allow the entry of further competitors. Furthermore, airline operators – particularly so-called "low-cost" operators – generally attach little or no value to the provision of facilities at airports other than essential facilities such as checking in baggage handling, and passenger embarkation.' By contrast, 'other categories of users, such as passengers, attach considerable value to the provision of ancillary provisions at airports, such as good transportation links, ample car-parking and adequate catering and retail facilities.'

Market dominance and dismantling a national airport monopoly

Table 9.1 shows that the Aer Rianta airports, Dublin, Shannon and Cork, had a 95.2 per cent market share of Irish airport passenger traffic in 2006. Dublin had 72.4 per cent of the market, Shannon had 12.6 per cent and Cork had 10.2 per cent. The largest non-Aer Rianta airport in 2006, Knock, had only a 2.1 per cent market share. Only two independent airports, Knock and Kerry, had runway capacity for jet aircraft.

Separating Shannon and Cork from Aer Rianta reduced the market share of the largest airport operator, the Dublin Airport Authority, to 75.9 per cent, based on the data in Table 9.1. Growth since 2002 has been strong at Dublin but stronger at Cork, Shannon, Knock, Galway and Waterford. Market shares are unlikely to have changed much with Dublin dominant. The separation of Shannon and Cork from the Aer Rianta group reduced its passenger numbers by 4.6 million, from 19.7 million in 2002 to 15.1 million, a fall of 24 per cent, However, the rapid growth in traffic at Dublin means that the Dublin Airport Authority (DAA), the successor of Aer Rianta, will quickly replace the number of passengers which the organisation lost when Shannon and Cork were made independent.

Breaking up a national airport monopoly is nonetheless a radical step. It contrasts, for example, with the policy of the UK government when the BAA was privatised as a single entity in 1987. The BAA market share of passengers at UK airports before privatisation was 80 per cent and the largest non-BAA airport Manchester had a 10 per cent market share (Starkie, 2004: 391). This contrasts with the Aer Rianta share of 97 per cent and the largest non-Aer Rianta airport share of 1 per cent in Ireland in 2002, as shown in Table 9.1. While the Irish monopoly concentration was greater than in the UK, the decision to dismantle Aer Rianta contrasts with the decision to retain the BAA as a single entity on privatisation. The contrast is examined in the next section.

Multiple versus single airport ownership: the UK and Ireland contrasted

The arguments of the BAA which persuaded the UK government not to dismantle the group in 1985 are shown in Table 9.7. The table combines three sets of arguments for the common ownership of airports. These were made in 1976 by the Department of Trade in support of a national airport company, in research by Foster and Boyfield for the BAA in 1984 and in the White Paper of 1985.

With the acknowledged benefit of hindsight and the experience of airline deregulation in the United Kingdom and Ireland market since 1986 the common ownership arguments for airports are much weaker than when made. The points made by the Department of Transport in 1985 have failed the test of time.

Table 9.7 The case for common ownership of UK airports

(a) Board of Trade (1976)

   (i) concentration of activity at a small number of airports;
  (ii) ownership by the BAA should ensure that there is no wasteful competition between airports;
 (iii) common ownership would ensure that the interests of the regions were taken into account when considering development in the London area;
  (iv) common ownership would mean a consistent charging and investment policy for the airports;
   (v) overall planning of the airport system to accommodate the growth of traffic might be less haphazard than if ownership remained in a number of different hands; and
  (vi) from the point of view of employees enhanced career opportunities and unified management control would attract the necessary quality of personnel to the benefit of the airport system as a whole.

(b) Foster and Boyfield (1984)

   (i) planning controls and long lead times preclude new entrants;
  (ii) product diversity reduces the impact of competition;
 (iii) the small share of airport costs in airline costs makes airport competition difficult;
  (iv) only a small number of airports can be viable given economies of scale in airport operation; and
   (v) market provision of airports risks underinvestment.

(c) Department of Transport (1985)

   (i) the volume of business switching airports for price or service reasons is, on past experience, very small;
  (ii) the effect of airport charges on airline costs is relatively unimportant; and
 (iii) separate ownership would introduce undesirable rigidity into the administration of government policy for route licensing.

Source: Barrett (2000, 2004).

Airlines and passengers have switched airports. The savings have resulted in lower fares. There is now no government control over route licensing within the EU.

Low-cost airlines and low-cost airports have competed successfully with traditional airports. The economic cost of increasing services at previously underused airports is low and market entry is swift. Passengers have gained from local air services, lower air fares, cheaper car parking charges, less waiting time and walking time at airports and easier surface access than if airport activity were in fact concentrated at a small number of locations. Competition has not been wasteful and there have been no personnel or management difficulties at the newly developing non-BAA airports. There are significant cost savings to airlines and passengers from airport competition as shown in Table 9.8.

The differences in airport charges between sections (a) and (b) of the above table were again highlighted in 2005 when the Commission for Aviation Regulation re-examined the efficiency of Dublin Airport. The 1999–2000 data show the contrast between claims of Aer Rianta that its charges were the lowest in their

Table 9.8 Airport charges at major airports ($) and
Ryanair airports charges index, Europe 1998–2000.

(a) Major airports	$
MAN	11.1
VIE	9.0
HAM	8.6
FRA	8.1
BAA	7.1
ADP	5.7
BRU	5.6
AMS	5.5
CPH	5.0
SEA	4.5
AENA	4.0
ADR	3.8
Aer Rianta	3.4
(b) Ryanair charges index (average = 100)	
Dublin	204
Gatwick	179
Birmingham	155
Manchester	122
Luton	119
Stansted	102
Leeds/Bradford	36
Cardiff	31
Bournemouth	>30
Liverpool	>30
Bristol	>30
Prestwick	>30
Teesside	>30
Derry	>30

Source: (a) Warburg Dillon Reed (1999) (b) University of
Westminster (2000).

benchmarking league and claims by Ryanair that Dublin was the most expensive
airport in its network.

Initial benefits of independent airport boards
at Cork and Shannon

The experience of the independent boards at Cork and Shannon in 2005, their first
full year of operation, was positive in terms of passenger and customer airline
reaction. The independent boards of Cork and Shannon quickly established good
working relationships with their customer airlines.

Passenger traffic at Cork grew by 21.1 per cent in 2005 to 2.7 million passengers.
Aer Lingus added routes from Cork to Warsaw, Rome, Munich, Nice and Faro

and Malev commenced a Cork–Budapest service. Aer Lingus services in 2006 to Berlin, Birmingham and Tenerife bring to 14 the number of its Cork routes. Ryanair established a base in Cork in November 2005 with a target of 1 million passengers per annum on routes to Stansted, Dublin, Gatwick and Liverpool.

Passenger numbers at Shannon grew by 35 per cent in 2005 to 3.3 million. There was growth of 67 per cent on routes to the UK to 1.2 million and growth of 48 per cent to mainland Europe to 0.7 million. Shannon became a Ryanair base with thirteen routes to mainland Europe and nine to the UK.

Supply-side problems in the transition to airport independence

These problems arise in two main categories: the attainment of full independence for Cork and Shannon from Dublin and the apportionment of past operating and capital cost decisions at Cork and Shannon between Dublin and the new companies. Cork and Shannon were to submit business plans on these issues to the government by the end of June 2006. This deadline was missed by over two years thus limiting the autonomy of Cork and Shannon.

The State Airports Act 2004, provides for 'a phased distribution of assets subject to conditions relating to the operational and financial readiness of the three airports' (Commission for Aviation Regulation 2005b: 55). The CAR notes also the 'withdrawal of previously projected staff reductions in Group and Shared Services (Head Office) in respect of Cork and Shannon Airports on foot of the State Airports Act, 2004. In other words, the DAA is of the view that it will need to maintain head office capability for the other airports' (2005b: 65).

In line with the BAA precedent, Aer Rianta/DAA has opposed independence of Cork and Shannon. It does not wish to hand over the assets of Cork or Shannon to the government until its cash reserves exceed the value of the two airports. This is claimed to protect the interests of creditors, lenders and bond holders. The Commission did not see a major impact on the weighted cost of capital from a reduced bond rating for the DAA.

At Cork the major issue in the transition to independence is the €180 million new terminal building opening in spring 2006. This is claimed by the airlines to be way in excess of the needs of airport customers for an airport with 2.7 million passengers. The project was not appraised by the Commission for Aviation Regulation and has the characteristics of 'gold-plating' and airports as prestige symbols rather than commercial investments. The case that the Cork terminal and the cost of surplus labour at Shannon should be borne by the DAA is that these decisions were taken by the parent body of the DAA. Ryanair adds that the DAA could cover these liabilities through the sale of subsidiaries Great Southern Hotels comprising nine hotels in Ireland, and Aer Rianta International comprising interests in airports and duty-free shops abroad. In August 2006, the DAA announced proceeds of in excess of €265 million from its sale of hotels. A compromise on the value of assets transferred reached between the Dublin and Cork airport authorities was reached in 2008.

A debt-free transfer of Cork and Shannon to independent ownership on the other hand would place the smaller competing airports at Waterford, Kerry, Galway and Knock at a competitive disadvantage. The private sale of Cork and Shannon which would put a market price on the assets of both airports is not on the political agenda. The issue of pricing at state airports with underused capacity has been the subject of lengthy dispute between the EU and Charleroi Airport but the issue did not arise at privatised airports such as Prestwick (Groteke and Kerber, 2004).

The competing terminals option at Dublin 2002–5

The Programme for Government sought proposals for an independent terminal at Dublin Airport in June 2002. Following an advertisement seeking expressions of interest in August, 13 expressions of interest were received and an assessment panel was established in November 2002. Table 9.9 shows the commercial groups of those who submitted the expressions of interest.

The Dublin Airport Review of Expressions of Interest in an Independent Terminal (2003) found that 'an independent terminal is a viable strategic option for the development of Dublin Airport and would elicit considerable interest' (2003: 85). On the implications for Aer Rianta the panel stated

> Aer Rianta would be profoundly impacted with the changing competitive landscape requiring them to continue their ongoing restructuring programme. Revenues and costs would come under pressure in the short term following the loss of any business to a new terminal. However the Panel believes that Aer Rianta would vigorously react to competition for the benefit of airlines and passengers at Dublin Airport. Aer Rianta would be able to capture a share of the forecast growth and grow their business in the medium term. This would require a quantum shift in company culture to react to a new competitive environment, a shift that would only be delivered through the combined efforts of staff and management.

Support for the independent terminal was expressed by the chief executive of Aer Lingus at the Oireachtas (Parliament) Committee on Transport on 14 January 2003. This included the transfer of Aer Lingus flights to the terminal which Ryanair

Table 9.9 Expressions of interest in an independent terminal at Dublin Airport, 2002

Airport companies	Grupo Dragdos (Mexico), Hoctief, Fichtner, (Germany), Morrison (UK, New Zealand, Australia), Peel (UK).
Construction companies	Vinci Park (France), Laing O'Rourke, Dublin Airport Terminal 2 (IRL).
Airport customers	Ryanair, Cityjet, Irish Association of International Express Carriers
Finance sector	Ambac Assurance (UK)

Source: Department of Transport announcement, 26 November 2002.

was then seeking to build. The independent terminal was opposed by Aer Rianta and the trade unions. The buyback by the Greater Toronto Airports Authority of the independent Terminal 3 at Toronto Airport in 1997 was claimed by the opponents of a Dublin independent terminal as evidence that competition between terminal operators was unworkable. The 38 per cent premium paid to the private investors at Toronto in the buyback and the political changes which caused the buyback were largely ignored in the Dublin discussion of competing terminals. Investor interest in the Dublin Airport independent terminal increased in early 2005 with the submission of an Ireland/UK consortium for Terminal West, with a capacity of 60 million passengers.

In May 2005 the independent Terminal 2 project was ended by the government award of the contract to commission Terminal 2 to the Dublin Airport Authority. An agreement between the Prime Minister and the Irish Congress of Trade Unions in June 2004 had supported the same pay and conditions at both the new and the existing terminals.

The wider implications of the government decision to seek international expressions of interest in a project and to then award the project to the existing state monopolist are negative. Given the lack of competition faced by the Dublin Airport Authority for 75 per cent of the Irish aviation market a major opportunity to introduce contestability at the airport has been rejected by the government. The refusal to use a market approach places an extra burden on the Commission for Aviation Regulation in the absence of competition. There will be a competitive tendering process for the operation of the DAA-commissioned Terminal 2. The disadvantages of this process are that the DAA has a bad record in capital expenditure appraisal and delivery and that this has consequences for operating costs. The trade union agreement will further limit the scope for savings in operating costs.

Airport regulation in Ireland, 2001–5

The Commission for Aviation Regulation (2005a) sanctioned a 25 per cent increase in charges at Dublin compared to the 50 per cent increase requested to fund a second terminal at Dublin. The request was a consequence of the rejection of the policy of seeking private sector provision of the terminal.

The Commission in 2005 found that the Dublin Airport Authority has 'met the Commission's targets' in a combination of 'substantial out-performance on non-payroll opex' and 'underperformance on payroll' (Commission for Aviation Regulation, 2005b: 64). The number of staff at the airport was 'approximately static' with increases in security and fire brigade staff and reductions in all other areas such as management, cleaning, car-parking, retail and support services. The Commission rejected a submission by Aer Lingus that the efficiency targets are 'insufficiently challenging' to the Dublin Airport Authority.

The Commission's view of efficiency gains at Dublin Airport since 2001 is based on commissioned work by Booz Allen Hamilton (BAH) (Booz Allen Hamilton, 2005). This work has been criticised by Aer Lingus and Ryanair.

In responding to criticism by Aer Lingus, BAH state frequently that they did not wish to support conclusions with supporting data because of 'commercial sensitivity'. For example, the Aer Lingus claims 'a significant increase in costs in 2003 and 2004' and that BAH 'do not properly analyse the reasons behind this increase'. BAH responds that 'considerable analysis was undertaken but, for reasons of commercial sensitivity, the detail was not made publicly available' (BAH, 2005: 8). Confidentiality was also invoked by BAH in response to criticisms that it failed to provide robust support for the current level of opex and the scope for future efficiency improvement, failed to compare processes between airports, and failed to examine service quality and productivity improvements combined. The Aer Lingus criticisms of Aer Rianta merited a more informative response since criticisms of one public body by another are rare in Ireland.

Research for the Commission by Transport Research Laboratory (TRL) found that in 2002 compared with Manchester, Copenhagen, Zurich, Brussels, Stockholm, Oslo and Vienna, Dublin's total core per passenger costs were 5 SDRs per passenger compared to an average of almost 9 per passenger and the lowest of 3.32. TRL also found that in a sample of 25 European airports the commercial revenue per passenger at Dublin in 2002 was 22nd (Commission for Aviation Regulation, 2005a). TRL did not however examine the growth of low-cost airports in Europe as indicated in section (b) of Table 9.8 and the development of both Ryanair and Aer Lingus as low-cost airlines with a combined total of over 40 million passengers in 2005.

The relevance of the TRL 7 benchmark airports to Irish airlines is limited. Compared to a possible fourteen services by the two airlines at the seven benchmark airports chosen there were only five services by Irish airlines. Ryanair served only Manchester on the benchmark list while Aer Lingus served four (Vienna, Brussels, Zurich and Manchester) in their 2005/2006 timetables. Ryanair had also reduced its exposure to the high charges at Manchester declining to use services such as airbridges and by developing services elsewhere in the northwest of England at four competing airports: Liverpool, Leeds/Bradford, Blackpool and Doncaster.

The competing airport option is available throughout the EU due to the large number of underused small airports developed from military airfields and airports built to promote city and regional development. The competitive option does not exist at Dublin where the airport has a monopoly in Ireland's most prosperous and populous province with 54 per cent of the population in 2002 in the EU's fastest growing economy. The Leinster (east) province has one airport, Dublin, for a 2.1 million population, compared with Munster (south) which has four airports for a 1.1 million population, and Connacht/Ulster (west/northwest) which has four airports for a population of 0.7 million.

The Air Transport Research Society (ATRS) database was used by the International Institute of Transport and Logistics to calculate productivity measures for the regulator (Commission for Aviation Regulation, 2005a). ATRS found that the number of employees at Dublin Airport, just below 1,500, was almost double the five airport average for other airports with 15 to 19 million passengers per annum. Excluding staff engaged in retailing, the Dublin head count of 1,250 is 67 per cent above the five-airport average.

ATRS also found Dublin Airport's passengers per employee well below the five-airport average, and also the nine-airport average, which includes the five plus Rome, Munich, Orly and Barcelona, and had between 14,500 and 15,500 passengers per employee.

ATRS found that Dublin's WLUs per employee and aircraft movements per employee (119 compared with 217) were well below the average of the European airports examined. Adjusting output to a measure combining passengers, air transport movements and non-aero output brought Dublin close to a five-airport average but only to 51 per cent of the best performer.

In terms of capital productivity ATRS found that Dublin's pax/gate rate is some two-thirds of the best performer; its pax/square metre of terminal is about one-third of the best performer; and that ATMs per runway are about three-quarters of the best performing airport in the European dataset. However, when all three runways are considered Dublin's ATMs per runway fall from 177.781 to 59,260, a quarter of the best performer. Oum (2005) notes the internal inconsistency of the Dublin Airport Authority response to the ATRS report because the DAA 'uses partial productivity or partial cost measures to claim they are efficient while cautioning the use of partial factor productivity when it is inconvenient for DAA'. Oum also noted that the ATRS measure of efficiency reflects airport management efficiency in the choice between franchising or in-house provision of commercial activities. 'Making a bad decision will make an airport less efficient whereas a good decision will improve efficiency of the airport in our measure' (2005: 10–11).

The problems concerning capital expenditure at Irish airports persisted in 2005. The Commission stated that 'a brief high level summary of the finalised capex programme was delivered to the Commission on 19 September 2005 – the fifty-first week of a process to which the Commission was allocated 52 weeks' (Commission for Aviation Regulation 2005a: 3).

Research by IMR for the Commission on Aviation Regulation analysed the capex proposals of the Dublin Airport Authority as submitted in May 2005. In a capex of €1 billion over the years 2005–14, IMR identified economies of €211 million in terminal and pier additions and accepted the other capex categories proposals for airside, other landside, other terminals and general capital expenditure. In relation to the later capital expenditure proposals IMR stated that 'the recommendation report does not include the level of detail of methodology and analysis necessary to support the size, location, specification and sequencing of major capacity-driven projects. It will be necessary to reappraise our findings in the light of detailed justification' (Ibid.: 2).

In assessing the various reports and representations the Commission decided that 'there remains scope for efficiency improvements in Dublin Airport' (Ibid.: 25). The appraisal of capital expenditure by the regulator is unsatisfactory because it was given so little time in which to carry out its task. The appraisal of opex lacks transparency to the degree that commercial confidentiality is frequently invoked as the reasons for failing to publish responses to vital questions on airport efficiency. Consultations with customer airlines are unsatisfactory as illustrated in the refusal to respond to issues raised by Aer Lingus and the benchmarking of Dublin Airport productivity using a sample of airports rarely used by either Aer Lingus or Ryanair, the major customer airlines of the Dublin Airport Authority.

Airport regulation in Ireland has been a contest between the airport monopoly and the airlines and has lacked both a consumer dimension and a macroeconomic context. Aviation costs are a vital part of Ireland's national productivity as an outer offshore island with large foreign trade and tourism components in GDP. The Irish economy has outperformed the OECD countries in terms of GDP per head, GDP growth rates, labour market performance and income growth. The Irish airlines reflect this superior performance. Ryanair is the leading low-cost airline in the EU and Aer Lingus as the leading legacy airline performer. In contrast to an economy outperforming the OECD, the Commission for Aviation Regulation has regulated the airport sector in Ireland at performance levels between 24 per cent and 26 per cent below that of the 'best performer' airport.

Employment in state commercial enterprises in Ireland fell from 7.8 per cent of total employment to 2.7 per cent between 1980 and 2002. This decline in employment share calls into question the appropriateness of the state company business model in the contemporary Irish economy. The Commission notes a complaint by Ryanair that its relatively benign view of Irish airport performance indicates regulatory capture of the Commission by the airports it regulates (Commission for Aviation Regulation 2005b: 59).

The future regulatory environment for Irish airports

The negative lessons from the first period of airport regulation in Ireland are the high level of legal costs; weak capital investment appraisal with little indication that the DAA has, even at the close of 2005, made any significant improvements in this field; and a lack of openness in the appraisal of operating cost efficiency. There remain sharp differences between regulator, airport and airlines on airport benchmarking. There has been a lack of consistency in the regulation of Irish airports by the Commission for Aviation Regulation. The IMG data series from 2001 was not continued through 2005 and a multiplicity of consultants was used in 2005.

A further problem in the regulation of Irish airports over the period 2001–5 has been the use of directives by the government to the regulator thus under-mining the independence of the regulator and losing the benefits sought when regulation of airports was moved from a government department to an independent regulator. Thus the government ordered in May 2005 that there should not be competing terminals at Dublin Airport without publishing any evaluations of the 13 expressions of interest by the groups shown in Table 9.9.

The 'triple lock' safeguards against inefficiencies in that decision were claimed to be:

(a) the requirements for consultation with the airlines servicing Dublin Airport;
(b) 'the independent verification of the final specifications and costings of Terminal Two by aviation experts'; and

(c) the regulation of airport charges to 'reflect costs appropriate to the building of an efficient terminal' (Commission for Aviation Regulation 2005b: 57/58).

Triple lock (a) offers little prospect for efficiency because consultation with the airlines has been unsatisfactory throughout the period. Triple lock (b) is likely to lead to further disputes because of the record in the field of rejecting the advice of independent aviation experts. Triple lock (c) assumes away the recurring problem of weak capital investment appraisal at Irish airports.

In his August 2005 directive to the Commission to give effect to the May 2005 decision, the Minister emphasised the problem of congestion at Dublin Airport. There is no acknowledgement in the directive that congestion at the airport may be due to weaknesses in capital investment appraisal procedures by Aer Rianta/Dublin Airport Authority over the years since 2001 or that it may be due to inefficiency in the airport's opex. CAR's research since 2001 and the views of the customer airlines provide much evidence that there are both capex and opex problems at the airport.

Summary and conclusions

Table 9.10 presents an agenda for airport competition in Europe based on the experience of the Irish case study since 2001 and presented above. The problem of airport monopoly in Europe is widespread. As the Davy report finds:

> Europe's airports have been shielded from competition by a structure that has preserved national and local multi-airport monopolies. These monopolies, public and private, dominate the European airports industry … Competition is preferable to regulation, which should be confined to unavoidable local monopoly in single-airport cities and to congested airports.
>
> (Davy Stockbrokers, 2004: 5)

Table 9.10 An agenda for airport competition in Europe

Problem	Instrument
Multi-airport groups	Demerger of potentially competing airports
Regulatory capture	Independent regulation
Dominant airports	Competing airport terminals
Efficient capex	Full publication
	Independent evaluation
	Better airline consultation
	Tackle gold-plating
Efficient opex	Wider benchmarking
	Unbundle services
	Full publication
	Better airline consultation

Prior to the Irish decision to dismantle Aer Rianta the only pro-competition decision on the structure of the airports market was the decision of the UK regulatory authorities to prohibit a merger between Belfast International and Belfast City airports in Northern Ireland. Demerging multiple airport groups serving the same city or region is a necessary in order to bring the airports sector to the same level of contestability as the airlines. In the United Kingdom case the Competition Commission determined in August 2008 that the BAA domination of airports in southeast England and Scotland is detrimental to passenger interests. The time taken to demerge Dublin, Cork and Shannon airports has exceeded expectations and the ability of Cork and Shannon to compete with Dublin is limited by their distance from Dublin. Competition at airports between terminals is also recommended in addition to the unbundling of services at airports in order to allow airlines to choose only the services they require. In addition, based on the Irish experience, measures are required to protect the independence of the regulator, to promote efficient regulation of capital and operating expenditures and to improve airport/airline consultation. Better consultation between airports and airlines is needed with an independent facilitator. Table 9.10 summarises an agenda for airport competition based on the Irish experience since 2001 based on a more competitive structure for Irish airports and improved regulation of airport efficiency.

The Appeals Panel (2008) decided that 'a detailed and transparent analysis of the capacity of Terminal 1' at Dublin was required along with 'a consequential assessment of the required capacity of Terminal 2'. The Panel stated that 'if Ryanair is correct, and on the submissions and oral hearing it would appear to be correct, Terminal 2 as proposed may well be oversized in an amount significantly in excess if that allowed by the Commission' (for Aviation Regulation).

Ireland was an innovator in airline deregulation and is an interesting case study in seeking to promote greater airport contestability. A pessimistic reading of the Irish record since 2001 is that the abandonment of competing terminals at Dublin in 2005 was a mistake, that Cork and Shannon will not be independent competitors with Dublin and that the regulator has failed to make any impact on capex at Irish airports while having minimal impact on opex. The optimistic reading of the Irish experience of airport regulation is that the lessons of airline deregulation are well known in Ireland and that the Table 9.10 agenda for airport competition will be implemented.

References

Aer Rianta CPT (2001) Statement grounding application for judicial review, High Court 2001/707.

Aviation Appeals Panel (2008) Decision on the Appeal of Ryanair Limited, Dublin.

Barrett, S.D. (1998) The importance of state enterprises in the Irish economy and the future for privatisation, in Parker, D. (ed.) *Privatisation in the European Union*. London: Routledge.

Barrett, S.D. (2000) Airport competition in the deregulated European aviation market, *Journal of Air Transport Management* 6: 13–27.

Barrett, S.D. (2004) How do the demands for airport services differ between full-service and low-cost carriers, *Journal of Air Transport Management* 10: 33–9.

Booz Allen Hamilton (2005) *Dublin Airport Bottom-up Efficiency Study*. Dublin: Booz Allen Hamilton.

Callaghan, J. (2002) High Court affidavit on behalf of Ryanair (notice party), Judicial Review 2001/707, dated 13 May.

Commission for Aviation Regulation (Ireland) (2001a) *Report on Determination of Maximum Levels of Airport Charges*, August. Dublin: Commission for Aviation Regulation.

Commission for Aviation Regulation (Ireland) (2001b) *IMG Recoverable Capex Programme*, Appendix 4. Dublin: Commission for Aviation Regulation.

Commission for Aviation Regulation (Ireland) (2005a) *The Performance of Dublin Airport: The Findings of the Comparative Reports of the TRL (Transport Research Laboratory (UK) and ATRS (Air Transport Research Society)*, May. Dublin: Commission for Aviation Regulation.

Commission for Aviation Regulation (Ireland) (2005b) Determination on maximum levels of airport charges, paper CP3/2005, Dublin: Commission for Aviation Regulation.

Department of Transport (2002) *Announcement of Expressions of Interest in Second Terminal at Dublin Airport*, November.

Department of Transport (2005a) *Aviation Action Plan*, May.

Department of Transport (2005b) *Directive to Commissioner for Aviation Regulation*, August.

Davy Stockbrokers (2004) *Late Arrival, a Competition Policy for Europe's Airports*. Dublin: Davy Stockbrokers.

Doganis, R. (2001) *The Airline Business in the 21st Century*. London: Routledge.

Dublin Airport Review of Expressions of Interest for an Independent Terminal (2003).

Groteke, F. and Kerber, W. (2004) *The Case of Ryanair – EU State Aid Policy on the Wrong Runway*, Ordo, Bd. 55. Stuttgart: Lucius and Lucius.

Infrastructure Management Group (2001) *Benchmarking Report for Commission for Aviation Regulation*. Bethseda, MD: Infrastructure Management Group.

IMR (2005) *Review of airport charges at Dublin Airport; Review of Capital Programme*. Ely: IMR.

Oireachtas (Parliament) Committee on Transport (2003) Minutes, 14 January.

Oum, T.H. (2005) Comments on the Dublin Airport Authority's response, International Institute of Transport and Logistics, Vancouver, pp. 10–11.

Prasifka, W. (2002) Aer Rianta CPT and the Commissioner for Aviation Regulation, Affidavit, High Court Judicial Review 2001/707, dated 14 February.

Starkie, D. (2004) Testing the regulatory model: the expansion of Stansted airport, *Fiscal Studies* 25: 4.

University of Westminster (2000) *Analysis of Ryanair Airport Charges*. London: University of Westminster.

Walsh. N. (2002) High Court Affidavit on behalf of Aer Lingus (notice party), Judicial Review 2001/707, dated May 13.

Warburg Dillon Read (1999) *Review of Strategic Options for Aer Rianta*, December, London.

10 Summary

A sector transformed

The transformation of European aviation from a series of bilateral agreements between governments and their national airlines to a single European market has had spectacular impacts on airline productivity and price. The airline product has been redefined by the unbundling of services such as business class as passengers chose price rather than service competition. The use of secondary airports has resulted in planes achieving quicker turnaround times with more rotations per day. Passengers have responded positively to the new, smaller, less congested airports. Point-to-point services from local airports have resulted in lower fares and reduced travel times compared with previous routings through hub airports.

National airlines in Europe remain identified with their home countries. The low-cost airlines, notably Ryanair and easyJet, have developed bases in other countries and developed third-country services. In summer 2006 only 19 of the Ryanair fleet of 107 aircraft were based in Ireland; 42 were based in Stansted; 17 elsewhere in the UK; 11 in Italy; 7 in Germany; 4 in Belgium; 4 in Scandinavia; and 3 in Spain. The LCC model in 2006 had 117 million passengers with Ryanair the market leader at 30 per cent of the market. easyJet was second at 26 per cent with strong market performance in the UK domestic, Czech Republic, French domestic, Hungary, Slovenia and Switzerland markets. Table 10.1 shows the composition of the low-cost airline market in Europe in 2006 for airlines with 2 million or more passengers. In addition there were seven smaller airlines with a total of 7.3 million passengers. The total market was 116.9 million with 56 per cent held by Ryanair and easyJet. The rapid growth of passenger numbers on the two main low-cost airlines projects 100 million passengers in 2008 comprising 58 million on Ryanair and 42 million on easyJet. The mid-2008 growth rate was 15.9 per cent on easyJet and 16 per cent on Ryanair. By contrast, in the full service airline sector the 30 member airlines of the Association of European Airlines had an increase in passenger numbers from 309 million in 2000 to 343 million in 2006, an increase of 11 per cent over seven years.

The new entrant airlines in Europe have overcome the region's long-standing problem of high costs. The ability of European airlines to provide low-cost travel was already demonstrated in the Cascade Studies. Table 10.2 shows the 2005/6 cost per seat km for Ryanair, easyJet, British Airways and four US airlines.

Table 10.1 European low-cost airlines
2006 (million passengers)

Ryanair	34.9
easyJet	30.3
Air Berlin	13.8
Flybe	5.5
Germanwings	5.5
Sterling/Maersk	3.8
bmibaby	3.5
dba	3.0
Hapag Lloyd Express	2.7
Vueling	2.5
Norwegian Air Shuttle	2.1
Virgin Express	2.0
Others (7)	6.0
Total	116.9

Source: Davy Stockbrokers (2006a) Table 11.

Table 10.2 Unit cost per available seat
km (€ cents) 2005/2006

Ryanair	4.0
easyJet	5.9
British Airways	7.8
American	8.8
Continental	8.5
Delta	9.7
US Airways	9.0

Source: Davy Stockbrokers (2006b) Table 12.

Table 10.3 shows similar data for 2001 showing the low-cost structures of easyJet, Ryanair and Southwest compared with US and EU full service airlines.

Table 10.3 shows earlier data from Gillen and Morrison showing a cost structure in 2001 which indicates that Southwest had a two-to-one cost advantage over US full-service airlines and that Ryanair and easyJet had a cost base lower than that attained by Southwest. The cost benchmarking of European airlines compared to those in North America has improved significantly compared with the studies in Chapter 2 of this volume covering the pre-deregulation era in Europe. The competitive response of Europe's legacy airlines to new low-cost entrants in Europe has strengthened their position in further liberalisations of the market such as the EU/USA open skies agreement which came into operation in 2008.

Deregulation in Europe has also redefined the airline product on short-haul routes. Chapters 4, 5, 6 and 7 describe this change in the airline product from a number of airline perspectives. Mason notes that while in 1998 'only 24 per cent of respondents believed business class products provided good value for money. This proportion had fallen to just 15 per cent in 2004' (2005: 22). Mason concluded

Table 10.3 Unit cost per available seat mile
(US cents), 2001

Frontier	5.6
Southwest	4.0
ATA	4.3
United	8.1
Continental	6.2
America West	6.2
US Airways	8.9
Delta	7.1
3 major EU flag carriers	8.3
Ryanair	3.3
easyJet	3.0

Source: Gillen and Morrison (2005b) Tables 1 and 2.

that 'business travellers do not need to change their tickets often and that when they do, low-cost carriers offer a more cost-efficient method of providing ticket flexibility' (2006: 92). Prior to deregulation in Europe business class combined two products, namely flexible ticketing and services such as in-flight food and beverages, newspapers, extra legroom, hub airport use, airport lounges, extra frequent-flyer points and interline connections. Unbundling these services will indicate which are most valued by passengers. In the case studies examined in this volume, Aer Lingus, in its transition to the low-cost model, retained only seat allocation and hub airport access to differentiate it from its low-cost main rival, Ryanair. The decline in emphasis on business class was dramatic. Doganis noted that as recently as 1999, some 28 per cent of Aer Lingus European traffic was in business class compared with an average of 14 per cent for all European carriers (2002: 297). In May 2006 Aer Lingus announced its decision to leave the One World alliance thus substituting point-to-point no-frills traffic for interline traffic at hubs such as Heathrow, Frankfurt, Amsterdam, Paris and New York.

In an interesting study of service-quality competition between US airlines Lee and Luengo-Prado (2004) contrasted the results of legroom improvements by both American and United in 2000. American increased seat pitch from 31/32 inches for all coach seats across its entire fleet while United increased pitch to 36 inches for the first 6–11 rows. They found that the American programme resulted in lower average fares for American while the United programme 'was effective in attracting passengers willing to pay higher fares for greater seat pitch when offered a choice of otherwise comparable service among competing full service carriers' (2004: 382).

The cost advantages of easyJet and Ryanair, shown in Table 10.3 above, including their scale economies in purchasing aircraft and other inputs such as airport services are expected to lead to concentration of the low-cost sector in its two leading airlines. Europe has some 60 low-cost airlines compared with a peak of 108 (Davy Stockbrokers, 2008). Similarly the 30 member airlines of the Association of European Airlines are expected to consolidate in three large groups based on Lufthansa, Air France–KLM and British Airways–Iberia. Airport competition in Europe has been facilitated by the plentiful supply of airports inherited from military uses and those built to promote regional and city development.

There are many more examples of airport competition in addition to the seventeen examples in Chapter 8. In 2006 the Dublin–London market of 4.3 million passengers, the busiest in Europe, was split between 47 per cent at Heathrow and 53 per cent at the combined rivals at Stansted, Gatwick, Luton and London City. The Heathrow share of Dublin–London has declined from 76 per cent in 1990. The share is likely to fall further given the opportunity cost of using 19 slot pairs, 13 by Aer Lingus and 6 by British Midland on a low-yield route, with passengers willing to pay only a small premium for Heathrow compared with the competing airports. In the total Ireland–London market of 6.8 million passengers in 2006 the Heathrow share was 40 per cent reflecting declining market shares going to Heathrow from Dublin, Cork and Shannon and services from new Irish airports to Stansted and Luton.

The closure of the Shannon–Heathrow route in January 2008 is likely to reduce the Heathrow share of Ireland–London passengers to 36 per cent. Slot pairs at Heathrow have sold for £10 million and are thus likely to be transferred from low-yield short-haul to longer routes with higher yields.

UK airport competition has increased since the 1998/1999 case studies in Chapter 8. In the north of England the competition on the Dublin route between Manchester, Liverpool, and Leeds-Bradford competition has been joined by Blackpool and Doncaster. Birmingham faces competition from Nottingham (East Midlands and Coventry). The Prestwick share of Dublin–Glasgow route is 60 per cent.

In 2006 two-thirds of passengers between Brussels and Dublin used Charleroi rather than Zaventem and the estimated total passenger numbers were 16 million at Zaventem and 2.5 million at Charleroi. Frankfurt Hahn exceeded 3.5 million passengers in 2006 and rapid growth is taking place at Skavsta, Bergamo, Girona, Pisa and Ciampino. Cross-border competition is seen in cases such as Malmo competing with Copenhagen and Bratislava competing with Vienna. In cases in which airlines are not satisfied with the price–service combination at Europe's airports airlines have moved, for example, from Rimini to Ancona and Shannon to Kerry. The emphasis by legacy airlines on hubs such as Frankfurt, Rome, Paris and Madrid has left many other cities open to the expansion of direct services bypassing connections through hubs.

The attractions of small airports for passengers include less waiting and walking times, easy local access, less confusion, more relaxed atmosphere and cheaper car parking. The attractions for the airlines include 20/25-minute turnaround, no airport congestion and lower charges. Many of the traditional hub airports have a long history of working with legacy airlines and exhibit the symptoms of distressed state airline syndrome such as losses, over-politicisation, strong unions, overstaffing, no clear development strategy, bureaucratic management and poor service quality (Doganis, 2002). The advent of low-cost airlines at previously unused airports has produced its own dynamic in a largely unforeseen result of European airline deregulation.

A study of the efficiency of the top 15 large, medium and small airports in the United States between 1996 and 2000 by Bazargan and Vasigh (2003) found that 'the small airports consistently outperform the large hubs based on their relative efficiency scores in all 5 years' (2003: 192).

The many under-utilised airports in Europe did not in the past attract legacy airlines to serve them because of high fares, high costs and the emphasis on hubs for interlining. The new airlines represented a market opportunity for the under-utilised airports. In the case of empty private sector airports, such as Prestwick, the price arrangement with an airline is a commercial decision. The under-used airport may decide to exit the aviation sector with its lands reverting to agricultural uses or to serve markets such as general aviation, flying clubs and private flying. At each stage of development the airport owner has to decide whether the marginal revenue from new aviation customers is at least equal to marginal cost.

Where underused airports are in public ownership their development raises the spectre of unfair competition and market distortion caused by state aid. The EU has ruled against Charleroi Airport and Ryanair in respect of their agreement which raised passenger numbers from 20,000 passengers a year before the agreement to 2.3 million passengers by locating five aircraft there serving 16 routes. The area experienced high unemployment and the Walloon government saw its development as a means of promoting employment and income growth in the region.

Following objections from competing airlines and airports the EU disallowed the agreement between Charleroi in 2004 on the grounds of lack of transparency, infringement of the private market investor principle, discriminatory exclusivity and the length of the agreement (Gillen and Morrison, 2005a: 47). Ryanair was required to refund €4 million of illegal state aid. The Commission states that airport contracts with airlines must be of limited duration, transparent, available to all carriers, used to develop new routes and be proportional to expected route revenue. The Ryanair defence is that the agreement has brought the airport into profit and that a new terminal with a capacity of 5 million passengers is planned. The project has generated almost 500 jobs at the airport and many more in the region. Charleroi is a long-established airport but no airline before Ryanair was willing to operate services there or invest in it. Since the agreement the number of non-Ryanair passengers at Charleroi has increased from some 20,000 to over 160,000. Ryanair successfully pleaded at the Court of First Instance in December 2008 that the agreement was publicised, open to other airlines long before Ryanair began to serve the airport, is not exclusive to Ryanair and has brought a loss-making airport into profit. In early 2009 the Commission decided not to appeal the decision of the Court of First Instance.

Gillen and Morrison (2005a) warn that low-cost airlines 'develop small markets and therefore need exclusive contracts' (2005a: 47). Extra traffic at a previously under-utilised airport benefits airports, airlines and passengers. 'An airport operating as a business has an incentive to ensure that its services are consistent with the business model of the airlines it serves.' A later study of the Charleroi decision found that subsidisation or lower airport charges benefit consumers and negatively affect incumbent airlines. They may be more affected by competition than by the subsidy. Ryanair charged lower fares to and from airports it dominates (Barbot, 2006). 'More competition, which is welfare enhancing, may be the main cause of its (the incumbent airline's) decline in profits. It is possible that the airport benefits more with the subsidy than the LCC, depending on its efficiency' (2006: 203).

The EU intervention in the Charleroi on behalf of legacy airlines and high cost airports rather than addressing the slot system at hub airports indicates an anti-contestability policy emphasis. Low-cost airlines face severe constraints in seeking to serve busy airports and face fines in seeking to serve under-utilised airports in the public sector. The EU has a poor record in airport matters such as ensuring efficiency in operations and investment at airports and examining the efficiency implications of multi-airport groups achieving control over several airports serving the same market. The EU has neglected for example the efficiency gains where low-cost airlines extract monopoly rents from previously non-competing airports. The duration of an airport/airline contract should not be limited by the EU without reference to the stage of development of the airport. Nor is it apparent that an under-utilised airport is better served by new routes than by the expansion of existing routes. Legislative changes in Europe have, however, reduced barriers to contestability such as ground handling monopolies and state aid to national airlines.

The development of the Internet allowed passengers direct access to airline information and booking. The Internet removed the advantages of incumbent airlines in controlling computer reservation systems (CRS) and travel agents as seen in the case study of Cityjet in Chapter 6. Since low-cost airline fares are lower than those charged by legacy airlines travel agents' commission at the same percentage of the retail ticket price gave the agents an incentive to sell higher priced tickets on behalf of legacy airlines rather than the products of low-cost airlines. Low-cost airlines in Europe have moved rapidly away from sales through travel agents. In a survey of 13 Asian airlines in the Asia-Pacific region in August 1999, Alamdari (2002) noted that 'all carriers indicated that the tendency to sell tickets through parallel channels could avoid over-dependence on travel intermediaries. Some 63 per cent pointed out that their companies could benefit from cost saving as the share of passenger revenue generated by travel agents declined' (2002: 346). The number of travel agents in the USA declined by 9 per cent, or 2,707 agents, between 1995 and 2000 (2002: 343). Passenger loyalty to airlines secured through frequent-flyer programmes was stronger in the world of non-competing airlines in the past and was weakened by the size of the fare reductions of the new market entrant airlines offering lower fares rather than incur the administration costs of frequent-flyer programmes.

Twenty-three years after Ryanair's entry to the Dublin–London route and twenty-five years after the parliamentary revolt which led to that market entry

European aviation has been transformed. New low-cost airlines have reduced the fares charged, redefined the product from non-price to price competition, dramatically increased the sector's productivity, secured direct access to passengers through the Internet rather than through travel agents and redefined the airport product from the perspective of both airlines and their passengers. The story of regulating Europe's skies over the last two and a half decades illustrates well that the more restrictive a cartel the more dramatic the results of a deregulation.

References

Alamdari, F. (2002) Regional development in airlines and travel agents relationship, *Journal of Air Transport Management* 8: 339–48.

Barbot, C. (2006) Low-cost airlines, secondary airports, and state aid: An economic assessment of the Ryanair–Charleroi agreement, *Journal of Air Transport Management* 12: 197–203.

Bazargan, M. and Vasigh, B. (2003) Size versus efficiency; A case study of US commercial airports, *Journal of Air Transport Management* 9: 187–93.

Davy Stockbrokers (2006a) *Ryanair as a Consumer Growth Company*. Dublin: Davy Stockbrokers.

Davy Stockbrokers (2006b) *Aer Lingus*. Dublin: Davy Stockbrokers.

Davy Stockbrokers (2008) *Airlines; Crisis points – where will the industry go from here?* Dublin: Davy Stockbrokers.

Doganis, R. (2002) *Flying off Course, The Economics of International Airlines*, 3rd edition. London: Routledge.

Gillen, D. and Morrison, W.G. (2005a) The economics of franchise contracts and airport policy, *Journal of Air Transport Management* 11: 43–8.

Gillen, D. and Morrison, W.G. (2005b) Regulation, competition and network evaluation in aviation, *Journal of Air Transport Management* 11: 161–74.

Lee, D. and Luengo-Prado, M. (2004) Are passengers willing to pay more for additional legroom, *Journal of Air Transport Management* 10: 377–83.

Mason, K.J. (2005) Observations of fundamental changes in the demand for aviation services, *Journal of Air Transport Management* 11: 19–25.

Mason, K.J. (2006) The value and usage of ticket flexibility for short haul business travellers, *Journal of Air Transport Management* 12: 92–7.

Index